Global Crises, Social Justice, and Education

Education cannot be understood today without recognizing that nearly all educational policies and practices are strongly influenced by an increasingly integrated international economy. Reforms in one country have significant effects in others, just as immigration and population tides from one area to another have tremendous impacts on what counts as official knowledge and responsive and effective education. But what are the realities of these global crises that so many people are experiencing and how do their effects on education resonate throughout the world?

Global Crises, Social Justice, and Education looks into the ways we understand globalization and education by getting specific about what committed educators can do to counter the relations of dominance and subordination around the world. From some of the world's leading critical educators and activists, this timely new collection provides thorough and detailed analyses of four specific centers of global crisis: the United States, Japan, Israel/Palestine, and Mexico. Each chapter engages in a powerful and critical analysis of what exactly is occurring in these regions and counters with an equally compelling critical portrayal of the educational work being done to interrupt global dominance and subordination. Without settling for vague ideas or romantic slogans of hope, *Global Crises, Social Justice, and Education* offers real, concrete examples and strategies that will contribute to ongoing movements and counter-hegemonic struggles already active in education today.

Michael W. Apple is John Bascom Professor of Curriculum and Instruction and Educational Policy Studies at the University of Wisconsin-Madison.

Global Crises, Social Justice, and Education

Edited by
Michael W. Apple

 Routledge
Taylor & Francis Group

NEW YORK AND LONDON

First published 2010
by Routledge
270 Madison Avenue, New York, NY 10016

Simultaneously published in the UK
by Routledge
2 Park Square, Milton Park, Abingdon, Oxon OX14 4RN

Routledge is an imprint of the Taylor & Francis Group, an informa business

© 2010 Taylor and Francis

Typeset in Minion by
Keystroke, Tettenhall, Wolverhampton
Printed and bound in the United States of America on acid-free paper by
Edwards Brothers, Inc.

Library of Congress Cataloging-in-Publication Data
Global crises, social justice, and education / edited by Michael W. Apple.
p. cm.
Includes index.
1. Education–Political aspects. 2. Education and state. 3. Social justice–Study
and teaching. 4. Conflict management–Cross-cultural studies. I. Apple, Michael W.
LC71.G54 2009
370.11'5–dc22
2009041564

ISBN 10: (hbk) 0–415–99596–5
ISBN 10: (pbk) 0–415–99597–3
ISBN 10: (ebk) 0–203–86144–2

ISBN 13: (hbk) 978–0–415–99596–2
ISBN 13: (pbk) 978–0–415–99597–9
ISBN 13: (ebk) 978–0–203–86144–8

Contents

Acknowledgments

Books such as this are often the result of a good deal of cooperative effort. This one is no exception. There were many meetings, intense discussions, and theoretical, political, and educational issues—and sometimes disagreements—that had to be talked through. Given the nature of a volume such as this one, this is to be expected, and also welcomed. By their very nature, the conflicts and tensions with which *Global Crises, Social Justice, and Education* deals can and do require that people take positions on matters of very real ethical and political importance. It may seem rather odd for me to thank the participants in this book. But Ross Collin, Keita Takayama, Assaf Meshulam, Jen Sandler, and Erika Mein worked very hard to embody the sensibility that serious critical work best goes on when people are free to supportively criticize and co-teach each other.

Many of these chapters were first presented at the Friday Seminar at the University of Wisconsin-Madison. This group has played a key role for many of us. It constantly exhibits a model of committed work; and through the years has demonstrated that even in universities that are being themselves transformed around neoliberal and managerial tendencies it is possible to live out a different and more collective reality.

A number of the issues dealt with in this volume, especially in the first and last chapters, benefited from discussions with Wayne Au, Stephen Ball, David Gillborn, Fatma Gok, Zhongjing Huang, Marie Lall, Amy Stambach, Carlos Alberto Torres, Guangcai Yan, Geoff Whitty, and Deborah Youdell. The final work on the book was completed during the time I was a World

Scholar at the Institute of Education, University of London. As usual, my colleagues at the Institute of Education helped create a fine environment for serious work.

Special thanks need to go to Catherine Bernard at Routledge. Once again, Catherine gave wise advice and provided constant support throughout the process of completing this book, as did Georgette Enriquez.

Finally, Mi Ok Kang served as the editorial assistant on this volume. Her careful attention to detail is much appreciated.

CHAPTER 1

Global Crises, Social Justice, and Education

MICHAEL W. APPLE

Globalizing Logics

If one were to name an issue that has come to be found near the top of the list of crucial topics within the critical education literature, it would be *globalization*. It is a word with extraordinary currency. This is the case not only because of trendiness. Exactly the opposite is the case. It has become ever more clear that education cannot be understood without recognizing that nearly all educational policies and practices are strongly influenced by an increasingly integrated international economy that is subject to severe crises, that reforms and crises in one country have significant effects in others, that the immigration and population flows from one nation or area to another have tremendous impacts on what counts as official knowledge and what counts as a responsive and effective education, and the list could continue for quite a while (see Burbules & Torres, 2009; Dale & Robertson, 2009; Peters, 2005; Rhoads & Torres, 2006). Indeed, as I show in *Educating the "Right" Way* (Apple, 2006) and *The State and the Politics of Knowledge* (Apple et al., 2003), all of these social and ideological dynamics and many more are now fundamentally restructuring what education does, how it is controlled, and who benefits from it throughout the world.

While localities and national systems inflect the processes of globalization differently and struggles are generated, convergences and homogenization of educational forms and modalities, driven by what de Santos (2003) calls "monocultural logics," are very clearly evident within and between settings. These logics are very visible in current education policies which privilege choice, competition, performance management and individual responsibility and risk management, and in a series of attacks on the cultural gains made by dispossessed groups (Apple, Ball, & Gandin, 2010). Neoliberal, neo-conservative and managerial impulses can be found throughout the world, cutting across both geographical boundaries and even economic systems. This points to the important "spatial" aspects of globalization. Policies are "borrowed" and "travel" across borders in such a way that these neoliberal, neoconservative, and managerial impulses are extended throughout the world, and alternative or oppositional forms and practices are marginalized or attacked (Gulson & Symes, 2007, p. 9).

The insight that stands behind some of the focus on globalization in general can perhaps best be summarized in the words of a character in a novel about the effects of the British Empire (Rushdie, 1981). If I may be permitted to paraphrase what he says, "The problem with the English is that they don't understand that their history constantly occurs outside their borders." We could easily substitute words such as "Americans" and others for "English."

There is a growing literature on globalization and education. This is undoubtedly important and a significant portion of this literature has pro-vided us with powerful understandings of the realities and histories of empire and postcolonialism(s), the interconnected flows of capital, populations, knowledge, and differential power, and the ways in which thinking about the local requires that we simultaneously think about the global.[1] But as I will argue in the next section of this chapter, a good deal of it does not go far enough into the realities of the global crises that so many people are experiencing or it assumes that the crises and their effects on education are the same throughout the world. Indeed, the concept of globalization itself needs to be historicized and seen as partly hegemonic itself, since at times its use fails to ground itself in "the asymmetries of power between nations and colonial and neocolonial histories, which see differential national effects of neoliberal globalization" (Lingard, 2007, p. 239).

This is not only analytically and empirically problematic, but it may also cause us to miss the possible roles that critical education and mobilizations around it can play in mediating and challenging the differential benefits that the crises are producing in many different locations. Any discussion of these issues needs to be grounded in the complex realities of various nations and regions and of the realities of the social, cultural, and educational movements and institutions of these nations and regions. Doing less than that means that we all too often simply throw slogans at problems rather than facing the hard realities of what needs to be done—and what is being done now.

Global Crises, Social Justice, and Education seeks to intervene into the ways we understand all this by getting more specific. And it seeks to intervene into the just as serious issue of what committed educators and other cultural activists can do to counter the relations of dominance and subordination that are currently having such tragic effects in so many countries.

Four specific areas have been selected: the United States, Japan, Israel/Palestine, and Mexico. Each has become a center of global crisis and each has shown the effects of neoconservative and neoliberal transformations and how identifiable people are being oppressed and marginalized. But as I noted earlier, the book is not content to simply critically analyze the crises and their effects in education, although that is indeed important. We also want to focus specifically on the ways in which critical and democratic educational and social movements and activists have sought to fight back.

Let me now say more about the areas and the reasons behind their choice.

1. The first case to be examined is the United States and the ways in which global economic and ideological forces have both led to fundamental changes in our definitions of important knowledge, literacy practices, and values in education *and* have provided spaces where serious counter-hegemonic educational work can be and is being done.
2. The second is Japan and the current reconstruction of educational policies and practices so that they support conservative nationalist impulses and favor the expressed needs of capital to impose neoliberal versions of marketization and weaker public power. Much of this set of neoliberal and neoconservative "reforms" has actually been borrowed from the United States and England. Yet these reforms have also opened up spaces for the rebirth of critically democratic movements around education.
3. The third example is Israel/Palestine with its status as a fault line of international conflicts and the struggles both over economic, political, and cultural autonomy and over a process of schooling that represents the possibility of diverse communities participating in addressing a just and shared solution to the social, cultural, and national conflicts in that region.
4. The fourth example is Mexico and the continuing attempts by social movements, especially by women's communities, to build community-based popular education at a local level that would counter the growing encroachment of neoliberal policies at all levels of society throughout Latin America. The growth of such popular education movements has been striking. They provide significant insights into what can be done.

These examples have been chosen for specific reasons. Many books on globalization and its influences on education are surveys of the general nature of the effects. Or they attempt to deal with a very large number of places, thereby risking making overly general statements about what is happening in each of these places and making all too general statements about what is possible to achieve to interrupt dominant power relations inside and outside of education. Many of these have been and are valuable books, but they do not push us far enough in terms of how these crises actually play out on the ground. And, even more importantly, they often do not go into enough detail on contradictory dynamics that may be emerging, on what can be done, and on what is actually now being done in education to act back against dominant neoliberal and neoconservative policies and practices. The reader, hence, is left with romantic hope perhaps, but with few concrete examples and strategies that may make a lasting difference.

I do not want to overstate these points, however. There are powerful examples that specify more critical moments and processes, of course, with the work of both Luis Armando Gandin on the justly well-known reforms in Porto Alegre, Brazil (see, e.g., Apple et al., 2003; Gandin, 2006) and Mario Novelli's discussion of the ways in which trade union activism led to critical learning and new identities in Columbia (Novelli, 2007) being among the more important. But the general point still remains.

These are not inconsequential issues, for they speak to unstated imperial assumptions that need to be challenged. One of the serious problems of learning from the experiences that have been tried outside of ones' home, so to speak, is that the all too usual brief treatments require authors to use considerable space providing relevant background information before getting to the core of the analyses. Constraints such as these and others often leave us with less than sufficient space to critically analyze both the situation and how it might be interrupted. This forces many critical authors to omit some of the key contextual information or, worse, to compromise on the depth and quality of our analyses. By allowing each analysis included in this volume more space than normally given in conventional books (and even in critically oriented journals), the volume challenges an unspoken mechanism in English-language publishing in critical education, one that at times has served to exclude the kinds of nuanced and careful treatments of educational struggles in other parts of the world. In this pattern, instead of acting to interrupt dominance, the crucial process of learning about those places where "our history occurred, and still occurs, outside our borders" is then itself interrupted (see Takayama, 2009). This is more than a little unfortunate.

Taking these challenges seriously is the task of *Global Crises, Social Justice, and Education*. Each of the four examples engages in a powerful and detailed critical analysis of what is happening in these varied areas and provides an equally compelling critical portrayal of the educational work that is being and can be done to interrupt dominance in a time of neoliberal and neo-conservative hegemony.

The analysis of the United States provides an example of an increasingly diverse society, one where major economic changes and the realities of multiculturalism, "race," "diaspora," and immigration play crucial roles, as does the fact that even with such policies as "No Child Left Behind," there is relatively weak central governmental control over education. Economic transformations, the creation of both paid and casualized and often racialized labor markets that are increasingly unequal, demands for new worker identities and skills—and all of this in a time of severe economic crisis—are having profound effects. The emerging structures of dominance and the role of movements around and inside education in partly interrupting these realities can give us crucial elements of how we might think about similar movements in other sites throughout the world—always remembering, of course, that we need to be very cautious of seeing the movements and struggles in other sites through taken-for-granted "parochial eyes" that center the Northern and Western gaze (Appadurai, 1996; Lingard, 2007).

Japan provides a different kind of example. Economic crisis, growing neoconservative and ultra-nationalist tendencies, strong central governmental control over education, and a somewhat more homogeneous society not only mean that dominance will be embodied in different ways (see, e.g., Nozaki, 2008). All of this also makes for a different set of movements and possibilities of counter-hegemonic challenges in education, possibilities that can provide important lessons on what can be done in those places where there is strong state control over education. But here, we do not wish to be romantic. As many of these chapters will show, the fact that there are possibilities does not at all guarantee that these possibilities can be acted upon; nor does it guarantee that they will last. Lasting transformations are *not* automatic. They require the formation of organized movements both nationally and internationally to support them against what will undoubtedly be concerted and equally organized attacks on demands for person rights in all of our institutions, including educational institutions.

In Israel/Palestine, the fault lines are very visible—and even more visible given the recent invasion of Gaza by Israeli armed forces. A history of severe tensions, occupation, expulsion, economic crises, being at the center of international disputes as well as national ones, and an educational system that is not only differentially based on one's ethnic, religious, and national identity but is also justifiably seen as a symbol of domination by many people—all of this creates even more difficult conditions for critically democratic educational work. But there are partial interruptions at the level of policy and practice there as well. If it is possible to build more critically democratic educational movements and institutions there, this can give us hope in other areas that now may look nearly hopeless. Here again, we are not romantic about this. Oppressive conditions, hegemonic power, the state's struggle for legitimacy and control, the "orientalization" of populations (Said, 1978), confinement, a racialization of state policy, murderous acts—these are not things that necessarily allow progressive educational institutions and practices to be built and defended.

And finally, Mexico—and especially rural Mexico—allows us to see how the crisis in local communities caused by a history of racialization and gendered inequalities and by the importation of neoliberal economic policies has had a profound impact on people's lives and futures in nearly all of their institutions. Yet, here too social movements among women's groups and indigenous and poor people in particular have established counter-hegemonic cultural and popular educational possibilities in civil society that have had important effects and run against the tide of neoliberal restructuring. As Hardt and Negri (2000) argue, population flows, the fact that significant portions of the world proletariat are now increasingly forced to be mobile, given the global economy and the growing immiseration that is so oppressive in nations throughout the world, and similar equally oppressive conditions, not only have powerful negative effects. These conditions also create spaces and movements for powerful counter-hegemonic activity both in the "center" and the "periphery." The analysis of popular educational movements in Mexico points this out quite clearly.

That the focus in this section of the book is on women is crucial in another way. In some of the critical literature, there seems to be an unstated assumption that class politics and labor conflicts are the driving engines of possible transformations. Gender and race are seen as partly epiphenomenal or as totally explained by class antagonisms. Class *is* indeed important, something I have argued for years. But the relatively autonomous dynamics of gender and race and their intersections with—not ultimately merging into or reducing to—class relations needs to be made an absolutely central part of any serious critical analysis (see Apple, 2000; Apple & Buras, 2006; Fraser, 1997; Gillborn, 2008; Leonardo, 2009; Rege, 2003; Stambach, 2000), as do the dynamics associated with postcolonial realities and struggles (see, e.g., Young, 2003).

Of course, there are those who would reject this more integrative approach, who believe that there is only one way a critical scholar/activist can be legitimately critical. For them, an approach that seeks to deal respectfully with and learn from critical theories and resources from multiple sources and multiple critical traditions is misguided. For me, however, and for all of the authors in this book, the key is to heed Fraser's absolutely imperative call for a politics of redistribution and a politics of recognition in ways that *do not interrupt* each other (Fraser, 1997). Such an approach, one in which one learns respectfully from each other and respectfully disagrees when necessary, is not an example of losing one's political soul. Indeed, as I have said before, while we need to be very cautious about theories that turn the world into simply discourses and that fly above the gritty materialities of real life, we are not in a church so we should not be worried about heresy (Apple, 1999, 2006). The key is the relationship between one's nuanced understanding and one's concrete political/educational action— and a willingness to build alliances and participate in the social agendas of other groups who suffer from the structures of this society.[2] This will require using theoretical/political resources that are varied, but still intensely political and committed.

By combining serious critical analyses of "the lay of the land" and the ideological terrain in different places where neoliberal and neoconservative policies are having profound effects, with the equally serious work of uncovering the concrete efforts of real people in real educational institutions and movements, the book helps to answer two of the most crucial questions facing educators and activists today: What do the realities that make it so hard to change education look like? And, what are the things we as educators and community members can do to alter these realities?

Facing Reality

Before we go further, however, it is important to face reality, both in terms of the ways many educators, even many progressives who say that they are committed to social justice in education, misrecognize the nature of educational reform and in terms of the daily lives of millions upon millions of people throughout the world.

Let us be honest. Much of the literature on educational reform, including some progressive literature, exists in something of a vacuum. It fails to place schooling sufficiently in its social and political context, thereby evacuating any serious discussion of why schooling in so many nations plays the complex roles that it does. Class and gender relations, racializing dynamics and structures, political economy, postcolonial struggles, and the connections between the state and civil society, for example, are sometimes hard to find.

But this absence is not the more mainstream literature's only problem. It is all too often romantic, assuming both that education can drive economic transformations and that reforming schools by only focusing on the schools themselves is sufficient. Or it limits our attention only to schools, thereby cutting us off from powerful interventions made in educational movements in communities among oppressed people. The naïveté of these positions is not only ahistorical; but it also acts as a conceptual block that prevents us from focusing on the real social, ideological, and economic conditions to which education has a dialectical and profoundly intricate set of connections (Anyon, 2005). A concern for social justice may then become more rhetorical than its proponents would like.

One of the most important steps in understanding what this means is to reposition oneself to see the world as it looks like from below, not above. Another step is to think internationally, to not only see the world from below, but to see the social world *relationally*.[3] In essence, this requires that we understand that in order for there to be a "below" in one nation, this usually requires that there be an "above" both in that nation and in those nations with which it is connected in the global political economy. Indeed, this demand that educators think relationally and face the realities of the global political, economic, and cultural context has been one of the generative impulses behind the growth of critical analyses of the relationship between globalization and education in the first place (Apple, Kenway, & Singh, 2005).

In *Cultural Politics and Education* (Apple, 1996), I spend a good deal of time discussing the relationship among "cheap French fries," the internationalization of the production of farm commodities, and the production of inequalities inside and outside of education. I focus on the connections between the lack of schools, health care, decent housing, and similar kinds of things in one particular Asian nation—all of which lead to immense immiseration—and the constant pressure to drive down the cost of labor in the imperial center. My basic point is that the connections between the exploitation of identifiable groups of people in the "Third World" and the demand for cheap commodities—in this case potatoes—may not be readily visible, but they are none the less real and extremely damaging.

Powerful descriptions of these relations are crucial and, as conditions worsen, some deeply committed scholars are bearing witness to these realities in compelling ways. Perhaps one particularly powerful author's work can serve as an example. If ever there was a doubt in anyone's mind about the growth of these truly distressing conditions, Mike Davis's volume *Planet of Slums* (2006) makes this reality crystal clear. At the same time, Davis also powerfully illuminates both the extent of, and what it means to live (exist is a better word) in, the immiserating conditions created by our need for such things as the "cheap French fries" that I pointed to. Let me say more about Davis's arguments, since many of them stand at the very root of a more adequate understanding of the realities that a vast number of people face throughout the world.

For example, I can think of few books that indict the development policies of the World Bank and the IMF as powerfully as *Planet of Slums* does. And it does this not simply by rhetorically challenging the economic, housing, ecological, and other policies that are advanced by such international bodies and by dominant groups within the "less developed" world. Rather, Davis draws together empirical and historical evidence that demonstrates time and again not only the negative effects of dominant policies, but also—given the realities of poor peoples' lives—*why* such policies cannot succeed (see also Apple, Au, & Gandin, 2009; Robertson & Dale, 2009). And he does this by placing all of these proposals for reform directly into the contradictory necessities of daily life in the increasingly large and growing slums throughout the "less developed" world. As you will see later on in *Global Crises, Social Justice, and Education*, like Davis a critical focus on institutions such as the World Bank will be a core element in a number of the discussions.

One third of the global urban population now lives in slums. Even more staggering is the fact that over 78 percent of urbanites in the least developed countries lives in slums (Davis, 2006, p. 23). The economic crisis in these slums is experienced by the people living there in ways that are extraordinarily powerful. Rather than thinking about "jobs" in the usual sense of that term, it is better to think of "informal survivalism" as the major mode of existence in a majority of Third World cities (Davis, 2006, p. 178).

Echoing the situation I described at the beginning of this section, Davis is clear on what is happening throughout the Third World. "As local safety nets disappeared, poor farmers became increasingly vulnerable to any exogenous shock: drought, inflation, rising interest rates, or falling commodity prices. Or illness: an estimated 60 percent of Cambodian small peasants who sell their land and move to the city are forced to do so by medical debts" (Davis, 2006, p. 15). This understanding allows him to show the dilemmas and struggles that people must face every day, dilemmas and struggles that should force us to recognize that, for the poor, certain words that we consider nouns are better thought of as *verbs*.

Take "housing" for example. It is not a thing. Rather it is the result of a complex and ongoing—and often dangerous—trade-off among contradictory needs. Thus, the urban poor who live in the slums "have to solve a complex equation as they try to optimize housing cost, tenure security, quality of shelter, journey to work, and . . . personal safety." And while the very worst situation "is a . . . bad location without [government] services or security" (Davis, 2006, p. 29), in many instances these people have no choice. As Davis documents, the role of the IMF in this process is crucial to point out. Its policies have constantly created these conditions and have made them considerably worse over time (Davis, 2006, pp. 66–69).

If all of this is so visible to Davis and many other committed people, why do the realities and very real complexities in this situation seem to be so readily ignored by governments, international agencies, and as Davis also demonstrates, a number of NGOs? Part of the explanation is that many Third World cities (and diasporic and poor populations of cities in the First World as well) exist in something like an epistemological fog, one that is sometimes willfully opaque. Most governments know least about the slums, about the housing in them, about the services that they need and (almost always) don't get, and so on. The lack of knowledge here provides an epistemological veil (Davis, 2006, p. 42). What goes on under the veil is a secret that must be kept from "public view." To know is to be subject to demands. Thus, the very *lack* of Foucault's panopticon (Foucault, 1977) constitutes a form of control. This is a political and conceptual intervention that is not overtly made by Davis, but it is a significant one. I hope that it causes some of those within the postmodern educational community who are uncritically wedded to Foucault as a theorist of new forms of control to raise questions about whether the *absence of knowledge* and the absence of the panoptican may be equally as important when we are talking about massive structural global inequalities such as those being discussed here.

It is important not to give the impression that the utter degradation that is being visited upon millions of people like the ones both Davis and I have pointed to—and much more could be said about the realities of poor people in rural areas—has led only to a politics of simple acceptance. Indeed, one of the major impulses behind the chapters in *Global Crises, Social Justice, and Education* is the agency of oppressed people inside and outside of education.

As Davis shows in his own accounts, the "informal proletariat" of these slums is decidedly *not* passive:

> Even within a single city, slum populations can support a bewildering variety of responses to structural neglect and deprivation, ranging from charismatic churches and prophetic cults to ethnic militias, street gangs, neoliberal NGOs, and revolutionary social movements. But if there is no monolithic subject or unilateral trend in the global slum, there are nonetheless myriad acts of resistance. Indeed, the future of human solidarity depends upon the militant refusal of the urban poor to accept their terminal marginality within global capitalism.
>
> (Davis, 2006, p. 202)

Such "militant refusal" will play a key role in the chapters in this book as well, as we look at the varied ways in which spaces of resistance are created and are taken up. Some of these will be in the formation of schools themselves, some in the formation of counter-hegemonic movements, and some in popular mobilizations that act back in daily life in local communities.

Davis's discussion of the ways in which resistance operates and its organizations and forms is thoughtful. It helps us think through the manifold and sometimes contradictory voices and identities taken up by subaltern groups (Apple & Buras, 2006). This is an absolutely crucial point. There has been a tendency to overly romanticize the agency of those whose lives are filled with "worlds of pain." One need not fall back into the political and conceptual traps associated with theories of "false consciousness" to understand that, as Gramsci and others have reminded us, there are always elements of both good and bad sense in subaltern consciousness (see, e.g., Apple, 2006; Gramsci, 1971; see also Pedroni, 2007). Without a better understanding of such contradictory elements, we are left with rhetorical politics, ones that are all too simple, given the transformations that global capitalism continues to undergo. Too many analyses from the left have been either reductive or romantic—or as I noted earlier have substituted rhetorical slogans for a seriously detailed analysis of the material and ideological conditions under which people actually live. This has been especially damaging in education, where it has proven to be distressingly easy to sloganize about a "return to *the* Marxist tradition" (as if there weren't various traditions, tendencies, and arguments within it) or a similar "purification," while at the same time eschewing the kinds of empirical and historical work that makes Davis's and others' efforts so compelling (Apple, Au, & Gandin, 2009).

All this does not mean that *Planet of Slums* is without faults. While empirically rich and synthetic, Davis's discussion is too brief to do more than suggest what this means for political and cultural mobilizations and struggle. It also does not specifically focus on education. Yet, it does confirm others' analyses of the limits and possibilities of subaltern agency (Apple & Buras, 2006). While his book is not a conscious response to Spivak's well-known question "Can the subaltern speak?" (Spivak, 1988), it does provide a number of insights into where and how we should look to recognize the agency that does exist. Such agency may be partial and even contradictory, but it is nearly always present. As I noted, discussing and documenting this is one of the tasks that we hope to take up in this volume.

Having said this, I do not want to give the impression that the conditions that *Planet of Slums* documents means that we can and should ignore education's role in challenging such immiseration in cities and rural areas. Although those reformers and economists wedded to human capital theories would do well to read Davis carefully, this does not mean that there is nothing that can be done. Indeed, as the aforementioned example of Porto Alegre in Brazil so clearly shows, when deeply connected to a larger project of critical social transformation, educational transformations can and do take on crucial roles in altering the relationship between the state and local communities, in the relationship between state and civil society, in radically challenging the unequal distribution of services, and in helping to create new activist identities for slum dwellers, and in using local resources to build new and very creative forms of oppositional literacy (see Apple et al., 2003; Apple & Buras, 2006; Fisher, 2009). Combining Davis's thoroughly unromantic picture of the conditions, struggles, and creative resilience of the poor with a recognition of the ways in which schools such as those in Porto Alegre can sometimes serve as arenas for building toward larger social transformations that has been done in previous volumes (see Apple et al., 2003; Apple, Au, & Gandin 2009; Apple, Ball, & Gandin, 2010; Apple & Buras, 2006) can provide us with some of the tools we need to go forward.[4] We hope to do the same here.

My discussion in this part of the introductory chapter has largely been on the Third World and the "Global South." But even given the immensity of the problems that are occurring in the slums to which Davis bears such eloquent witness, we also need to focus a good deal of our attention on what is (perhaps too arrogantly) called the "First World." We need to do this for a number of reasons. First, there is ever-growing immiseration within this part of society, stimulated by exploitative economic conditions and the international divisions of labor and border crossing populations that accompany this, by the move toward what have been called "knowledge economies" and new definitions of what are "required skills,"[5] and of who does and does not have them (Lauder, Brown, Dillabough, & Halsey, 2006), by the severe economic crisis so many nations are experiencing, and by the fact that in essence "the Empire has come home" (Centre for Contemporary Cultural Studies, 1982).

Second, as I mentioned earlier, we need to think relationally. There are extremely important connections between crises in the "center" and those on the "periphery." Of course, even using such words to describe these regions is to reproduce a form of the "imperial gaze" (see, for example, Bhabha, 1994; Said, 1993). Yet, not to focus on what is too easily called the center, can lead us to forget something else. Not only do economic, political, and ideological crises in those nations "at the center" have disastrous consequences in other nations, but the more privileged lives of *some* people in these more advantaged nations also require that other people living there pay the costs in the physical and emotional labor that is so necessary to maintain that advantage.

As Pauline Lipman has clearly demonstrated, the advantages of the affluent in global cities depend on the availability of low paid—and gendered and raced—"others" who are "willing" to do the labor that underpins the affluent lifestyles of those higher up on the economic ladder (Lipman, 2004). No analysis of the realities of schooling in cities in the United States or of the relations between cities, suburbs, and rural areas in the United States can be complete without an understanding of how schooling is implicated in these relations. And this too serves as a guiding thread behind our analysis here.

Each of the chapters included in *Global Crises, Social Justice, and Education* is guided by a recognition of the tense relations between global and local, affluence and impoverishment, oppressive economic, social, and cultural conditions, and resistance to them. Each is committed to employing serious critical approaches in both understanding these conditions and interrupting them. And all of them want to employ a range of critical theoretical, historical, political, and empirical resources to do this.

The Uses of "Powerful" Theory

In order to fully understand this, I need to say more about the word "theoretical" in the previous paragraph and its place both in critical work and in this book. In so doing, I want to ground this section of the introductory chapter in what may seem a somewhat odd, and partly auto-biographical, way. When I was being trained as a teacher (I use the word trained consciously), I went to a small state teachers college at night. Nearly every course that I took had a specific suffix—"for teachers." I took "Philosophy for Teachers," "World History for Teachers," "Mathematics for Teachers," "Physics for Teachers," and so on. The assumption seemed to be that since I had attended inner city schools in a very poor community—a community that had been rocked by economic decline caused by the mobility both of capital and of its factories as they moved to nations where labor was less organized and could be more completely exploited—and was going back to teach in those same inner city schools, I needed little more than a cursory understanding of the disciplines of knowledge and the theories that stood behind them. Theory was for those who were above people such as me.

There were elements of good sense in this. After all, when I had been taught particular kinds of theory both at that small state teachers college and even at times later on in my graduate studies, it was all too often totally disconnected from the realities of impoverishment, racism, class dynamics, gendered realities, decaying communities and schools, cultural struggles, and the lives of teachers and community members. But the elements of bad sense, of being intellectually marginalized because of my class background and of being positioned as a "less than," were palpable. For me and many others who grew up poor and who wanted to more fully understand both our own experiences and why schooling, the economy, and indeed the world itself, looked the way they did, the search for adequate explanations became crucial. Learning and using *powerful* theory, especially powerful *critical* theories, in essence, became a counter-hegemonic act. Getting better at such theories, employing them to more fully comprehend the ways in which differential power actually worked, using them to see where alternatives could be and are being built in daily life, and ultimately doing all this in what we hoped were non-elitist ways gave us two things.

First, all of this made the realities of dominance both sensible—and at times depressing. But, second, it also provided a sense of freedom and possibility, especially when it was connected to the political and educational actions in which many of us were also engaged. These same experiences could be and are spoken of by members of many other groups who have been marginalized by race, by sex/gender, by class, by colonialism, and by an entire array of other forms of differential power.

I say all this at the outset of this section because the chapters included in this book bring back these memories to me and remind me of some of the reasons why critical theoretical, historical, political, and empirical resources are so essential to creating a richer and more detailed understanding of the society in which we live and the role of education in it. This same sensibility of making sense of dominance and of seeing possibilities guides the authors in this book.

First Principles

But how are these theoretical, historical, political, and empirical resources to be mobilized? There are some key principles that are significant in this regard. Over the past four decades, I and many others have argued that education must be seen as a political act. We have suggested that in order to do this, as I stated earlier in this chapter, we need to think *relationally*. That is, understanding education requires that we situate it back both into the unequal relations of power in the larger society and into the realities of dominance and subordination—and the conflicts—that are generated by these relations. Take the issues surrounding the curriculum, for example. Rather than simply asking whether students have mastered a particular subject matter and have done well on our all too common tests, we should ask a different set of questions: Whose knowledge is this? How did it become "official"? What is the relationship between this knowledge and the ways in which it is taught and evaluated and who has cultural, social, and economic capital in this society? Who benefits from these definitions of legitimate knowledge and from the ways schooling and this society are organized and who does not? How do what are usually seen as "reforms" actually work? What can we do as critical educators, researchers, and activists to change existing educational and social inequalities and to create curricula and teaching that are more socially just (Apple, 1995; Apple, 1996; Apple, 2000; Apple & Beane, 2007; Au, 2009; Buras, 2008; Gutstein, 2006; Lipman, 2004; Valenzuela, 2005)?

At the very root of these concerns is a simple principle. In order to understand and act on education in its complicated connections to the larger society, we must engage in something else I noted earlier, the process of *repositioning*. That is, we need to see the world through the eyes of the dispossessed and act against the ideological and institutional processes and forms that reproduce oppressive conditions. This repositioning involves a commitment to both political and cultural policies and practices that embody the principles of critical education; but it also has generated a large body of critical scholarship and theory that has led to a fundamental restructuring of what the roles of research and of the researcher are (Apple, Au, & Gandin, 2009; Smith, 1999; Weis & Fine, 2004). These roles have been defined in many ways, but perhaps the best descriptions center around what the Italian political activist and theorist Antonio Gramsci (1971) called the *organic intellectual* and the cultural and political historian Russell Jacoby (2000) termed the *public intellectual* (see also Burawoy, 2005).

The restructured role of the researcher—one who sees her or his task as thinking as rigorously and critically as possible about the relations between the policies and practices that are taken for granted in education and the larger sets of dominant economic, political, and cultural relations, and then connects this to action with and by social movements—is crucial to what we are doing in this book. In order to more fully understand this, I need to say more about the specific tasks of the critical scholar/activist in education. Although some of these arguments are developed in more detail elsewhere (see Apple, Au, & Gandin, 2009), detailing the complexities of this role will enable us to see more clearly the contribution that *Global Crises, Social Justice, and Education* makes.

The Tasks of the Critical Scholar/Activist in Education

In general, there are nine tasks in which critical analysis (and the critical analyst) in education must engage.

1. It must "bear witness to negativity."[6] That is, one of its primary functions is to illuminate the ways in which educational policy and practice are connected to the relations of exploitation and domination—and to struggles against such relations—in the larger society.[7]

2. In engaging in such critical analyses, it also must point to contradictions and to spaces of possible action. Thus, its aim is to critically examine current realities with a conceptual/political framework that emphasizes the spaces in which more progressive and counter-hegemonic actions can, or do, go on. This is an absolutely crucial step, since otherwise our research can simply lead to cynicism or despair.

3. At times, this also requires a broadening of what counts as "research." Here I mean acting as "secretaries" to those groups of people and social movements who are now engaged in challenging existing relations of unequal power or in what elsewhere has been called "nonreformist reforms," a term that has a long history in critical sociology and critical educational studies (Apple, 1995) and one that also stands behind some of the thoughtful discussions in the book you are reading here. This is exactly the task that was taken on in the thick descriptions of critically democratic school practices in *Democratic Schools* (Apple & Beane, 2007) and in the critically supportive descriptions of the transformative reforms such as the Citizen School and participatory budgeting in Porto Alegre, Brazil (see Apple et al., 2003; Gandin, 2006).

4. When Gramsci (1971) argued that one of the tasks of a truly counter-hegemonic education was not to throw out "elite knowledge" but to reconstruct its form and content so that it served genuinely progressive social needs, he provided a key to another role that "organic" and "public" intellectuals might play. Thus, we should not be engaged in a process of what might be called "intellectual suicide." That is, there are serious intellectual (and pedagogic) skills in dealing with the histories and debates surrounding the epistemological, political, and educational issues involved in justifying what counts as important knowledge and what counts as an effective and socially just education. These are not simple and inconsequential issues, and the practical and intellectual/political skills of dealing with them have been well developed. However, they can atrophy if they are not used. We can give back these skills by employing them to assist communities in thinking about this, learning from them, and engaging in the mutually pedagogic dialogues that enable decisions to be made in terms of both the short-term and long-term interests of dispossessed peoples (see Borg & Mayo, 2007; Burawoy, 2005; Freire, 1970).

5. In the process, critical work has the task of keeping traditions of radical and progressive work alive. In the face of organized attacks on the "collective memories" of difference and critical social movements, attacks that make it increasingly difficult to retain academic and social legitimacy for multiple critical approaches that have proven so valuable in countering dominant narratives and relations, it is absolutely crucial that these traditions be kept alive, renewed and, when necessary, criticized for their conceptual, empirical, historical, and political silences or limitations.

This involves being cautious of reductionism and essentialism and asks us to pay attention to what Fraser has called both the politics of redistribution and the politics of recognition (Fraser, 1997; see also Anyon et al., 2009). This includes not only keeping theoretical, empirical, historical, and political traditions alive but, very importantly, extending and (supportively) criticizing them. And it also involves keeping alive the dreams, utopian visions, and "non-reformist reforms" that are so much a part of these radical traditions (Apple, 1995; Jacoby, 2005; Teitelbaum, 1993).

6. Keeping such traditions alive and also supportively criticizing them when they are not adequate to deal with current realities cannot be done unless we ask "For whom are we keeping them alive?" and "How and in what form are they to be made available?" All of the things I have mentioned above in this taxonomy of tasks require the relearning or development and use of varied or new skills of working at many levels with multiple groups. Thus, journalistic and media skills, academic and popular skills, and the ability to speak to very different audiences are increasingly crucial (Apple, 2006). This requires us to learn how to speak in different registers and to say important things in ways that do not require that the audience or reader do all of the work.

7. Critical educators must also *act* in concert with the progressive social movements that their work supports or in movements against the rightist assumptions and policies they critically analyze. This is another reason that scholarship in critical education implies becoming an "organic" or "public" intellectual. One must participate in and give one's expertise to movements surrounding efforts to transform both a politics of redistribution and a politics of recognition. It also implies learning from these social movements (Anyon, 2005) and being expressly open to criticism of one's taken-for-granted perspectives from movements outside of one's national boundaries. This means that the role of the "unattached intelligentsia" (Mannheim, 1936), someone who "lives on the balcony" (Bakhtin, 1968), is not an appropriate model. As Bourdieu (2003, p. 11) reminds us, for example, our intellectual efforts are crucial, but they "cannot stand aside, neutral and indifferent, from the struggles in which the future of the world is at stake."

8. Building on the points made in the previous paragraph, the critical scholar/activist has another role to play. She or he needs to act as a deeply committed mentor, as someone who demonstrates through her or his life what it means to be *both* an excellent researcher and a committed member of a society that is scarred by persistent

inequalities. She or he needs to show how one can blend these two roles together in ways that may be tense, but still embody the dual commitments to exceptional and socially committed research and participating in movements whose aim is interrupting dominance.

9. Finally, participation also means using the privilege one has as a scholar/activist. That is, each of us needs to make use of one's privilege to open the spaces at universities and elsewhere for those who are not there, for those who do not now have a voice in that space and in the "professional" sites to which, being in a privileged position, you have access. This can be seen, for example, in the history of the "activist-in-residence" program at the University of Wisconsin Havens Center for Social Structure and Social Change, where committed activists in various areas (the environment, indigenous rights, housing, labor, racial disparities, education, and so on) were brought in to teach and to connect our academic work with organized action against dominant relations. Or it can be seen in a number of Women's Studies programs and Indigenous, Aboriginal, and First Nation Studies programs that historically have involved activists in these communities as active participants in the governance and educational programs of these areas at universities.

The list is not meant to be a final one. But it suggests a range of responsibilities with which I and the other authors involved in this book are deeply concerned. Of course, no one person can do all of these things simultaneously. These are *collective* responsibilities, ones that demand a cooperative response. But these varied tasks are constantly on the minds of the authors included here.

Some Final Thoughts

As you will see, the chapters that follow engage in a critical dialogue with a complex reality. Because of this, they employ political and theoretical resources from a range of critical traditions to illuminate the importance of the connections between economic and cultural/ideological struggles, the state, the relations among imperial powers, the politics of policy "borrowing," and the ways in which these things can be better understood and interrupted. They also think *strategically* about how existing ideological affiliations can be changed, about how issues can be disarticulated from one set of political positions and rearticulated to another and sometimes more progressive one, about the formation of new counter-hegemonic alliances, about working across differences (see, e.g., Apple, 2006). In doing so, they take seriously the point I made earlier of thinking both redistribution and recognition simultaneously. But they also are grounded in something that Ricardo Rosa has articulated. As he has said, "For new structures to come into being and new political engagements to be nurtured, it is necessary that we have a language to bring it into existence – a lexicon of change, so to speak" (Rosa, 2008, p. 3).

These languages speak to the dialectic of old and new, of residual and emergent economic, political, ideological, and educational forms (Williams, 1977), and of the constant struggles both to more fully understand the forces of dominance and to keep them from preventing or destroying an education worthy of its name. As this book shows, these struggles for what I have elsewhere called *thick democracy* occur both inside and outside of schools (Apple, 2006). They signify the continuation of what Raymond Williams (1961) so felicitously called "the long revolution," the ongoing movements in so many nations to create a vision of radical democracy that responds to the best in us. Again in Rosa's words:

> Radical democracy is not just born out of our option to participate in the ordinary political infrastructure. It is a process involving the ongoing democratization of civil society, the constant interrogation of how exclusion on the grounds of multiple markers occurs even when progressive projects are unfolding, and the problematizing of conditions that fail to call into question the various ways in which economic systems undermine political cultures. The term encodes democracy as unfinished. Educators need more exposure to such language given the reality of schools as highly undemocratic spheres where various oppressive ideologies converge in front of a captive audience. A democratic political system cannot come to fruition if the institutions of that society are undemocratic, anti-democratic, or fail to (re)create the structures and conditions that lead to further democratization. Democracy flourishes when democratic cultures are the norm.
>
> (Rosa, 2008, p. 4)

Both I and the other authors included in this book are certainly aware that the regions discussed in what follows cannot represent the immense complexities of education and its connections to the relations of dominance and subordination and to the struggles against these relations throughout the world. Nor can these chapters engage with all of the ways in which radically democratic movements and, say, cultural mobilizations can and do participate in these struggles (see, e.g., Boler, 2008). The inclusion of popular education movements speaks to some of these issues. Again, Rosa articulates this well:

The literature and examples of popular education help us under-stand how we may be able to step in institutions and remain con-nected to social movements outside and build new and more effective movements (particularly in the North). Exposure to this literature and language is sorely lacking in schools of education. Instead, too great a focus is placed on reductionistic curriculum theory and practice, managerial discourses, and on the like. Political projects that are housed only inside schools too often translate to forms of "furniture moving" and "window dressing" capable of winning small battles, but unable to sustain long term liberatory structures.

(Rosa, 2008, p. 3)

Let me say one final thing. This book was held back from publication for a number of months because of the tragic situation in Israel/Palestine. Given the volatility of this region and the hardening of positions, and above all the invasion of Gaza and the continuation of repressive policies and violence, we needed to take stock of what could be said. After waiting for months, we had to go forward and made the decision that the chapter on Israel/Palestine still needed to be published. This reminded us of one thing that is absolutely essential in a book such as this. Things are in constant motion. Overly romantic understandings of "solutions" that keep hegemonic powers in place and that continue processes of marginalization and misery are exactly that—romantic.

A key here is what I mentioned in my taxonomy of tasks in this chapter: *non-reformist reforms*. Reforms—such as building and defending schools that can be jointly controlled by all of the people involved and that may partly interrupt dominance—should be engaged in *if and only if* they expand the space of further interruptions. Given the ongoing situation in Israel/Palestine, it remains to be seen whether the examples given in that chapter are simply "reformist" or whether than can indeed provide spaces for more powerful possibilities and transformations.

The ongoing relations among education and dominance/subordination and the struggles against these relations are exactly that, the subject of struggles. Thus, this book cannot be the "final word" on any of the areas we discuss. Indeed, we would be distressed if that were the case. The constant attempts by real people in real movements in real economic, political, and ideological conditions to challenge their circumstances—and the ensuing actions by dominant groups to regain their hegemonic leadership and their control of this terrain—makes any statement about a final conclusion meaningless. What we can do is to help ensure that these movements and counter-hegemonic activities in education are made public and that we honestly ask ourselves what our roles are in supporting the struggles toward the long revolution.

Much more needs to be done than one book can accomplish, of course. What we do hope, however, is that the critical theoretical, educational, and political resources employed here can "bear witness," illuminate spaces for counter-hegemonic work, and act as secretaries for the tendencies, movements, and people who demand something better both for themselves and for their children in a world filled with both pain and possibility.

Notes

1   The journal *Globalization, Societies, and Education* is a particularly valuable resource in this regard.
2   As I argue in *Educating the "Right" Way* (Apple, 2006), this is exactly what the Right did. Its ability to form alliances across differences and to understand that *every site counts* have been crucial to its success in many nations. In essence, the Right has often understood Gramsci's points about the necessity of "wars of position" much better than many on the Left.
3   Such relational understanding is also based in a recognition of the importance of Bourdieu's comment that "Intellectual life, like all other social spaces, is a home of nationalism and imperialism" (Bourdieu, 1999, p. 220).
4   Combining these analyses with the work that has been done on the powerful counter-hegemonic literacy practices that have been built in racialized and minoritized communities is also a very significant step. Maisha Fisher's critical investigations of this in the United States and the Caribbean are essential to this project. See Fisher (2009).
5   The concept of "skill" is not a neutral word. It is an ideological and political concept. For example, the work that women and minoritized people have historically done has had a much harder time being labeled as skilled labor.
6   I am aware that the idea of "bearing witness" has religious connotations, ones that are powerful in the West, but may be seen as a form of religious imperialism in other religious traditions. I still prefer to use it because of its powerful resonances with ethical discourses. But I welcome suggestions from, say, Muslim critical educators and researchers for alternative concepts that can call forth similar responses. I want to thank Amy Stambach for this point.
7   Here, exploitation and domination are technical not rhetorical terms. The former refers to economic relations, the structures of inequality, the control of labor, and the distribution of resources in a society. The latter refers to the processes of representation and respect and to the ways in which people have identities imposed on them. These are analytic categories, of course, and are ideal types. Most oppressive conditions are partly a combination of the two. These map on to what Fraser (1997) calls the politics of redistribution and the politics of recognition.

References

Anyon, J. (2005). *Radical possibilities: Public policy, urban education, and a new social movement.* New York: Routledge.
Anyon, J., Dumas, M., Linville, D., Nolan, K., Perez, M., Tuck, E., and Weiss, J. (2009). *Theory and educational research: Toward critical social explanation.* New York: Routledge.
Appadurai, A. (1996). *Modernity at large.* Minneapolis: University of Minnesota Press.
Apple, M. W. (1995). *Education and power* (2nd ed.). New York: Routledge.
Apple, M. W. (1996). *Cultural politics and education.* New York: Teachers College Press.
Apple, M. W. (1999). *Power, meaning, and identity.* New York: Peter Lang.
Apple, M. W. (2000). *Official knowledge: Democratic education in a conservative age* (2nd ed.). New York: Routledge.
Apple, M. W. (2006). *Educating the "right" way: Markets, standards, God, and inequality* (2nd ed.). New York: Routledge.

Apple, M. W. (in press). Theory, research, and the critical scholar/activist, *Educational Researcher.*

Apple, M. W. & Beane, J. A. (Eds.). (2007). *Democratic schools: Lessons in powerful education* (2nd ed.). Portsmouth, NH: Heinemann.

Apple, M. W. & Buras, K. L. (Eds.). (2006). *The subaltern speak: Curriculum, power, and educational struggles.* New York: Routledge.

Apple, M. W., Au, W., & Gandin, L. A. (Eds.). (2009). *The Routledge international handbook of critical education.* New York: Routledge.

Apple, M. W., Ball, S., & Gandin, L. A. (Eds.). (2010). *The Routledge international handbook of sociology of education.* London: Routledge.

Apple, M. W., Kenway, J., & Singh. M. (Eds.). (2005). *Globalizing education: Policies, pedagogies, and politics.* New York: Peter Lang.

Apple, M. W., Aasen, P., Cho, M. K., Gandin, L. A., Olvier, A., Sung, Y-K., Tavares, H., & Wong, T-H. (2003). *The state and the politics of knowledge.* New York: Routledge.

Au, W. (2009). *Unequal by design: High-stakes testing and the standardization of inequality.* New York: Routledge.

Bakhtin, M. M. (1968). *Rabelais and his world* (H. Iswolsky, Trans.). Cambridge, MA: MIT Press.

Bhabha, H. (1994). *The location of culture.* New York: Routledge.

Boler, M. (Ed.). (2008). *Digital media and democracy: Tactics in hard times.* Cambridge, MA: MIT Press.

Borg, C. & Mayo, P. (Eds.). (2007). *Public intellectuals, radical democracy, and social movements.* New York: Peter Lang.

Bourdieu, P. (1999). The social conditions of the international circulation of ideas. In R. Shusterman (Ed.), *Bourdieu: A critical reader.* Oxford: Blackwell.

Bourdieu, P. (2003). *Firing back: Against the tyranny of the market 2.* New York: New Press.

Buras, K. L. (2008). *Rightist multiculturalism: Core lessons on neoconservative school reform.* New York: Routledge.

Burawoy, M. (2005). For public sociology. *British Journal of Sociology of Education*, 56, 259–294.

Burbules, N. & Torres, C. (Eds.). (2009). *Globalization and education: Critical perspectives* (2nd ed.). New York: Routledge.

Centre for Contemporary Cultural Studies. (1982). *The empire strikes back: Race and racism in 70s Britain.* London: Hutchinson.

Dale, R. & Robertson, S. (Eds.). (2009). *Globalisation and Europeanisation in education.* London: Symposium Books.

Davis, M. (2006). *Planet of slums.* New York: Verso.

Fisher, M. (2009). *Black literate lives: Historical and contemporary perspectives.* New York: Routledge.

Foucault, M. (1977). *Discipline and punish: The birth of the prison.* New York: Pantheon.

Fraser, N. (1997). *Justice interruptus.* New York: Routledge.

Freire, P. (1970). *Pedagogy of the oppressed.* New York: Continuum.

Gandin, L. A. (2006). Creating real alternatives to neoliberal policies in education: The citizen school project. In M. W. Apple & K. L. Buras (Eds.), *The subaltern speak: Curriculum, power, and educational struggles* (pp. 217–241). New York: Routledge.

Gandin, L. A. & Apple, M. W. (2003). Educating the state, democratizing knowledge: The citizen school project in Porto Alegre, Brazil. In M. W. Apple et al., *The state and the politics of knowledge* (pp. 193–219). New York: RoutledgeFalmer.

Gillborn, D. (2008). *Racism and education: Coincidence or conspiracy.* New York: Routledge.

Gramsci, A. (1971). *Selections from the prison notebooks* (Q. Hoare & G. N. Smith, Trans.). New York: International Publishers.

Gulson, K. & Symes, C. (Eds.). (2007). Knowing one's place: Educational theory, policy, and the spatial turn. In K. Gulson & C. Symes (Eds.), *Spatial theories of education: Policy and geography matters* (pp. 3–16). New York: Routledge.

Gutstein, E. (2006). *Reading and writing the world with mathematics.* New York: Routledge.

Hardt, M. & Negri, A. (2000). *Empire.* Cambridge, MA: Harvard University Press.

Jacoby, R. (2000). *The last intellectuals: American culture in the age of academe* (2nd ed.). New York: Basic Books.

Jacoby, R. (2005). *Picture imperfect: Utopian thought for an anti-utopian age.* New York: Columbia University Press.

Lauder, H., Brown, P., Dillabough, J., & Halsey, A. H. (Eds.). (2006). *Education, globalization and social change.* New York: Oxford University Press.

Leonardo, Z. (2009). *Race, whiteness, and education.* New York: Routledge.

Lingard, B. (2007). Deparochializing the study of education: Globalization and the research imagination. In K. Gulson & C. Symes (Eds.), *Spatial theories of education: Policy and geography matters* (pp. 233–250). New York: Routledge.

Lipman, P. (2004). *High stakes education: Inequality, globalization, and urban school reform.* New York: Routledge.

Mannheim, K. (1936). *Ideology and utopia.* New York: Harvest Books.

Novelli, M. (2007). Trade unions, strategic pedagogy and new spaces of engagement: Counter-knowledge economy insights from Columbia. In K. Gulson & C. Symes (Eds.), *Spatial theories of education: Policy and geography matters* (pp. 250-271). New York: Routledge.

Nozaki, Y. (2008). *War memory, nationalism, and education in post-war Japan.* New York: Routledge.

Pedroni, T. (2007). *Market matters: African American involvement in school voucher reform.* New York: Routledge.

Peters, M. (Ed.). (2005). *Education, globalization, and the state in the age of terrorism.* Boulder: Paradigm.

Rege, S. (Ed.). (2003). *Sociology of gender: The challenge of feminist sociological knowledge.* Thousand Oaks, CA: Sage.

Rhoads, R. & Torres, C. A. (Eds.). (2006). *The university, state, and market: The political economy of globalization in the Americas.* Stanford: Stanford University Press.

Robertson, S. & Dale, R. (2009). The World Bank, the IMF, and the possibilities of critical education. In M. W. Apple, W. Au., & L. A. Gandin (Eds.), *The Routledge international handbook of critical education* (pp. 23–35). New York: Routledge.

Rosa, R. (2008). Savage neoliberalism and subaltern responses, *Education Review,* 11, 1–17.

Rushdie, S. (1981). *Midnight's children.* New York: Knopf.

Said, E. (1978). *Orientalism.* New York: Pantheon.

Said, E. (1993). *Culture and imperialism.* New York: Vintage.

Santos, B. S. (2003). *Towards a counter-hegemonic globalisation.* Paper presented at the XXIV International Congress of the Latin American Studies Association, March, Dallas, USA.

Smith, L. T. (1999). *Decolonizing methodologies.* New York: Zed Books.

Spivak, G. C. (1988). Can the subaltern speak? In C. Nelson & L. Grossberg (Eds.), *Marxism and the interpretation of culture* (pp. 271–313). Urbana: University of Illinois Press.

Stambach, A. (2000). *Lessons from Mount Kilimanjaro: Schooling, community, and gender in East Africa.* New York: Routledge.

Takayama, K. (2009). Progressive struggle and critical educational scholarship in Japan: Toward the democratization of critical educational studies. In M. W. Apple, W. Au, & L. A. Gandin (Eds.), *The Routledge international handbook of critical education* (pp. 354–367). New York: Routledge.

Teitelbaum, K. (1993). *Schooling for good rebels.* Philadelphia, PA: Temple University Press.

Valenzuela, A. (Ed.). (2005). *Leaving children behind.* Albany: State University of New York Press.

Weis, L. M. & Fine, M. (2004). *Working method: Research and social justice.* New York: Routledge.

Williams, R. (1961). *The long revolution.* London: Chatto & Windus.

Williams, R. (1977). *Marxism and literature.* New York: Oxford University Press.

Young, R. (2003). *Postcolonialism.* New York: Oxford University Press.

CHAPTER 2

New Literacies and New Rebellions in the Global Age

ROSS COLLIN AND MICHAEL W. APPLE

I. Changing Times, Changing Literacies

Introduction

One of the great victories of capital[1] in recent times is its winning active consent among disparate publics for its account of globalization. In this "official" story, globalization is portrayed as the inevitable and irresistible process of corporate-led integration and reconstitution of world economies, cultures and political orders. Central to this process, goes the corporate narrative, is the emergence and expansion of a high-technology informational economy that, though disruptive of certain traditional social, cultural and economic practices, generates work that is more intellectually engaging (or at least more remunerative) than work in the industrial and agricultural eras. Schools figure prominently in particular versions of this story as sites where societies develop the human capital necessary for both the running of the informational economy and, relatedly, the steerage of the unfolding processes of globalization.

So dominant, so "natural," is this story of irresistible corporate-led globalization that even those sympathetic to the worldwide expansion (globalization) of social justice often refer to the resistance to corporate domination as the "anti-globalization movement." Taking a different tack, we work in this chapter to denaturalize corporate-led globalization and to examine particular struggles through which it was/is constructed, thereby broadening our conceptions of the possibilities for global movements that subordinate profits to people. As there exist multiple, evolving and often-contradictory dynamics of globalization in a range of fields, however, we endeavor to study globalization through a conjunctural analysis in which we situate current transformations of literacy and schooling in shifting economic and political spheres in the US and other advanced economies. Through this more focused analysis, we work to clarify how certain dynamics of globalization (e.g. pressures to restructure economies for informational labor) shape and are shaped by specific processes and practices (e.g. public schooling and literacy development).

We focus on literacy and schooling for a number of specific reasons. First, all too many analyses of globalization have remained at too general a level. Second, in many instances, practices of literacy and processes of schooling are functioning more and more as flows in important global networks and as means by which workers add or learn to add value in economies driven in powerful ways by the generation, assessment and application of new knowledge (see Apple, 1995; Carnoy, 2000; Castells, 1996; Hardt & Negri, 2000; Reich, 1991). Third, transformations in literacy practices can serve as markers for the specificities and differences that occur in different contexts undergoing the multiple (not singular) effects of globalizing processes and dynamics. Finally, by examining the specifics of two interacting sets of transformations, we are much more able to think through the issues associated with a politics of *interruption*. That is, we can begin to point to ways in which the politics of globalization might be altered at both the macro and micro levels. Overly general portraits of globalization—those that do not focus directly on the nuances and details of particular dynamics—make this more difficult.

In the following exploration of these issues, then, we take as our basic context the ongoing and conflict-ridden shift in the US and similar nations from welfare state industrial economies to neoliberal state informational economies. As explained below, by "informational economy," we do not mean a state of affairs wherein agricultural and industrial labor has disappeared and all workers employ cutting-edge technologies to engage in intellectually challenging endeavors. Rather, we refer to an economy in which value is added in labor processes increasingly through the generation, assessment and application of new knowledge and disparate aspects of production are reorganized accordingly (see below; see also Apple, 1995; Carnoy, 2000; Castells, 1996; Hardt & Negri, 2000; Reich, 1991). Furthermore, though in the interest of specificity we focus on developments within the US and similar capitalist economies, we must emphasize that in the emerging informational economy, both the processes and components of production, consumption and circulation are organized more or less directly in networks that are global in scope. To cite but one implication of these arrangements, laborers are pressured both to undercut the wages of all other workers around the world and to offer capital full access to their resources (material, intellectual and spiritual), lest their regions be "switched off" from worldwide networks of power and transformed into economic "black holes" such as the *favelas* around São Paulo, the slums of Kolkata, or the South Side of Chicago (see Apple, 1996; Castells, 1996; Davis, 2006). Thus, when we examine how educators and employers produce workers and literacies "necessary" for the currently constituted global economy, we must see this production as bound up with—*indeed, dependent upon*—the exploitation of billions of women, men and children around the world.

Against this background we render an analysis of how, in the emerging informational economy and social order of the United States and similar nations, both workplace and school-based literacies and the literacy sponsorship offered by employers and state-run schools change, compete, increase and decrease in value, and interact with differential power relations in society. Though we draw upon work carried out in economics, history, sociology, and political science, we ground our investigation largely in analyses developed in the areas of literacy studies (Brandt, 2001, 2005; Gee, Hull, & Lankshear, 1996; New London Group, 2000) and critical education studies (Apple, 1995, 2006; Gee, 1996; Robertson, 2000), a field with a long history of examining the production, commodification and leveraging of knowledge in educational and economic systems (see Apple, 1982; Bourdieu & Passeron, 1977; Willis, 1977). Working in these traditions, we place in dialogue socio-cultural practice accounts of literacy and literacy sponsorship (Brandt, 2001) and Michael Hardt and Antonio Negri's (2000) conception of biopolitical production.

Globalization and "Biopolitics"

In their analysis of the emerging informational economy and its social and political contexts, Hardt and Negri (2000) posit that this global economic system is driven by what they term biopolitical production, "the production of social life itself, in which the economic, the political, and the cultural increasingly overlap and invest one another" (p. xiii). Though at times overstating the case, Hardt and Negri argue that fast capitalist firms[2] call upon workers in all sectors to reshape and engage their hearts and their minds so as to stand as mediators between different nodes within networked firms and between firms and various niche markets (often organized in part by marketing agencies and other fast capitalist interests). Afforded by their employers the (bounded) freedom to respond to shifting economic, political and cultural dynamics, workers in fast capitalist firms transform themselves again and again so as to generate new knowledge and engage in cooperative labor with other employees and with customers. Thus, as they produce new commodities and provide new services (indeed, *in order to do this*), fast capitalist firms create "agentic subjectivities within the biopolitical context: they produce needs, social relations, bodies, and minds—which is to say, they produce producers. In the biopolitical sphere, life is made to work for production and production is made to work for life" (Hardt & Negri, 2000, p. 32).

To place this analysis of the workings of biopolitical production in dialogue with socio-cultural practice accounts of literacy (Barton, 1994; Heath, 1983; Scollon & Scollon, 1981; Scribner & Cole, 1981; Street, 1984), we draw upon Gee's (1996) argument that literacy is the control of a secondary (non-home-based) discourse. Gee (1996) defines discourses as

> ways of being in the world, or forms of life which integrate words, acts, values, beliefs, attitudes, and social identities, as well as gestures, glances, body positions, and clothes. A Discourse is a sort of identity kit which comes complete with the appropriate costume and instructions on how to act, talk, and often write, so as to take on a particular social role that others will recognize.
>
> (p. 127)

Furthermore, integrating into our argument Brandt's (2001) work on literacy sponsorship, we observe that literacies "exis[t] only as part of larger material systems, systems that on the one hand enable acts of reading or writing"—or, as per Gee's definition of literacy, performances of particular discourses—"and on the other hand confer their value. Changes in these systems change the meaning and the status of individual literacy" (p. 1). Thus, Brandt (2001) writes:

> To treat literacy this way is to understand not only why individuals labor to attain literacy but also to appreciate why, as with any resource of value, organized economic and political interests work so persistently to conscript and ration the powers of literacy for their own competitive advantage.
>
> (p. 5)

Synthesizing the arguments of Brandt and Gee, then, we may note that in shifting material systems, performances of different discourses, or forms of life, are valued in different and evolving ways. Indeed, in the emerging fast capitalist system of the US, the UK, and elsewhere, competing interests struggle ceaselessly in workplaces, schools and other sites to sponsor and/or engage in the development of "newer" and "more valuable"[3] forms of life and thereby gain social, political and economic advantage. Troublingly, though, we may observe that the market values of particular forms of life are determined in part by their potential for exploitation by capital, rendering less valuable the discourses of those who resist the demands of the market and/or those with access to few "high-value" resources (Apple, 2006; Apple & Buras, 2006).

Drawing together these lines of analysis, we conclude that many of the literacies and patterns of literacy sponsorship valued in welfare state industrial economies are being reshaped and repositioned as new forms of life and new systems of literacy sponsorship rise in value with the emergence of neoliberal state informational economies (even as changes in literacy practices reshape the social, political and economic contexts in which they occur). Disconcertingly, however, powerful fast capitalist and neoliberal interests operating in such economies recruit forms of life and endorse patterns of literacy sponsorship that are in many ways antithetical to principles of social justice and strong democracy (Barber, 2003). In opposition to this, we argue that citizens can and should seek out opportunities for intervention in and across nation states and should work together through disparate channels to help each other shape and adapt to the new realities of the emerging socio-economic order. As we shall argue, a crucial step in this process is the widening of opportunity within and across educational institutions for diverse learners to collaborate in developing powerful literacies necessary both for securing productive, rewarding labor in fast-moving informational economies and for reshaping socio-economic orders according to principles of justice and strong democracy. However, it is important to note that the prospects for such collaboration have narrowed over the past few decades due to radical transformations in the relationships among globalizing processes, states, schooling, and economies.

Literacies and the Fordist Keynesian Welfare State Settlement

To understand how certain kinds of literacies—the control of certain forms of life—have come to be valued in particular ways in the emerging socio-economic order and to appreciate the difficulties that students and workers face in acquiring, reshaping or challenging these literacies, it is necessary to investigate the changes both in the material systems that enable and confer value upon different literate practices and in the social settlements of which these material systems are part. We will examine first the Fordist Keynesian welfare state settlement of the industrial age, understood here as the moment in capitalist development in which profit was ultimately realized by firms through the provision of large quantities of standardized goods and services to more or less stable markets, not through the manipulation of forms of life (see below). We will then turn to a discussion of the emerging settlement of the neoliberal state informational economy, focusing throughout on the ways particular literacies are recruited, put to work and traded upon.

In the Fordist Keynesian welfare state settlement of the post-Second World War era, notes Gary Teeple, the state strengthened its hand in arranging "social policy, programs, standards and regulations in order to mitigate class conflict and to provide for, answer or accommodate certain social needs for which the capitalist mode of production in itself has no solution or makes no provision" (as cited in Robertson, 2000, p. 95). In return for social and worksite protections (e.g., relatively stable employment for considerable portions of the white male workforce) and access to affordable consumer goods, many laborers accepted jobs in workplaces run on the command-and-control model in which: orders flowed from a small top to a wider base (pyramidal logic); departments within companies were clearly marked off from one another; new projects were generated, refined and executed in-house by full-time employees; much work was highly routinized; management exhibited low trust of workers' decision-making abilities; and the amount of higher-order thinking required in work decreased the further one moved down the chain of command (see Brown & Lauder, 2001; Carnoy, 2000; Castells, 1996; Gee, 2000; Hardt & Negri, 2000; Reich, 1991; Taylor, 2001).

Relative to the forms of life recruited by capital in the informational era, then, the forms of life sponsored among workers in the industrial age were prescribed, bounded, stable, and less consuming. Explaining this state of affairs, Hardt and Negri (2000) argue that the industrial era was driven primarily by disciplinary forms of power which

> fixed individuals in institutions but did not succeed in consuming them completely in the rhythm of productive practices and productive socialization; it did not reach the point of permeating entirely the consciousnesses and bodies of individuals, the point of treating and organizing them in the totality of their activities.
>
> (p. 24)

Thus, while industrial-era workers may have struggled to control particular literacies, the extent to which they internalized and could reconfigure and draw upon new forms of life was of less consequence than it would be for workers in the informational era of fast capitalism.

Furthermore, due to a range of factors, including the modicum of power won by organized labor in the welfare state settlement, some full-time workers (especially white males) were provided within-firm training to help them acquire valuable literacies. Public sponsorship of literacy development also expanded with the growth of the welfare state as organized groups of citizens (e.g., the African American Civil Rights Movement, the Trade Union

Movement, and the Women's Movement) worked collectively in the widened public sphere to press their demands for better and more inclusive public education.

These popular calls for better provision of literacy training through more equitable public schooling, we must note, interacted with other demands made on the welfare state, in general, and on public schools, in particular, by powerful business interests and by conservative social groups (see Apple, 2006). The state, seeking to "integrate many of the interests of allied and even opposing groups under its banner" (Apple, 1995, pp. 26–27), struggled continuously through its educational apparatus to engage certain of these groups and meet certain of their needs. Thus, while the state responded to popular pressure and made limited efforts to equalize participation in public schooling, it also endeavored, as it had since the late nineteenth century, to meet the needs of industry by moving high-cost and high-risk research and worker-training processes into the educational apparatus (this included colleges and universities) (see Althusser, 1971). Public schools, then, came to play central roles in the production of both high-status technical/administrative knowledge and the workers who manipulated this knowledge in more-or-less routinized ways for the corporate interests of the industrial economy. Importantly, through this and other processes, the state also (re)created (in part) and won the active consent of a white middle class whose children in schools could filter to the top of their classes (in part) by virtue of their possession of and orientation toward dominant groups' "valuable" literacies (including the workplace literacies of their parents, many of whose jobs involved the manipulation of technical/administrative knowledge) (Apple, 1995; Bourdieu & Passeron, 1977).

Thus, while allowing that they are complicated institutions shaped by myriad forces, we may note that industrial era public schools, for a number of complex reasons characterized by both "good sense" and "bad sense" (Apple, 2000), developed standardized work processes, grid-like organizational forms, and white, middle-class institutional cultures that served, at least partially, to (re)produce through struggle both a stratified labor force (privileging the white middle class) and the disparate literacies "necessary" for the functioning of the industrial economy (see Apple, 1995; Katz, 1975; Tyack, 1974; Willis, 1977).

What, though, were the characteristics of the dominant literacies sponsored by industrial era public schools and that, among other things, greased the wheels of the industrial economy and perpetuated the advantage of the white middle class? As with all literacies, these involved the control of certain discourses that call upon individuals to draw upon particular technologies and particular systems of knowledge in particular ways so as to take on identities recognizable to others. In general, these school literacies were characterized by a view of knowledge as stable, standard, decon-textualized, bounded, and situated in clear hierarchies that privileged the "official knowledge" of dominant groups (Apple, 2000). Furthermore, these literacies advanced a conceptualization of work as involving de-raced, de-classed and de-gendered individuals laboring alone to carry out the more-or-less routinized tasks handed down to them by authorities. These features of dominant school literacies were strengthened by and helped strengthen the institutional structures and practices of industrial era schools, including: rigid departmentalization; individual (vs. collaborative) teaching; adherence to local and state standards; use of uniform mass-marketed textbooks and pre-packaged curricula; grading of individual students; tracking; standardized testing; 30-to-1 student-to-teacher ratios; and factory-like time management (Apple, 1995).

These structures, practices and processes of literacy sponsorship, we may note, worked well enough to help (re)produce the technical/administrative knowledge and the differently literate and differently oriented workers "necessary" for the US industrial economy of the twentieth century. As Gee (2004) argues, though, industrial era literacies and literacy sponsors (e.g. standard public schools) are becoming more and more outmoded as *parts* of the economies of the US, the UK, and many other nations come to be powered in important ways by non-standard knowledge, "learning to learn," flexibility, diversity, networking, teamwork, and total commitment. It is to an analysis of this emerging order that we now turn.

Literacies and the New Settlement: The Emergence of the Informational Economy

While many firms and state institutions (e.g., public schools) established in or reconstituted for the industrial era remain prominent in these nations, there are underway profound changes in the social, political and economic arenas in which these organizations are situated. So dramatic are these changes, in fact, that the Fordist Keynesian welfare state settlement and its accompanying institutions and systems of literacy sponsorship have arguably been strained to the breaking point, and certain fractions of capital, labor and the state are struggling to establish a new settlement, new institutions and new systems of literacy sponsorship appropriate for the informational era.[4]

In his analysis of the emergence of global knowledge economies and network societies, Castells (1996) observes that with advances in both information technology and transportation—advances often subsidized by governments—and with the global diffusion of sophisticated manufactur-ing instruments, greater numbers of firms around the world have become able to provide services and produce large volumes of inexpensive, high-quality goods for international markets. Given both the number of new firms in global competition and the remarkable diversity of emerging international markets, many companies may no longer plan to realize profit simply by providing standardized services and producing large numbers of standardized goods. Instead, these companies now work to engage (and, in part, form) niche markets of customers through the design and provision of competitively priced products and services that are both innovative and customized for particular lifestyles—distinct from all the other inexpensive, high-quality services provided and goods produced around the world. In part to facilitate the generation, processing and application of new knowledge, including "the continuous discovery of new linkages between solutions and needs" (Reich, 1991), ideal fast capitalist firms operating in the US and other advanced capitalist economies have flattened out parts of their old industrial-model hierarchies and reorganized certain of their operations according to network logic.

Many laborers in networked firms, then, are afforded by employers the (bounded) freedom to generate, process and apply new knowledge by reworking and mobilizing their literacies—their control of particular forms of life—in such ways as to forge or strengthen connections within and between firms' shifting networks and between networked firms and evolving niche markets. Thus, as Hardt and Negri (2000) write, in the informational economy, "life is made to work for production and production is made to work for life" (p. 32) and "productivity, wealth, and the creation of social surpluses takes the form of cooperative interactivity through linguistic, communicational, and affective networks" (p. 294). More specifically, they argue, workers in fast capitalist firms perform one or more of the three types of labor that drive the informational economy:

> The first is involved in an industrial production that has been informationalized and has incorporated communication technologies in a way that transforms the production process itself. Manufacturing is regarded as a service, and the material labor of the production of durable goods mixes with and tends toward immaterial labor. Second is the immaterial labor of analytical and symbolic tasks, which itself breaks down into creative and intelligent manipulation on the one hand and routine symbolic tasks on the other. Finally, a third type of immaterial labor involves the production and manipulation of affect and requires (virtual or actual) human contact, labor in the bodily mode.
>
> (Hardt & Negri, 2000, p. 293)

While there exist significant differences between types of labor in the informational economies of advanced capitalist nations (see below), we may nonetheless identify some common features characteristic of work in each of Hardt and Negri's three categories of labor. Indeed, more so than many industrial-era laborers, workers engaged in each of these forms of labor[5] must be willing and able to: commit heart, mind and body to the vision of the firm employing them at the moment; develop and perform new and constantly evolving literate practices (see Brandt (2001) and Carnoy (2000) for discussions of rising standards of literacy for many forms of labor in the US); work as part of a team; manage their affect in such ways as to facilitate teamwork and, for some workers, evoke in customers a sense of well-being; and utilize information technology to carry out multiple tasks communicated to the workplace team through intra-firm networks (these tasks are more or less pre-determined, depending on the worker's position within a firm's network). Moreover, these workers are expected to invest their hearts and minds in their labors and, oftentimes through writing, feed information about the work process—including ideas about innovations that could make their work faster and more efficient—back into the network for the consideration of symbolic analysts who ultimately set the routes for work (see Carnoy, 2000; Castells, 1996; Gee et al., 1996; Reich, 1991).

In her study of writing in knowledge economy workplaces, Brandt (2005) discusses how laborers situated in particular positions within their organizations' networks carry out the crucial work of mediation and synthesis by reshaping and enlisting their hearts and minds:

> Mediation and synthesis refer to the ways that writers serve as tools of production, transforming complex organizational histories and interests, needs, and constrains into textual form and smelting their awareness of specialized knowledge, regulation, and multiple audiences, constituencies, and competitors into their work processes and products. . . . Workplace writers can be likened to complex pieces of machinery that turn raw materials (both concrete and abstract) into functional, transactional, and valuable form, often with great expenditures of emotional, psychological, and technical effort. As securities dealer George Carlisle observed in answer to a question about whether he used boilerplate formats in his writing, "you better write with your heart and your brain if you expect to win."
>
> (p. 176)

A central and multi-layered concern of workers who engage in mediation and synthesis, Brandt (2005) writes, is the matter of integrity: the integrity of the multiple interests they represent and address, the integrity of the heteroglot texts they produce, and their own personal integrity. Literacy theorists Suzanne and Ron Scollon (1981) might discuss this matter of integrity by noting that to the extent that the values endorsed by the entities they represent and address in their writing conflict with their own personal values, writers may find it difficult to commit their hearts and minds to the mediation and synthesis of those disparate views. Thus, we may observe, workers whose values and beliefs align most closely with those of capital (often workers from dominant social groups) may be more comfortable than other workers (often workers from marginalized groups) with investing themselves fully in mediating and synthesizing on behalf of capital (Bernstein, 1990). Moreover, new conflicts may arise again and again for workers in the fast capitalist economy as companies seek constantly to link up with new firms and constitute and engage new niche markets.

These observations cast light on one of the most troubling aspects of unfairly regulated informational economies. With literacies and identities so central to all aspects of production and without progressive laws regulating hiring and labor practices, only those workers possessing what capital considers the "right" literacies—the "proper" control of powerful discourses, the "correct" understanding of how to maneuver through and mediate important networks—stand to be hired for rewarding work by fast capitalist firms that demand from their workers total commitment in exchange for short-term employment (see below). Gee, Hull, and Lankshear (1996) note:

> Work in the old capitalism was alienating. Workers were forced to sell their labor, but often with little mental, emotional, or social investment in the business. Today they are asked to invest their hearts, minds, and bodies fully in their work. They are asked to think and act critically [but not *too* critically], reflectively, and creatively. While this offers a less alienating view of work and labor, in practice it can also amount to a form of mind control and high-tech, but indirect coercion.
>
> (p. 7)

Moreover, because the ideal "lean and mean" fast capitalist firm (supposedly) operates with flattened hierarchies, *all* workers must commit themselves fully to the enterprise and to their projects. *All* workers must draw upon the "right" literacies for their jobs.

Literacies and the New Settlement: The Contested Formation of the Neoliberal State

While more and more companies around the world, mindful of trans-formations in the global informational economy, are reorganizing themselves so as to make greater use of their workers' literacies, it must be noted that the particular organizational forms and practices that companies adopt—and thus the channels through which workers develop particular literacies—will always be determined in part by the cultures and politico-legal structures of the nations in which they operate. Indeed, in the global economy, argue Carnoy (2000) and Castells (1996), states, through their economic and educational policies, play critical roles in the transformation of corporations operating in their territories and, relatedly, in the sponsorship of citizens' literacies.

In the US, ascendant neoliberal politicians, like their counterparts in the UK, Australia, and New Zealand, have endeavored since the late 1970s to dismantle the welfare state and its modes of literacy sponsorship and to construct a "competitive state" that would work, in part, to create economic, political and social environments in which shareholder capitalism could flourish. In this form of capitalism, note Brown, Green, and Lauder (2001), executives are pressured to generate substantial short-term profits, often "through takeovers, mergers, and buyouts, rather than through value added production" or long-term investment in the development of workers' literate skills (p. 232). Neoliberals in many nations argued that welfare state settlements had run their course and that government-directed social service providers such as public schools had become financial drains and had grown overly bureaucratic and unresponsive to the needs of disparate citizens.

Moreover, working to shift "commonsense" understandings of equity, neoliberals insisted that because the missions of welfare state public service providers are determined in part through the collective deliberations of the citizenry, the needs of "minority" groups were going unmet (Apple, 2006).[6] A more equitable solution, they posited, is a market system in which individual consumers select from a range of private service providers that suit their particular needs. Furthermore, contended neoliberals, the state's provision of welfare services, concessions to labor, and limited support for "off-market" hiring of women and "minority" workers inhibited citizens' entrepreneurship and fostered "cultures of dependency." Also, as economic globalization proceeded throughout the 1980s and 1990s, neoliberals argued that because corporations could move production sites and jobs from nations that taxed firms at levels necessary for the maintenance of welfare states, there was no alternative but to cut or privatize programs that soaked up "excessive" public funding (Greider, 1997).

The cure for these ills, insisted neoliberals, was the building of a "competitive state" that would place the nation and its workers at the forefront of the global informational economy through the pursuit of policies based on selective deregulation, competition and privatization (Robertson, 2000). Many services once provided by public agencies would be offered by private companies. Remaining public agencies providing "off-market" services would provide only "the basics," lest they "waste" taxpayer money and encourage among citizens dependency on the state.[7] Citizens, for their part, would no longer work collectively through government to shape the work of the public agencies that served the nation as a whole, but would act as individual consumers selecting the services (e.g., education and training) that place them in favorable positions in a range of markets where they compete against other individuals (e.g., labor markets). Responsibility for the receipt of poor services, then, would rest with citizens who chose poorly, not with the state. And despite talk of getting government off the backs of its people, neoliberals envisioned for the competitive state an active role in arranging and overseeing markets through auditing the performances of both service providers and citizens. In this respect, writes Mark Olssen, the competitive state may be understood as a regulatory state which sees to it that citizens are "perpetually responsive" to key markets and are making "continual enterprises of [them]selves" (as cited in Apple, 2001, p. 72).

Insofar as the neoliberal project of deregulation, competition and privatization removes certain governmental and union "interferences" from the economy and subjects individual citizens more directly to the demands of markets, we may note, it facilitates a certain form of biopolitical production. That is, the competitive state under construction in these nations works in certain ways to create forms of life that may be exploited by fast capitalist interests. Indeed, the competitive state's project of requiring individual citizens to make "continual enterprises of themselves" by shopping around for services that fit their shifting lifestyles helps create niche markets for fast capitalist firms perpetually seeking new kinds of consumers. Furthermore, individual citizens' efforts to purchase newer and better services (e.g., education and training) so as to occupy more favorable positions in different markets (e.g., labor markets) play to the strategies of fast capitalist companies that call upon workers to labor constantly to develop newer and more powerful literacies that can help firms win competitive advantages in important and emerging markets.[8]

Though neoliberals in the advanced capitalist nations have come to dominate many areas of policymaking over the past twenty-five years (see Apple, 2006), they have been unable (and in certain cases unwilling) to marketize *all* sectors of the state. For instance, there remain tens of thousands of government-run K-12 public schools in the US, though they are involved more and more in private sector initiatives and are increasingly subject to market forces (see Apple, 2006). Despite the lack of total success of their project, however, neoliberals have, through their advocacy for selectively deregulated markets, shareholder capitalism, a reduced and privatized public sector, and a small, strong competitive state, helped create in a growing number of countries what Brown, Green, and Lauder (2001) call a "high skills/low skills" informational economy. This model of informational economy, they write,

> bases competitiveness on high levels of innovation and productivity in some hi-tech and innovation-led manufacturing and service sectors as well as on flexible labor markets and capital productivity. The skills formation system which articulates this generates a polarized combination of low skills and high skills elites, typically mirrored by high levels of income inequality.
>
> (Brown et al., 2001, p. 143)

Indeed, in the "high skills/low skills" informational economy of the US, for example, particular versions of Hardt and Negri's (2000) three forms of labor are compensated at different rates, depending in part upon the extent to which they can be performed by minimally expensive workers and/or in minimally regulated areas in the US or around the world. Thus, workers face a situation in which: a small number of creative symbolic analysts enjoy relatively steady work and high compensation (Brown and Lauder (2006) note, though, that this may change as more and more "low cost" students and workers in "developing" nations such as India and China acquire the literacies and credentials to perform symbolic-analytic work); a small percentage of skilled laborers engage in steady-paying work in informationalized manufacturing (a form of manufacturing that compromises managers' abilities to produce large short-term gains through labor flexibility, thereby making this form of production ill-suited to the shareholder capitalism of the US (Brown et al., 2001)); many workers perform routine symbolic tasks, though their numbers, pay and job security are diminishing as advances in communications technologies make it possible for this work to be performed by minimally expensive laborers in "developing" economies; large numbers of laborers compete with one another for increasingly unsteady work in the low-paying routine service sector; and considerable numbers of citizens are unemployed or incarcerated.[9]

Turning our attention to how this system is created and sustained, we may note that while one of the widely accepted functions of public schools is to help students acquire the literacies necessary for securing steady employment, contemporary public schools that are run on the industrial model of individuated and standardized work fail to prepare students for employment in *any* level of the informational economy. Indeed, even in the "low skills" routine service sector, employees are called upon to work in shifting teams and to commit their hearts and minds to performing the affective labor that helps firms engage niche markets of customers.

Ironically, perhaps, many of the school reforms proposed and implemented by business-friendly figures in the neoliberal state, including high-stakes standardized testing, school choice programs, and slowed growth in governmental spending on K-12 public education, may work to create situations in which *less* emphasis is placed by the school on fostering the kinds of powerful, non-standard literacies valued in the new economy and *increased* attention is given by the school to improving its students' test scores (and thus its market position) through standard, traditional instruction and through the use of basic curricula aligned with high-stakes tests (see Apple, 2006; Au, 2009; Hartley, 2003; Lipman, 2004; Valenzuela, 2005; Whitty, Power, & Halpin, 1998). Furthermore, evidence suggests that the expansion of school choice programs and educational markets correlates with increased segregation of schools by race and class and thereby works against the development in students of understandings of how to collaborate with diverse co-workers in the production of new knowledge (see Apple, 2006; Gewirtz, Ball, & Bowe, 1995; Lauder & Hughes, 1999).

This partial disarticulation of the public school system with important sectors of national and international economies becomes more understandable when we recall that the state, through its apparatuses, must continuously "integrate many of the interests of allied and even opposing groups under its banner" and engage in an ongoing "process of compromise, conflict, and active struggle to maintain hegemony" (Apple, 1995, pp. 26–27). In this case, we may note that state-run schools are pulled in (somewhat) different directions by groups including certain fast capitalist interests that want flexible, creative and cooperative workers and white middle-class parents who support the (re)establishment of systems that privilege their children and allow for social closure.[10] These parents may support a national education system in which, on the one hand, schools or tracks serving mostly working-class students of color emphasize the standardized knowledge measured on high-stakes tests and, on the other hand, schools or tracks serving mostly white middle-class students stress abstraction, system thinking, experimentation, and collaboration, what Reich (1991) calls the new "basic skills" of the informational economy.

Moreover, white middle-class parents know that even when their students' "off-market" public schools provide only "the basics" (as required in neoliberal philosophy), more-affluent families can use their economic, social and cultural capital to help their children enjoy the experiences, attain the credentials and develop the literacies and identities valued in the higher education market and the small "high skills" labor market of the US, UK, and elsewhere (see Apple, 2006; Ball, 2003; Power, Edwards, Whitty, & Wigfall, 2003). Finally, research indicates that in expanded systems of school choice (proposed by neoliberal politicians in many nations), white middle-class parents tend to deploy their economic, social and cultural capital and tap into *informal* networks to secure for their children positions in schools that cultivate images of prestige in part through the selection of student bodies that are predominantly white and affluent (see Apple, 2006; Gewirtz, Ball, & Bowe, 1995; Lauder & Hughes, 1999). Again, while systems of educational markets and high-stakes standardized testing may (re)create for white middle-class students environments in which they can maintain their privileges and close out students from marginalized groups, such systems interfere in certain ways with the workings of the forms of biopolitical production that drive the informational economy.

What Is to Be Done?

Though they overstate the case to a degree, in their book *The New Work Order: Behind the Language of the New Capitalism,* Gee, Hull, and Lankshear (1996) argue that certain fast capitalist interests, concerned with the growing disarticulation between public schools and the informational economy, will heighten their call for schools to adopt "progressive" practices such as fostering diverse communities of practice and encouraging the development of new, non-standard literacies. They write:

> In its attempts to create new kinds of workers/partners, the new capitalism will put pressure on other learning-centered Discourses to help produce such kinds of people. In particular, the new capitalism will progressively recruit schools to produce suitable "subjects" or "citizens" for new-capitalist Discourse in general and its manifestations in specific Discourses.
>
> (Gee et al., 1996, p. 22)

Some progressive educators may see real potential for strengthening social justice in reforms that aim to increase economic growth by leaving intact current economic structures and fostering among *each individual student and worker* the development of the literacies most valued in fast capitalist markets. Brown and Lauder (2006) warn, however, that such efforts lead to dead ends. They note that this "magnet economy" approach of leaving untouched economic structures while (re)training every student and worker for employment in the "high skills" sector is based on a number of faulty assumptions, including both overestimations of the number of high-paying knowledge jobs available in presently constituted labor markets and underestimations of the abilities of employers to weaken knowledge workers' labor power through the routinization of knowledge work. Furthermore, by developing students' and workers' creative capacities, their hearts and their minds, in ultimate accordance with market demands, educators reify the present economic system, forbidding meaningful critique of capitalist relations and engaging in what Gee, Hull, and Lankshear (1996) consider "mind control and high-tech, but indirect coercion" (p. 7).

Rather than beginning with the question of what skills and literacies the informational economy requires, argue Brown and Lauder (2001), we must ground our analyses and efforts in a vision of a society that is egalitarian, just and within reach. With this in mind, they write:

> Marx suggested that in the womb of the old there is the germination of something new, but at this moment in history it is not the overthrow of capitalism, but the potential for a new form of post-industrial cooperation which reflects the growing importance of human collaboration, knowledge, skills and talents in raising economic productivity, enhancing democracy and improving the quality of life.
>
> (Brown & Lauder, 2001, p. 205)

Indeed, though possibilities for creating new forms of social organization are not opened solely through shifts in the economy, we may note that capital's growing need for biopolitical production creates opportunities (fraught with conflict) for people to work with diverse others in recreating forms of life and recreating societies.

Continuing, Brown and Lauder (2001) argue that a new social settlement and new structures and institutions can and should be formed on the basis of collective intelligence, the

> empowerment through the *development and pooling of intelligence* to attain common goals or resolve common problems. It is inspired by a spirit of cooperation rather than a Darwinian survival of the fittest. In a society that eulogizes the virtues of competition, self-interest and acquisitiveness, rather than cooperation, common interests and the quality of life, it is difficult to maximize human potential or to coordinate opportunities for intelligent action in an efficient manner. The struggle for collective intelligence therefore involves more than a democratization of intelligence, it involves making a virtue of our mutual dependence and sociability which we will need to make a dominant feature of post-industrial society based on information, knowledge and lifelong learning.
>
> (pp. 218–219; original emphasis)

Although it is at least somewhat difficult to imagine in this era of market individualism, we may note that the formation of a social settlement based on collective intelligence may help solve the problems of key interests: workers in need of evolving, non-standard literacies; citizens requiring means for addressing problems that require collective efforts (e.g., environmental crises); employers looking for workers who can reconstitute themselves for shifting modes of labor; and governments in need of new strategies for strengthening their workforces.

Critical to the progress of a society organized around knowledge and lifelong learning, we may note, are institutions such as reconfigured public schools that provide spaces for diverse citizens of all ages to work together in creating strong, inclusive communities and rich social networks that, among other things, help workers from traditionally marginalized groups to find employment and training opportunities (see Carnoy, 2000). Moreover, in these spaces, citizens can collaborate in developing the non-standard literacies that will stand them in good stead in knowledge economy labor markets and, more importantly, enable critical analyses of how social, political and economic spheres function and how they might be changed. Drawing upon theories of design that center humans' creative, socially situated constructions of environments and practices, the literacy scholars of the New London Group (2000) argue that such information age schools must embrace a reflexive, four-part "pedagogy of multiliteracies" consisting of:

> Situated Practice based on the world of learners' Designed and Designing experiences; Overt Instruction through which students shape for themselves an explicit metalanguage of Design; Critical Framing, which relates meanings to their social contexts and purposes; and Transformed Practice in which students transfer and re-create Designs of meaning from one context to another.
>
> (p. 31)

Thus, as opposed to the *market-driven* pedagogy endorsed by certain fast capitalist interests (see above), the New London Group's pedagogy of multiliteracies bases education on *human* experiences and needs and takes as central components of education the critique and purposeful transformation of social, political and economic relations.

Finally, we may note that educators working in public schools, citing both the existence of problems that require the collective efforts of all citizens and the informational economy's emphasis on the creation of diverse forms of life through biopolitical production, may claim a strong mandate for centering in curricula the experiences and epistemologies of diverse social groups. While the most powerful case for public schools engaging the traditions of different groups will always be based on ethical arguments—it is most ethical for public institutions to engage all social groups openly and respectfully—educators mindful of large-scale socio-economic trans-formations may argue with greater emphasis that an education based in engagement with diverse traditions is becoming more and more of an economic, political and social necessity for every citizen. Indeed, as the literacy scholars of the New London Group (2000) argue,

> cultural and linguistic diversity is a classroom resource just as powerfully as it is a social resource in the formation of new civic spaces and new notions of citizenship. This is not just so that educators can provide a better "service" to "minorities". Rather, such a pedagogical orientation will produce benefits for all. For example, there will be a cognitive benefit to all children in a pedagogy of linguistic and cultural pluralism, including for "mainstream" children. When learners juxtapose different languages, discourses, styles, and approaches, they gain substantively in metacognitive and metalinguistic abilities and in their ability to reflect critically on complex systems and their interactions.
>
> (p. 15; see also Carnoy, 2000)

While such a pedagogy of multiliteracies runs counter to the dominant logics of traditional schooling and neoliberal reform, educators committed to helping students develop literacies necessary for social, political and economic engagement in our "new times" need not start with empty drawing boards. Indeed, beginning at a conceptual level, educators may develop understandings of the possibilities for and limitations of critical education in emerging socio-economic orders by drawing from rich theoretical traditions including those of poststructuralism and neo-Marxism. By selectively utilizing parts of poststructural theory, critical educators may better understand the nature and implications of a number of phenomena central to current transformations in social, political and economic spheres: the dissolution of the unified modernist subject; the (re)constitution of subjects (in part) through the workings of discourse(s); the emergence of non-disciplinary forms of power; and the rise of informational economies. In order to clarify how these phenomena shape and are shaped by the fields of power in which they occur (e.g., fields of power of the state), and in order to conceptualize how actors might create counter-hegemonic mobilizations that take advantage of the contradictions in these shifting fields of power, however, analyses of emerging social, political and economic orders must place in dialogue with poststructural arguments the insights of neo-Marxist theory. That is, we posit that when educators draw from both poststructural *and* neo-Marxist theory, they can break through conceptual impasses characteristic of both approaches and clarify the workings of and possibilities within emerging orders. (see Apple, 1999; Apple et al., 2003).

Guided in part by theoretical orientations of poststructuralism and neo-Marxism, critical educators may find workable models for powerful, forward-looking education in existing initiatives such as those pursued in the Citizen Schools of Porto Alegre, Brazil and in the classrooms of teachers throughout the world working in the democratic schools movement (Apple & Beane, 2007). Consistent in many ways with the recommendations of the New London Group (2000), students in these schools and classrooms develop powerful literacies in part through identifying and responding to the real concerns of their communities. In Porto Alegre's Citizen Schools, for instance, students carried out action research in their communities and determined that poverty should be their object of study and cause for social action (see Apple & Gandin, 2002; Apple et al., 2003; Apple & Buras, 2006).

Similarly, students and educators working in Chicago's underfunded Richard E. Byrd Community Academy banded together and engaged in widely noted counter-hegemonic mobilizations to challenge the realities of their daily experiences and to change the material conditions in their school (see Schultz, 2007). Once they identified community concerns to address, students in Citizen Schools and at the Byrd Academy worked in shifting networks of educators, community members, political figures, media workers, and other learners to engage both local and dominant ways of knowing in order to generate, assess and apply knowledge relevant to the interests of their communities. Through these processes, we may note, students: shifted between identities valued in myriad contexts (e.g., community worker, "good" student, lobbyist, concerned citizen, etc.); employed Reich's (1991) "new basic skills" of abstraction, system thinking, experimentation, and collaboration; developed facility with a range of discourses and genres (including "high status" discourses of city planning and "high status" genres of political testimony); and strengthened their understandings of how discourses and genres work differently for actors positioned in disparate locations in fields of power.

Though such activity, powered by biopolitical production and characterized by flexibility and multimodality, resonates in some ways with the fast capitalist pedagogy described above by Gee, Hull, and Lankshear (1996), work carried out in Porto Alegre's Citizen Schools and in democratic classrooms throughout the world is fundamentally different from fast capitalist work because it subordinates profits to people and builds capacity in communities for mobilizations around issues of social and economic justice. Indeed, to appropriate the words of Porto Alegre's Municipal Secretariat of Education, educators working in Citizen Schools and democratic classrooms insist that, contra the neoliberal definition of democracy as individual consumer choice,

> to democratize is to construct, with participation, a project of education that has social quality, is liberating and transformative, where the school is a laboratory of practice, exercise and achievement of rights, of formation of autonomous, critical and creative historic subjects, full citizens, identified with ethical values, willing to construct a social project that has as a center of attention the practice of justice, of freedom, of respect and fraternal relationship among men and women and a harmonic relationship with nature.
>
> (As cited in Apple & Gandin, 2002, pp. 263–264)

Such democratic vistas, along with depictions of progressive educational practice (see Apple & Gandin, 2002; Apple & Buras, 2006; Apple & Beane, 2007; Apple, Au, & Gandin, 2009) and precise delineations of the spaces open for struggle in our "new times" (see Brown et al., 2001; Castells, 1996; Hardt & Negri, 2000), show us that even amidst the dangers of emerging global orders, ideals of democracy persist and real victories in campaigns for social and economic justice are still possible. We cannot ensure, of course, that the development among students around the world of critical literacies and the dispositions and values that accompany them will contribute to the subversion of the global biopolitics we have discussed in this chapter. But we can be certain that without struggling to build and defend them, capital in its multiple forms will press on, with predictable effects on the lives and hopes of billions of people throughout the world. We cannot afford to let this happen. The next section of this chapter points to equally powerful ways in which many people take advantage of new literacies and are engaged in actions that indeed "will not let this happen."

II. New Interruptions

Introduction

> Inspired by the plight of friends who are illegal [*sic*] immigrants, Elizabeth Vasquez and her sister Bess recently used text messages and MySpace.com to orchestrate a recent school walkout of 1,500 students in South Florida.
>
> That put the Vasquez sisters, 15 and 14 respectively, at the forefront of the movement to give immigrants legal status. And last

weekend, it put Elizabeth on a 16-hour bus ride from South Florida to Nashville [for activist training].

"My friend that helped me with the walkout, she was born in Mexico but she has lived here all her life," said Vasquez. "She was text-messaging me, 'You think this will change things?' I said, 'I think so.'"

(Cardenas, 2006, pars. 10–12)

Throughout the spring of 2006, the cycle of pro-immigration[11] actions in which the Vasquez sisters participated jolted the social, political and economic systems of the United States. Even foes of progressive immigration policy such as CNN's Lou Dobbs acknowledged these actions, focused against legislation restricting immigrants' rights and animated more generally by Latinos/as' assertion of their presence on the national stage, transformed ongoing debates over work, citizenship and justice (Dobbs, 2007). Crucial to this transformation, as suggested above, were the efforts of students such as Elizabeth and Bess Vasquez who advocate for immigrants' rights and who interrupt reactionary discourses framing undocumented workers and their families as "illegal aliens" overrunning public schools and other state institutions.

While it is of great significance *that* students are working to promote equitable immigration policies, it is also of real interest to educators and activists alike *how* students are carrying out this work. In numerous accounts of the pro-immigration actions of the spring of 2006, students are described using digital tools to circulate information and link together shifting networks of students for participation in both long-planned and spontaneous events (Cardenas, 2006; Navarro, 2006; Shapira, 2006b). Intrigued by these developments and concerned about the dearth of critical educational scholarship on digital literacies (but see Warschauer, 1999), we present in this section a conjunctural analysis of student activists' uses of digital tools, considering how these practices shape and are shaped by: corporate globalization; the uneven diffusion of digital tools throughout the world; conservative modernization; transformations of public schools; and patterns of immigration into the United States. In so doing, we endeavor to understand how students and educators may appropriate the tools of high-tech global capitalism for use in the construction of more just orders.

The Autonomist Tradition

In developing this analysis, we deploy and rework several concepts associated with autonomist Marxism, a tradition that emphasizes subaltern groups' efforts to control their own affairs and organize themselves into non-hierarchical communities (see Cleaver, 1979; Dalla Costa & Dalla Costa,

1995; Dyer-Witheford, 1999; Virno & Hardt, 1996). Elaborating on themes introduced in our discussion of biopolitics (see above), we take up the autonomist concept of the social factory—the society-wide network of relations and practices required for capitalist production, distribution and consumption and for the reproduction of labor power—and consider how, in the US and in other post-industrial orders, economic activity relies increasingly on labor and processes of subject formation carried out beyond the walls of industrial-era workplaces.[12] Indeed, as noted in the previous section, workers are called upon more and more to draw upon all of their personal resources and commit themselves fully to capitalist enterprise. In this state of affairs, then, the cultivation of workers' hearts, minds and bodies—through, for example, teaching, child care, medical assistance, and cultural expression—is linked more directly into networks of capitalist control, control that is made even more powerful, given the threat of job loss under which so many millions of paid workers live.

One indication of this fuller subsumption of daily life under the rule of capital, we may note, is the expansion in the US of the service industry, an economic sector driven by social interaction and powered in important ways by the labor of immigrants and women (Dalla Costa & Dalla Costa, 1995; Hardt & Negri, 2000). While this tighter integration of everyday activities and ways of being into circuits of capitalist control is hardly worth celebrating, we consider the autonomists' claim that this process nonetheless broadens the field of struggle against capitalist domination beyond the economic and political and into the social and cultural. This expanded terrain, we observe, is the very field of struggle in the conflict over immigration.

Relatedly, we deploy Marx's concept of "general intellect," redefined by autonomist theorists as the forms of knowledge one acquires, reproduces and develops through engagement in the everyday life and institutions of a society. With corporate profits increasingly dependent upon the generation, assessment and application of new knowledge, with growing numbers of laborers and students called upon to acquire flexible literacies and facility with digital tools, and with low-cost digital instruments flooding consumer markets, those living in media-saturated informational orders are pressed to develop as forms of general intellect understandings of how to manipulate digital tools.[13] Indeed, writes Nick Dyer-Witheford (1999),

> [T]he new communicative capacities and technological competencies manifesting in the contemporary work force, while most explicit among qualified workers, are *not* the exclusive attributes of this group, but rather exist in "virtual" form among the contingent and unemployed labor force. They are not so much the products of

a particular training or specific work environment but rather the premises and prerequisites of everyday life in a highly integrated technoscientific system permeated by machines and media.

(p. 84; original emphasis)

Though capital works to channel and profit from such general knowledge, we observe, student activists are applying this knowledge in struggles for immigrants' rights.

Finally, in accord with autonomist theory, we view the dynamism and creativity of subaltern groups as primary factors in social, political and economic change. That is, we understand these groups' creative efforts to control and improve their own lives as motivating capital to revolutionize the means of production so as to harness and capitalize upon the vitality of the subaltern. With each revolution, though, subaltern groups find new lines of struggle and new possibilities for creative work even as they build upon and extend longstanding traditions of resistance. Moreover, in each new order, liberatory struggles may spiral from group to group as the subaltern recognize common—though not identical—conditions of experience and common possibilities for resistance (Hardt & Negri, 2004). In the era of globalization and the expanded social factory, autonomists argue, capital's networking together of more and more elements of everyday life into global circuits of production, distribution and consumption means that a greater range of subaltern groups may recognize common conditions of experience and may support each others' struggles against domination.

Furthermore, the wiring together of the world and the spread of digital literacies means that increasing numbers of workers and activists are able to communicate rapidly and at little cost both within and across groups. Thus, feminists struggling against healthcare policies that exploit women's unpaid labor may work online to alert and enlist the help of environmentalists committed to creating healthier living conditions for all families. These groups, in turn, may circulate information posted to the web by immigrants' rights groups fighting industrial pollution of immigrant communities (see Desert Mirage High School & F.I.R.M.E. Productions, 2006). In forging such connections and developing shared knowledge, then, subaltern groups destabilize and press ahead of reactive systems of domination.

Globalization and Immigration

To understand the current balance of forces and to comprehend the tensions in high-tech global capitalism that student activists and others in the immigrants' rights movement are exploiting, it is necessary to chart some of the social, political and economic trends of the past forty years. More specifically, we must consider how various developments in multiple domains shaped and were shaped by the creation of a high-tech, corporate-led global economy dependent on immigrant labor. To begin, we follow Hardt and Negri (2000, 2004) in observing that the anti-establishment rebellions that circulated across Western societies throughout the 1960s and 1970s set off or contributed to numerous transformations in capital. In the face of waged workers' resistance to factory discipline, women's resistance to unpaid reproductive labor, students' resistance to educational inequality, and diverse racial and ethnic groups' resistance to racist hierarchies and practices, capital, at times following the spearhead of the United States military, pressed deeper into "Third World" societies in search of new sites for production, distribution and consumption.

Capital's creation of global supply chains, we may note, was made possible by breakthroughs in the development of transportation and communications technologies. Many of these efforts, including the development of the internet, satellites, lasers, robotics, and container shipping, were subsidized by taxpayer dollars funneled through the Pentagon system and other arms of the state (Reich, 2007). These publicly financed inventions were, in turn, handed over to capital, which deployed them in the linking together of a command and control system for the nascent corporate-run global economy.

With the worldwide integration of high-tech communications and transportation systems, corporations came to require at certain nodes in their networks laborers able to use digital tools to coordinate and carry out the activities of global chains of production, distribution and consumption. Responding to these and other pressures, including marginalized communities' demands for both increased educational opportunities and access to technical/administrative knowledge (Apple, 1995), the state expanded its system of technical and community colleges and wired many public schools to facilitate students' acquisition of digital literacies (Kasper, 2002/2003). Importantly, however, we must note the state's distribution of digital instruments to public schools was uneven and favored schools serving more affluent communities. Nonetheless, the diffusion of digital tools throughout society, along with the growth of mass media and the expansion of consumer markets for personal computers and other low-cost digital goods, thickened the electronic ether of everyday life in the United States and strengthened the high-tech dimension of forms of general intellect in the population (Dyer-Witheford, 1999). Student activists in the immigrants' rights movement would later draw upon this collective knowledge and reappropriate the tools of high-tech capitalism in resistance to the global order.

Though corporations came to rely increasingly on workers' control of powerful literacies, business groups, mindful of shrinking margins of profit, lobbied the state to roll back corporate taxes used to fund schools, libraries and other public sponsors of literacy (Apple, 2006; Brandt, 2001). Thus did corporations shift the burden for literacy sponsorship more squarely on to the state and through the state on to the shoulders of local communities. At the same time as they worked to reduce their contributions to the funding of domestic programs, corporate interests pressed the federal government to negotiate business-friendly international trade pacts such as the 1994 North American Free Trade Agreement (NAFTA), which opened Mexico to giant retailers such as Wal-Mart and which flooded Mexican markets with the underpriced products of heavily subsidized US-based agricultural companies. As a result, small farms and small and medium-sized firms in Mexico went under, sending waves of displaced workers and families to Mexican cities and to the US, where "low skill" jobs were available in construction, in the growing service industry, and in the remnants of US agricultural and manufacturing sectors (Faux, 2006). Similar processes of economic restructuring and displacement have occurred throughout the world and especially in Latin American countries such as El Salvador and Guatemala.

Thus, as noted by student protestors and others in the immigrants' rights movement, entry into the US by workers and families with or without full documentation has much to do with the push provided by the destruction in Latin America of longstanding economic practices and the pull generated by the creation of "low skill" work in the US. These phenomena, writes economist Geoffrey Faux (2006), were the predicted and partly intended results of NAFTA and other economic policies backed by corporate interests and made possible by the wiring together of the global economy.

While many US citizens, motivated by altruistic or pecuniary impulses, welcomed Latin American immigrants into the country, others railed against the "invasion" of the US by "aliens" interested only in stealing jobs and availing themselves of social services such as public education (MacGillis, 2006; Minutemen back on border patrol, 2006; Minutemen Project, 2007).

Much as nativist and traditionalist groups in Japan and Israel bolstered their political standing by speaking to citizens' anxieties over social and economic change, neoconservative and authoritarian populist groups in the US addressed the well-founded concerns of workers anxious about changes in global labor markets and endeavored to convince them that their troubles were ultimately attributable to the influx into the US of dark-skinned, non-English-speaking "aliens" and not to, say, unfair trade policies. In pursuing this strategy, nativist groups in the US succeeded in building a real base of support, though they found themselves in a difficult situation politically in that the anti-immigration proposals they favored would shrink the low-wage workforce desired by powerful business groups, key allies of the nativists in the contemporary conservative bloc (Apple, 2006).

Despite challenges in the political field, nativists have had some success in passing measures designed to punish undocumented workers (while leaving intact economic structures creating the push/pull dynamics compelling many "unskilled" immigrants to seek work in the US). In 1994, for instance, voters in California approved Proposition 187, the so-called "Save Our State" initiative designed to curtail undocumented immigrants' access to public education and other social services. Though the measure was eventually overturned in the courts, voters' initial approval of Proposition 187 demonstrated the political power of anti-immigration discourse. Over a decade later, US Representative F. James Sensenbrenner (R-WI) once again stoked fears of "illegal aliens" overwhelming labor markets and public institutions when he introduced House Resolution 4437, the Border Protection, Anti-Terrorism, and Illegal Immigration Control Act of 2005. As with Proposition 187, Sensenbrenner's bill failed to stand as law, but succeeded in circulating and further popularizing nativist ideology. Unlike Proposition 187, however, H.R. 4437 met stiff resistance from an emerging immigrants' rights movement comprised of students and others living and laboring in the social factory of global capitalism.

The 2006 Pro-Immigration Actions

Week after week during the spring of 2006, millions of women, men and children in cities large and small marched, walked out, sat in, and boycotted in solidarity with immigrants living in the US. Though united in opposition to H.R. 4437, these millions comprised a diverse and decentered alliance of groups with disparate goals, beliefs and motivations. Nonetheless, we may still identify as prominent themes of the actions several important ideas: immigrant labor, "legal" and "illegal," waged and unwaged, inside the factory and out, is indispensable to the functioning of the domestic and global economy (immigrant laborers demonstrated their importance by participating in the Day Without Immigrants and other work stoppages, shutting down businesses in the service industry and other economic sectors); immigrants utilize public schools and other state-run institutions in large part to sustain and develop their abilities to contribute to the greater good (students and educators walked out of schools to protest the threatened withholding of public education from students without full documentation); rigid delineations such as (US) American vs. Salvadoran and documented vs. undocumented are ever more untenable in a world increasingly integrated across national boundaries by economic, social and cultural networks (many marchers displayed US flags alongside flags from other nations, privileging neither and holding open possibilities for still other identifications).

Thus, in the terminology of autonomist theory, demonstrators emphasized that the social factory, the web of relations and practices necessary for the functioning of the capitalist order, relies for its operation upon immigrant labor. Indeed, by deploying in their messages images and sounds of Latino/a traditions (see below), activists called to public attention how immigrants' social and cultural practices prepare and sustain immigrant and non-immigrant workers and families and contribute to the storehouse of general intellect from which the global economy draws its power. While capital depends upon immigrants' social and cultural practices for the cultivation of labor power and for the development of general intellect, however, it cannot create or fully control these practices and always faces the possibility of communities organizing themselves through cultural, political and economic actions carried out against and potentially beyond its rule. Thus, activists' citations of Latino/a cultural forms may be read as underscoring the fact that immigrant families and communities produce that which both powers the current system and threatens its very existence.

Such multivalent messages were generated by Latino/a students working through the "I Am Orange County" digital storytelling project, a joint endeavor linking together public schools and the Orange County Human Relations Commission and the Community Therapeutic Arts Center of Orange County, California. Students who participated in the project during the 2005/2006 school year learned how to create powerful narratives and how to use video cameras and computers to produce digital films that interrupt exclusionary discourses and emphasize the social, political and economic contributions of immigrant communities. The project's website states:

> Despite an ethnically diverse population, Orange County is a flashpoint for anti-immigrant movements and legislation. Media portrayals of Orange County consistently depict a wealthy paradise, which is devoid of ethnic or class diversity. The "I Am Orange County" digital stories enable students to exercise social justice leadership skills, while promoting a sense of empowerment, accomplishment and belonging in their primarily immigrant communities. These stories also foster social justice dialogues that strengthen students' voices and also find and share positive solutions to common problems facing youth today.
>
> (Orange County Children's Therapeutic Arts Center &
> Orange County Human Relations Commission, 2006)

Like students at the Byrd Academy in Chicago and in the Citizen Schools of Porto Alegre (see above), then, students working through the "I Am Orange County" project developed powerful and valuable literacies by employing Reich's (1991) "new basic skills" of abstraction, system thinking, experimentation, and collaboration and by engaging diverse technologies to create texts that speak to wide audiences and mobilize support for justice-oriented projects.[14]

While several of the stories and scenes presented in "I Am Orange County" address overtly political matters of immigration policy, others focus on immigrant communities' cultural practices and the importance of these practices for sustaining those who make possible the functioning of the socio-economic order of the United States. Put in autonomist terms, then, these stories expose the social factory's reliance upon immigrant communities' social and cultural practices. Student filmmakers convey this idea by matching their stories of growing up in hardworking, vibrant communities with video montages of neighborhood parks, mariachi bands, Catholic weddings, local schools, and children at play. In her account of her community's traditions and practices, student filmmaker Yessenia Gomez speaks over an image of her uncle's rough, reddened hands, saying, "It is a community where we have the hands of construction workers, giving the children the opportunity to have a better education, a better life." Ending her story, Ms. Gomez juxtaposes her uncle's hands against the small hands of her young cousin, stating, "I'm a young woman who wants to be someone—a doctor, a psychologist. I am part of this beautiful community, born of the hands of *mi gente*. I am Orange County" (Orange County Children's Therapeutic Arts Center & Orange County Human Relations Commission, 2006). Thus, more than just announcing their presence, student filmmakers like Yessenia Gomez proclaim they and their immigrant communities are the very lifeblood of Orange County, California and of the United States.

More generally, it is the case that students who use digital tools to participate in the pro-immigration movement—whether through digital storytelling or by using mobile phones or networked computers to disseminate information about rallies and walkouts—acquire and further develop aspects of the general intellect of technologically advanced socio-economic systems and enlist this knowledge in a project that challenges these systems in part by exposing their dependence on the waged and unwaged labor of immigrant groups and other marginalized communities. In pursuing such strategies, then, immigrant students and other activists exploit key tensions in high-tech global capitalism so as to advance causes of social justice. To review, many immigrant students and their families, pushed from countries "restructured" by neoliberal policies and pulled to the US by the prospect of work in "low skill" economic sectors widened by domestic fiscal initiatives, find themselves living in electronically saturated environments of key hubs of networks of global capitalism. In these environments, a growing percentage of the population makes increasing use of digital tools to mediate disparate practices at work, at school and in their homes and neighborhoods. Thus does the general intellect of many communities in the

United States take on a distinctly high-tech quality. Students who live in impoverished neighborhoods and who attend under-resourced schools, therefore, are nonetheless able to access forms of high-tech knowledge and reappropriate the tools of global capitalism to organize themselves for social justice work.[15]

Crucially, students involved in the pro-immigration movement draw upon high-tech knowledge not simply to organize those within their own groups, but also to coordinate with, support and learn from those working in other groups in other locations. Paralleling the actions of corporate agents who utilize digital tools to link together far-flung nodes of production, distribution and consumption (thereby shifting prospects for work and setting off flows of migration), students in the immigrants' rights movement use digital tools to network with and win support from groups and individuals in their own regions, across the US and around the world. Indeed, in the spring of 2006, students gathered information about H.R. 4437 from internet sites, forwarded this information to their friends, watched and read coverage of marches and school walkouts, organized events through social networking sites such as MySpace.com, and text-messaged each other about the shifting details of pro-immigration actions (Cardenas, 2006; Navarro, 2006; Shapira, 2006b). Additionally, students engaged "old" media both to learn about others' efforts in the movement and to disseminate information about their own endeavors: student filmmakers working through the "I Am Orange County" project publicized their work by granting interviews to CNN, *The New York Times*, and *The Los Angeles Times* (Delson, 2006; Navarro, 2006; Orange County Children's Therapeutic Arts Center & Orange County Human Relations Commission, 2006); other students, along with older members of the movement, tuned into Spanish language radio stations, where disc jockeys such as Los Angeles' Eddie Sotelo and Renan Almendarez Coello circulated information about times, locations and themes of particular actions (Balz & Fears, 2006; Shapira, 2006).

By engaging both "old" and "new" media, then, students across the US were able to learn of, organize and publicize pro-immigration actions and thereby intensify and widen the circulation of struggles over immigration. Much as Dyer-Witheford (1999) notes of young Italian activists' utilization of media, the efforts of students in the immigrants' rights movement in the US display "the generational characteristics of subjects who, having come of age in a media environment, are capable of shaping this terrain for their own political purposes, rather than merely being passively exploited as objects of spectacular display" (pp. 227–228). That is, rather than acquiescing to mainstream media's casting of immigrants as "illegals" or "undesirables," student activists appropriated the tools of media so as to create themselves as agentic subjects working to bring about a more just order.

Conclusion

Though student activists in the immigrants' rights movement conducted much of their work outside of the "official" spaces of school, teachers may support students' efforts by providing them with opportunities both to network with potential allies and to acquire literacies useful for activism. Educators might, for instance, help students working in the immigrants' rights movement forge connections with student organizations focused on other issues related to globalization and social justice: environmental clubs; student anti-sweatshop groups; and high school chapters of Amnesty International. Through networking with other groups, students may develop nuanced understandings of how their concerns overlap with the concerns of others, learn of different strategies and tactics for activism, and expand their list of allies who may be mobilized for ad hoc rallies such as those organized during the spring of 2006.

Additionally, following the example of educators who worked with student filmmakers on the "I Am Orange County" project, teachers might provide students with opportunities to develop digital literacies for activist work. While students may, by virtue of their acquisition of the general intellect of the informational order, understand how to manipulate certain digital tools, they may have few ideas about how to apply digital literacies in social justice work. Teachers therefore might engage students in explorations of how to use the digital tools in their environments to investigate and address concerns in their own communities. More specifically, educators and students might consider how digital tools' affordances (e.g., many-to-many communication) open new possibilities for activism (e.g., building support across the country and around the world by posting to the internet on-the-scene audio and video of rallies).

Finally, educators interested in supporting students working in the pro-immigration movement should consider the dangers of pressing activist students to organize themselves into traditional school-based organizations or clubs. Insofar as such school-sanctioned organizations take on hierarchical structures and establish boundaries between members and non-members, the formation of such groups may slow down and rigidify a movement that thrives on speed and fluidity. Indeed, in an ironic twist, the endorsement and absorption of activist groups by schools may undercut these groups' abilities to press forward with their projects.

In this chapter, we have critically analyzed the production and use of new literacies and identities that are contradictory. They are part of an emerging global biopolitics of capitalism that demand heart and mind. As such, they are clearly associated with relations of exploitation and domination that lead to differentiation and immiseration. Yet, as we showed in our second section that goes beyond the act of bearing witness to negativity, there are spaces of action and movements engaged in such action that challenge these relations. While our focus has been on the example of mobilizations around immigration, this is but one example that can and must be multiplied. Counterhegemonic actions and agents exist in every sphere. And we can act as secretaries in making their struggles visible.

Acknowledgments

We would like to thank Scot Barnett for his work on the initial draft of this article. We would also like to thank the Friday Seminar at the University of Wisconsin-Madison, as well as Deborah Brandt, for their comments on earlier drafts of this piece. A briefer analysis of the issues we treat here can be found in Gallegos, Tozer, and Henry (in press).

Notes

1   We use "capital" here as a stand-in for more-or-less organized business interests. While different factions within this group have different concerns and commitments, we argue that it is possible to identify *basic* and *general* similarities in the sub-groups' beliefs and objectives. For differently accented and differently nuanced articulations of the dominant corporate narrative of globalization and the emergence of the informational economy, see Friedman (2006), Norberg (2003), and Wolf (2004). For versions of this narrative that emphasize the role of schooling in developing human capital, see The Committee on Science, Engineering and Public Policy and Policy and Global Affairs (2006), Friedman (2006), and Gates (2005). For critiques of such accounts, see Apple (2006), Brown and Lauder (2001), Lauder, Brown, Dillabough, and Halsey (2006), and Lipman (2004).

2   Throughout this paper, we describe the structures and performance of *ideal* industrial and fast capitalist enterprises doing business in advanced industrial nations. The structures and performance of *actual* firms, of course, are always shaped through interactions of dominant, residual and emergent organizational forms.

3   Such forms of life are not *inherently* valuable, but valuable because they can be exploited for profit by capital. That is, as argued below, valuable forms of life—the control of which may be considered valuable literacies—are those forms of life that help workers generate new, profitable knowledge and engage in cooperative labor with other employees and with customers.

4   Although in the following analysis of these changes and struggles we discuss first economic transformations, we do not argue that changes in the economy *wholly determine* changes in social and political spheres (nor vice-versa). Rather, we argue that activity in each of these spheres has relative autonomy from, yet interacts with, activity in other spheres.

5   These analyses, argue Hardt and Negri (2000), apply to a range of workers in the informational economy: symbolic analysts collaborating in ad hoc teams and mining and synthesizing information from disparate semiotic domains to create and design new products for new niche markets; laborers engaged in informationalized manufacturing who work in shifting teams with diverse colleagues to produce and to refine processes for making customized goods; and service workers embodying the 'official' values and interests of their companies so as to create senses of well-being in customers from particular niche markets.

6   There is some truth to the argument that welfare state public service providers were not/are not responsive to the needs of marginalized groups. Indeed, neoliberals have achieved success in the political realm in part through speaking to citizens' real concerns (e.g., the unresponsiveness of welfare state public service providers to marginalized groups) and providing seemingly practical solutions (e.g., the privatization of public services). We argue that progressives must interrupt such rightist discourses and must provide alternate solutions

7   that are both practical and consistent with principles of strong democracy (see Apple, 2006). Certain neoliberals are "willing to spend more state and/or private money on schools, if and only if schools meet the needs expressed by capital. Thus, resources are made available for 'reforms' and policies that further connect the education system to the project of making our economy more competitive" (Apple, 2001, p. 41). See the final section of this paper for a discussion of school reform proposals premised on enhancing competitiveness in the emerging informational economy.

8   These trends within the neoliberal state informational economy are consistent with Anthony Giddens' (1991) observations that in late modernity, citizens in post-industrial and post-traditional states are called upon more and more to engage in "reflexive life planning." Giddens (1991) argues that "because of the 'openness' of social life today, the pluralization of contexts of action and the diversity of 'authorities,' lifestyle choice is increasingly important in the constitution of self-identity and daily activity. Reflexively organized life-planning, which normally presumes consideration of risks as filtered through contact with expert knowledge, becomes a central feature of the structuring of self-identity" (p. 5; see also Gee, 2004)[0].

9   The International Centre for Prison Studies (2005) notes in its World Prison Population List for 2005 that in the US, 714 out of every 100,000 citizens are imprisoned. This gives the US the highest imprisonment rate in the world.

10   Also involved in the struggle over public schools' endorsement of non-standard knowledge and practice are groups on the Right, including: neoliberals in favor of constructing a competitive regulatory state that audits schools through measuring students' control of standardized knowledge; social conservatives and authoritarian populists who endeavor to standardize in public schools' curricula and instructional processes their own (and at least slightly different) forms of "traditional" knowledge, values and habits; and managerial workers with professional commitments to measuring disparate work practices.

We wish to emphasize here the importance of analyzing the actions of multiple groups working in the political sphere (as well as other spheres) to shape processes of schooling. Too much of the educational literature on fast capitalism, we argue, fails to theorize the role of the state as a set of institutions serving in part to mediate social and economic dynamics. Indeed, much of this work neglects to take up the important matter of how the occupation of particular positions within the state by actors of certain classes helps (re)create "official" networks of sponsorship for certain classed modes of identity formation and literate practice (see Apple, 2006).

11   We focus in this chapter on working-class families and individuals who immigrate to the United States from Latin American countries. The experiences of these families and individuals, of course, do not represent the experiences of *all* immigrants from Latin American countries.

12   Of course, capitalism has always depended upon the unpaid labor of women for the reproduction of the workforce (Dalla Costa & Dalla Costa, 1995).

13   As we note further into our analysis, particular forms of high-tech knowledge are distributed unevenly throughout society.

14   El Puente Project of Indianapolis, IN also works with Latino/a youth, providing opportunities for students to develop powerful and valuable literacies through social justice work (Puente Project, 2007). Visit El Puente Project's website at http://www.elpuenteproject.com to watch student-produced "Varriomentaries" (digital stories similar in many ways to the stories produced by students working through the "I Am Orange County" project).

15   This in no way mitigates concerns about the unequal funding of public schools. If anything, students' and educators' resourcefulness in under-funded and under-equipped schools underscores the need for a fairly funded system in which currently marginalized communities can more fully realize their potentials.

References

Althusser, L. (1971). Ideology and ideological state apparatuses. In *Lenin and philosophy, and other essays* (B. Brewster, Trans., pp. 127–186). London: New Left.

Apple, M. W. (Ed.). (1982). *Cultural and economic reproduction in education: Essays on class, ideology and the state.* London: Routledge & Kegan Paul.

Apple, M. W. (1995). *Education and power.* New York: Routledge.
Apple, M.W. (1996). *Cultural politics and education* (2nd ed.). New York: Teachers College.
Apple, M. W. (1999). *Power, meaning, and identity.* New York: Peter Lang.
Apple, M. W. (2000). *Official knowledge: Democratic education in a conservative age* (2nd ed.). New York: Routledge.
Apple, M. W. (2001). *Educating the "right" way: Markets, standards, God and inequality.* New York: RoutledgeFalmer.
Apple, M. W. (2006). *Educating the "right" way: Markets, standards, God and inequality.* (2nd ed.). New York: Routledge.
Apple, M. W. & Beane, J. A. (Eds.) (2007). *Democratic schools: Lessons in powerful education.* (2nd ed.). Portsmouth, NH: Heinemann.
Apple, M. W. & Buras, K. L. (Eds.). (2006). *The subaltern speak: Curriculum, power, and educational struggles.* New York: Routledge.
Apple, M. W. & Gandin, L. A. (2002). Challenging neo-liberalism, building democracy: Creating the Citizen School in Porto Alegre, Brazil. *Journal of Education Policy, 17*(2), 259–279.
Apple, M. W. et al. (2003). *The state and the politics of knowledge.* New York: RoutledgeFalmer.
Au, W. (2009). *Unequal by design.* New York: Routledge.
Ball, S. (2003). *Class strategies and the education market.* London: RoutledgeFalmer.
Balz, D. & Fears, D. (2006). "We decided not to be invisible anymore"; Pro-immigration rallies are held across country. *The Washington Post,* April 11, p. A01. Retrieved November 26, 2007 from http://www.washingtonpost.com.
Barber, B. R. (2003). *Strong democracy: Participatory politics for a new age.* Berkeley: University of California.
Barton, D. (1994). *Literacy: An introduction to the ecology of written language.* Oxford: Blackwell.
Bernstein, B. (1990).*The structuring of pedagogic discourse.* New York: Routledge.
Bourdieu, P. & Passeron, J. C. (1977). *Reproduction in education, society and culture.* London: Sage.
Brandt, D. (2001). *Literacy in American lives.* New York: Cambridge University Press.
Brandt, D. (2005). Writing for a living: Literacy and the knowledge economy. *Written Communication, 22*(2), 166–197.
Brown, P. & Lauder, H. (2001). *Capitalism and social progress: The future of society in a global economy.* New York: Palgrave.
Brown, P. & Lauder, H. (2006). Globalization, knowledge and the myth of the magnet economy. *Globalization, Societies and Education, 4*(1), 25–57.
Brown, P., Green, A., & Lauder, H. (2001). *High skills: Globalization, competitiveness, and skill formation.* Oxford: Oxford University Press.
Cardenas, J. (2006). Young immigrants raise voices, hopes. *St. Petersburg Times* (Florida), May 13, p. 1A. Retrieved November 26, 2007 from http://www.sptimes.com.
Carnoy, M. (2000). *Sustaining the new economy: Work, family, and community in the information age.* Cambridge: Harvard University Press.
Castells, M. (1996). *The rise of the network society* (Vol. 1): *The information age: Economy, society and culture.* Malden, MA: Blackwell.
Cleaver, H. (1979). *Reading capital politically.* Brighton, UK: Harvester.
Committee on Science, Engineering and Public Policy & Policy and Global Affairs. (2006). *Rising above the gathering storm: Energizing and employing America for a brighter future.* Prepublished edition. Washington, DC: National Academies Press. Retrieved September 19, 2006, from http://www.nap.edu/catalog/11463.html#orgs.
Dalla Costa, M. & Dalla Costa, G. F. (Eds.) (1995). *Paying the price: Women and the politics of international economic strategy.* London: Zed.
Davis, M. (2006). *Planet of slums.* London: Verso.
Delson, J. (2006). Their 'O.C.' is about striving, not glitz; The student documentary covers immigrant marches, life in working-class neighborhoods—and hope. *The Los Angeles Times,* May 22, p. B3. Retrieved November 26, 2007, from http://www.latimes.com/.
Desert Mirage High School & F.I.R.M.E. Productions (Producers & Directors). (2006). *Contaminated valley: Thermal, CA* (Motion picture). (Available from F.I.R.M.E. Productions and El Puente Project at http://www.elpuenteproject.com/?pageId=160#contaminated_valley.
Dobbs, L. (2007). *War on the middle class: How the government, big business, and special interest groups are waging war on the American dream and how to fight back* (2nd ed.). New York: Penguin.

Dyer-Whitheford, N. (1999). *Cyber-Marx: Cycles and circuits of struggle in high-technology capitalism.* Urbana, IL: University of Illinois.

Faux, G. (2006). *The global class war: How America's bipartisan elite lost our future—and what it will take to win it back.* Hoboken, NJ: Wiley.

Friedman, T. L. (2006). *The world is flat: A brief history of the twenty-first century.* New York: Farrar, Straus & Giroux.

Gallegos, B., Tozer, S., & Henry, A. (Eds.) (in press) *Handbook on social foundations research.* Mahwah, NJ: Lawrence Erlbaum.

Gates, B. (2005). Keynote address presented at the National Education Summit on High Schools, February, Washington, DC. Retrieved September 19, 2006, from http://www.gatesfoundation.org/MediaCenter/Speeches/BillgSpeeches/BGSpeechNGA-050226.htm.

Gee, J. P. (1996). *Social linguistics and literacies: Ideology in discourse.* Philadelphia, PA: Falmer.

Gee. J. P. (2000). New people in new worlds: Networks, the new capitalism and schools. In B. Cope & M. Kalantzis (Eds.), *Multiliteracies: Literacy learning and the design of social futures* (pp. 43–68). Routledge: New York.

Gee, J. P. (2004). *Situated language and learning: A critique of traditional schooling.* New York: Routledge.

Gee, J. P., Hull, G., & Lankshear, C. (1996). *The new work order: Behind the language of the new capitalism.* Boulder, CO: Westview.

Gewirtz, S., Ball, S.J., & Bowe, R. (1995). *Markets, choice and equity in education.* Buckingham, UK: Open University Press.

Giddens, A. (1991). *Modernity and self-identity: Self and society in the late modern age.* Stanford, CA: Stanford University Press.

Greider, W. (1997). *One world, ready or not.* New York: Simon & Schuster.

Hardt, M. & Negri, A. (2000). *Empire.* Cambridge, MA: Harvard University Press.

Hardt, M. & Negri, A. (2004). *Multitude: War and democracy in the age of Empire.* New York: Penguin.

Hartley, D. (2003). New economy, new pedagogy? *Oxford Review of Education,* 29(1), 81–94.

Heath, S. B. (1983). *Ways with words: Language, life and work in communities and classrooms.* Cambridge: Cambridge University Press.

International Centre for Prison Studies. (2005). World prison population list (6th ed.). London: Walmsley, R. Retrieved July 25, 2006, from http://www.kcl.ac.uk/depsta/rel/icps/world-prison-population-list-2005.pdf.

Kasper, H. T. (2002/2003). The changing role of the community college. *Occupational Outlook Quarterly,* 46(4).

Katz, M. B. (1975). *Class, bureaucracy, and schools: The illusion of educational change in America.* New York: Praeger.

Lauder, H. & Hughes, D. (1999). *Trading in futures: Why markets in education don't work.* Philadelphia, PA: Open University Press.

Lauder, H., Brown, P., Dillabough, J., & Halsey, A. H. (Eds.). (2006). *Education, globalization and social change.* Oxford: Oxford University Press.

Lipman, P. (2004). *High stakes education: Inequality, globalization, and urban school reform.* New York: RoutledgeFalmer.

MacGillis, A. (2006). Minutemen assail amnesty idea. *The Washington Post,* May 13, p. B.03. Retrieved November 26, 2007 from http://www.washingtonpost.com.

Minutemen back on border patrol. (2006). *Chicago Tribune,* April 2, p. 6. Retrieved November 26, 2007, from http://www.chicagotribune.com.

Minuteman Project. (2007). *The official website for the Minuteman Project.* Retrieved November 26, 2007 from http://www.minutemanproject.com.

Navarro, M. (2006, June 11). Taking to the streets, for parents' sake. *The New York Times,* sec. 9, p. 1. Retrieved November 26, 2007 from http://www.nytimes.com.

New London Group. (2000). A pedagogy of multiliteracies: Designing social futures. In B. Cope & M. Kalantzis (Eds.), *Multiliteracies: Literacy learning and the design of social futures* (pp. 9–37). Routledge: New York.

Norberg, J. (2003). *In defense of global capitalism.* Washington, DC: Cato Institute.

Orange County Children's Therapeutic Arts Center & Orange County Human Relations Commission (Producers) (2006) and Rosa, J. (Director). "I Am Orange County" (Motion picture). (Available from Orange County Therapeutic Children's Arts Center, 2215 N. Broadway, Santa Ana, CA, 92706-2615).

Power, S., Edwards, T., Whitty, G., & Wigfall, V. (2003). *Education and the middle class.* Philadelphia, PA: Open University Press.

Puente Project. (2007). El Puente Project homepage. Retrieved November 26, 2007, from http://www.elpuenteproject.com.

Reich, R. (1991). *The work of nations.* New York: Knopf.

Reich, R. (2007). *Supercapitalism: The transformation of business, democracy, and everyday life.* New York: Knopf.

Robertson, S. L. (2000). *A class act: Changing teachers' work, the state, and globalization.* New York: Falmer.

Schultz, B. D. (2007). "Feelin' what they feelin'": Democracy and curriculum in Cabrini Green. In M. W. Apple & J. A. Beane (Eds.), *Democratic schools: Lessons in powerful education* (2nd ed., pp. 81–105). Portsmouth, NH: Heinemann.

Scollon, R. & Scollon, S.W. (1981). *Narrative, literacy, and face in interethnic communication.* Norwood, NJ: Ablex.

Scribner, S. & Cole, M. (1981). *The psychology of literacy.* Cambridge, MA: Harvard University Press.

Shapira, I. (2006a). Hispanic students step into spotlight: Teen activists could grow to exercise political influence, some observers say. *The Washington Post,* April 2, p. C14. Retrieved November 26, 2007, from http://www.washingtonpost.com.

Shapira, I. (2006b). Cause transforms Woodbridge teen into activist leader. *The Washington Post,* April 17, p. A01. Retrieved November 27, 2007, from http://www.washingtonpost.com.

Street, B. (1984). *Literacy in theory and practice.* Cambridge: Cambridge University Press.

Taylor, M. C. (2001). *The moment of complexity: Emerging network culture.* Chicago: University of Chicago Press.

Tyack, D. (1974). *The one best system: A history of American education.* Cambridge, MA: Harvard University Press.

Valenzuela, A. (Ed.). (2005). *Leaving children behind: How "Texas-style" accountability fails Latino youth.* Albany, NY: State University of New York.

Virno, P. & Hardt, M. (1996). *Radical thought in Italy: A potential politics.* Minneapolis: University of Minnesota.

Warschauer, M. (1999). *Electronic literacies: Language, culture and power in online education.* Mahwah, NJ: Lawrence Erlbaum Associates.

Whitty, G., Power, S., & Halpin, D. (1998). *Devolution and choice in education: The school, the state, and the market.* Philadelphia: Open University Press.

Willis, P. (1977). *Learning to labour.* Farnborough, UK: Saxon House.

Wolf, M. (2004). *Why globalization works.* New Haven: Yale University Press.

CHAPTER 3

From the Rightist "Coup" to the New Beginning of Progressive Politics in Japanese Education[1]

KEITA TAKAYAMA

Introduction

Japan is currently undergoing a radical transformation of its education system. Much in the same way that the New Right challenged the postwar social-democratic, state welfarist settlement on public education in Anglo-American nations (Brown & Lauder, 2001; Whitty, Power, & Halpin, 1998), Japanese conservatives attempt to restructure public education by attacking the postwar democratic and egalitarian settlement of their education system. As seen elsewhere, the current Japanese education restructuring is part of the larger transformation of the postwar hegemonic configuration and its shift towards the post-postwar socio-political and economic arrangement. This perspective is absent in the current English language discussion of Japanese education reform (see Takayama, 2008a, 2009b) which tends to isolate education reform from what Stephen Ball (1997) calls "the generic quality of reform" (p. 27)—the general projects and ideologies of contemporary social policy and the changing relationship between the state and civil society.

One of the pillars of the postwar settlement in Japanese education is the Fundamental Law of Education (FLE). Promulgated in 1947 during the US occupation period (1945–1952), the law replaced the 1890 Imperial Rescript on Education (*kyōiku chokugo*), which was central to the imperial state's ideological project. Preaching to children that "should emergency arise, offer yourselves courageously to the State" (The Imperial Rescript on Education, as cited in Horio, 1988, p. 399), the Rescript defined education as one of imperial subjects' *obligations* to the state, along with military service and tax payment. Japanese educational leaders drafted the FLE in the immediate aftermath of the Asia Pacific War to mark a clear break from this regrettable past, redefining education as one of citizens' inalienable human rights. Closely linked with the postwar pacifist Constitution, the 1947 law proclaimed the democratic and pacifist idealism of new Japanese education.

Since its inception, the FLE has consistently faced conservative attacks. The early sign of conservative dissatisfaction with the democratic educational principle was already visible even when the US occupation's demilitarizing effort was still pursued both in and outside education. The Ministry of Education (MoE) officials and conservative politicians fought to keep the Imperial Rescript, insisting that it was compatible with the democratic principle of the newly instituted Constitution (Horio & Yamazumi, 1976). In addition, the US occupation was not keen on demolishing the Imperial Rescript, either, because it wanted to use Japanese people's blind loyalty to the emperor as its occupation strategy (Fujioka, Nakano, Nakauchi, & Takeuchi, 1987, pp. 53–4; see also Dower, 1999). No sooner had Japan gained the political independence from the Allies (US) occupation in 1952 than conservatives started fiercely attacking the FLE. Far-right politicians within the ruling Liberal Democratic Party (LDP), which achieved the half-century conservative political reign from 1955 to 1993, were nostalgic for the prewar elitist and imperial education system. To them, the postwar democratic and egalitarian principles were the "US imposition"—the symbol of Japan's defeat and "emasculation." In their mind, the democratic FLE went too far in embracing "Western" educational values such as individuality and human rights at the expense of teaching Japanese tradition, history, and patriotism. Despite their relentless attacks, however, the law was kept intact till the early 2000s—though the MoE consistently infringed upon its democratic values by strengthening its administrative control over curriculum, teachers, and textbooks. Postwar progressives fought to demand the substantiation of the FLE's idealism, resorting to the law and Constitution in a series of court battles to challenge the state abuse of power in education.

In the late 1990s, for the first time in postwar history, the revision of the FLE was taken up in an official policy deliberation, a fact indicating the demise of the postwar democratic settlement in education. As the media featured youth violence, bullying, and declining academic standards and morality as "educational" problems, rightist LDP politicians capitalized upon the pervasive sense of public fear about these issues to legitimize the inclusion of teaching moral values, tradition and patriotism in the revised FLE, while at the same time appraising the Imperial Rescript (Namimoto, 2000). The revisions were first proposed in December 2000 by the National Commission on Educational Reform (NCER), a private advisory panel to then Prime

Minister Yoshirō Mori (LDP) who was one of the most vocal proponents of the FLE revision. It was Mori and his associates who brought in the FLE revision as an agenda for the NCER deliberations (Fujita, 2001). The revision was further debated at the MoE's Central Council of Education which issued in March 2003 its final proposal to the law amendments that aimed to nurture the "Japanese with rich heart" (*kokoro yutakana nihonjin no ikusei*) (MoE, 2003).

After six years of deliberations at top governmental councils, the ruling LDP and its coalition partner New Kōmeitō drafted the FLE revision proposal in April 2006. Under the strong initiative of then Prime Minister Shinzō Abe (2006–2007), the LDP-led coalition government passed the proposal through the Diet in December 2006. The half-century-old symbol of postwar democracy (to progressives) and war defeat (to conservatives) was thus revised for the first time since its 1947 inception. The most controversial of all the revisions was the inclusion of the expression "cultivating an attitude that respects tradition and culture and love of the national homeland that has fostered them" (Japan Times, 2006). The mainstream progressive media and intellectuals challenged this addition, seeing it as a retrogressive move to return to the prewar and wartime state intervention in education, often analogizing the proposed revision with the 1890 Imperial Rescript. They warned that the amendment would render education "a means of producing children who lack autonomous judgment and a critical mind, just following the will of the state" (Japan Times, 2006; see also, Namimoto, 2000; Narushima, 2006; Nishihara, 2003; Nishihara & Ogi, 2006; Ōuchi, 2003; Sanuki, 2003; Takahashi, 2003, 2004).

This chapter chronicles the recent rise of conservative politics culminating in the 2006 FLE revision, or what progressive scholars call "the coup in education" (Nishihara & Ogi, 2006). In so doing, I articulate contradictory spaces in the current conservative dominance of education reform and strategies for progressive political gains. The first part of this chapter "witnesses negativity"—"to illuminate the ways in which education policy and practice are connected to the relations of exploitation and domination in the larger society" (Apple, 2006b, p. 681)—over the conservative revision of the FLE. Situating the FLE revision within the neoliberal economic restructuring and neoconservative cultural backlash in the early 2000s, I closely examine two agents who played a critical role in the conservative mobilization towards the revision.

First, I look at the cultural politics of crisis borrowing by conservative intellectuals and politicians. They borrowed crisis discourse from the United Kingdom in changing the people's common sense about the law and the new role of the state in education. This analysis draws on postcolonial literature to advance a reconceptualization of educational borrowing from a non-

Western perspective. Second, the chapter examines the role of the MoE in the revision, paying particular attention to the Ministry's legitimacy crisis in the time of the relentless neoliberal attack against its bureaucracy. These analyses lead to another task that Apple proposes for critical education— "identifying the contradictory spaces for counter-hegemonic actions" (Apple, 2006b, p. 681). As Henry, Knight, Lingard, and Taylor (1990) point out, "it is crucial to have clear understanding of the totality of the forces which surround any 'arena' of action in order to develop appropriate strategies to resist the hegemonic and at times coercive processes" (p. 14). Building on the earlier analysis of "the totality of the forces" involved in the controversial FLE revision, the last section of this chapter then identifies the tensions within the rightist forces and articulates strategies to ply open and take advantage of the tensions towards more progressive ends.

Conceptually, this chapter takes a globalization approach to the discussion of Japanese education reform. It situates the FLE revision within the common global structural transformation of the state, economy, and education and the associated change in the technology of state control in many advanced capitalist nations. Borrowing Dale and Robertson's expression, I argues that "it is not possible to make sense of Japanese education policy in terms of Japan alone" (1997, p. 209).[2] I concur with Dale and Robertson and others about the structural convergence of education among advanced industrial nations (Ball, 1997; Whitty, Power, & Halpin, 1998). However, the discussion of global policy convergence must be differentiated from the "globalization without a subject" thesis (Dale & Robertson, 2002, p. 11). Changes in economy, civil society, and state institutions do not travel around the world as if no human and institutional agencies and domestic mediations are involved. As Dale and Robertson (2002) points out:

> The installation of global processes and practices is not totally determinative in its needs and expectations; on the contrary, it can live alongside a range of existing (national and local) institutions and combine with them in a range of ways to obtain the desired ends. More than this, local structures and institutions, processes and practices, are crucial to, even the medium necessary for, the spreads of global practices.
>
> (p. 12)

Taking seriously the notion of "globalization with a subject," this study identifies in the FLE revision the situated, specific articulation of similar structural changes in Japanese state and education that are also under way in other advanced capitalist nations. I begin by discussing the "bigger picture"

(Whitty, 2002)—the neoliberal economic transformation and the subsequent neoconservative backlash both of which rendered the cultural politics of crisis borrowing a particularly effective ideological tool at the turn of the Millennium.

The Bigger Picture

In the late 1990s Japan underwent a series of radical socio-economic and political reforms. The economic recession in the aftermath of the early 1990s bubble burst, along with the intensification of global economic competition, led the Japanese business and state elites to break away from the postwar socio-economic and political arrangements that have sustained Japan's postwar stability since the 1960s, thus the "regime shift" (Pempel, 1998). The radical neoliberal turn in both state and corporate capital accumulation strategies resulted in the disappearance of corporate welfarism (lifetime employment, incremental salary scale, family wage) and the termination of developmentalist state intervention in the economy, both of which had been central to Japan's postwar economic nationalism (Gotō, 2002; see also Collin & Apple, this volume). Japanese corporations aggressively pursued capital flight and corporate downsizing to increase their global competitiveness, while the state "reformed" its tax and social welfare policies along the logic of "upward economic distribution" (Duggan, 2003), further reducing the already minimal social spending in comparison to other advanced industrial nations (Ninomiya, 1999). Prime Minister Junichirō Koizumi (2001–2006) further neoliberalized the Japanese state under his slogan "the small and efficient state." His cabinet's aggressive pursuit of privatization of social services and his massive reduction of corporate taxes further promoted the widening economic disparity among the populous.

Indeed, disparity (*kakusa*), winners (*kachigumi*), losers (*makegumi*), and working poor (*wōkingu pua*) have become the keywords of the time (e.g., Kariya, 2001; Sato, 2001; Yamada, 2004). The unemployment rate reached the record high 5 percent in 2004, but this number still hides the rapid increase of irregular contract laborers who are exposed to an unstable work environment and minimum wages. The unemployment rate is particularly higher among young adults, roughly around 10 percent with a substantial number of them working full-time but barely making ends meet.[3] Companies have turned increasingly to temporary workers, once hired almost exclusively for short-term specialized jobs, to perform general office work, which used to be performed by full-time employees (Ministry of Health, Labor and Welfare, 2006). These temporary workers rarely become full-time regular employees, leaving millions of young adults in unstable economic conditions. According to the Ministry of Health, Labor and

Welfare's White Paper (2006), non-regular employees (part-time, temporary, and contract workers) comprised 33 percent of the entire workforce, the highest percentage ever recorded.[4] In 2006, the majority of male non-regular workers (56.8 percent) made an annual salary of 1.99 million yen (Yomiuri News, 2007, March 2), approximately "40 percent as much per hour as full-time workers."

This dualism in the labor market is one of the primary factors causing the rise in inequality and poverty in Japan (OECD, 2006). OECD's (2006) *Economic Survey of Japan 2006* confirms that Japan's widening disparity is worrisome when viewed from an international comparative perspective. The report points out the significant rise in the Gini coefficient measure "since the mid 1980s from well below to slightly above the OECD average" and further indicates that Japan's rate of relative poverty is now one of the highest among the OECD nations. Clearly, Japan is no longer "a classless society" (Sato, 2001) of which the nation used to pride itself.[5]

Since the early 1990s, it has been a remarkably unstable time in terms of politics and ideology, as well. During the cold war period, there was a clear binary structure of ideological conflicts both domestically and internationally. Internationally, Japan had long allied with the Western capitalist bloc led by the United States as opposed to the Soviet Union's communist bloc. Domestically, the all-time-ruling LDP and the all-time opposition Japan Socialist Party (JSP) had formed the binary ideological poles. The same ideological polarization existed in the political contestation between the MoE on the one hand and the Japan Teachers Union (JTU) on the other. The cold war context thus provided people with a clear sense of belongingness and singular identity which allowed them to situate themselves politically.

This picture of political predictability changed in the early 1990s. In 1994 the LDP and the JSP formed an unprecedented alliance along with New Party *Sakigake* in a coalition government. The JSP chairman Tomiichi Murayama discarded the party's long-held policy and declared support for the Japan–US Security Treaty, accepted the constitutionality of the Self-Defense Forces and supported international defense cooperation. Corresponding to this unprecedented move, the JTU and the MOE agreed in 1995 to collaborate and thus announced the end of a half-century-long political contestation. Around this time many scholars agreed on the emergence of a risk, postmodern society where people's social identities are increasingly in flux (Oguma, 2003b; Oguma & Ueno, 2003; Yamada, 2004). The pervasive sense of confusion, stagnation, and disintegration which are the consequence of the 1990s regime shift, prepared the ground for the popular acceptance of the neoconservative call for *the* national *history*, traditional gender norm, patriotism, and "back to basics" in schools (Ida, 2006; Kaizuma, 2005; Oguma, 1998).

"Progressive" Gains During the 1990s Flux

Behind the recent rise of neoconservativism is the series of modest "progressive" gains in the 1990s. In the early 1990s, then Prime Minister, Morihiro Hosokawa (1993–1994), the first non-LDP prime minister since the 1955 formation of the LDP, for the first time in history expressed an apology as a state head to former "comfort women" and his official recognition of wartime atrocities committed by the Japanese imperial army.[6] In 1995, the Diet adopted the "resolution of apology" and the House of Representatives adopted a no-war resolution to mark the 50th anniversary of the end of the Asia Pacific War. Following the official apologies and recognition about the wartime crimes, the MoE's textbook screening accepted textbook references to the dark side of Japanese history during the war.

This shift in the Japanese power bloc's attitude toward the contentious past corresponded with Japanese global capital's relocation of its manufacturing facilities to other Asian neighbors, particularly China. The official apology for the past imperial aggressions was driven by capital's needs to "clean" the past and secure its vital access to rapidly growing Asian market and "economical" manufacturing bases. Along with multinational corporations' interests joined progressive political struggles over the nation's "foundational narrative" (Igarashi, 2000) which had long concealed Japan's memories of colonial ambition in the neighboring Asian nations.[7] Grassroots organizations in Japan and other Asian nations collaborated to bring the media attention to former sex slaves, forced the Japanese government to acknowledge its past wrongdoing, and pressured the MoE to accept more textbook references to these women (Nozaki, 2002).

The 1990s also marked the incorporation of feminist ideas into a series of national and regional laws both in and outside education. At the 1995 Fourth World Conference on Women and the NGO Forum in Beijing it was pointed out that the use of gender-segregated student rolls in Japanese schools that place boys ahead of girls would perpetuate the latter's secondariness to the former. This further augmented the ongoing grassroots mobilizations of citizens and educators to promote gender equality in education (see Hasegawa, 2006; Kimura, 1999, 2005). The grassroots mobilizations were quickly given the official endorsement by state bureaucrats who invented the term "gender-free" in collaboration with scholars of gender studies and promoted gender-free education that aimed to eliminate gender bias in schools (Yamaguchi, 2006). While feminist scholars critique the ambiguous definition of "gender free" and its tendency to reduce gender discrimination as issues of people's attitude and stereotypes (see Ueno, 2006; Yamaguchi, 2006), the term served progressive political ends in that it problematized both subtle and overt forms of discrimination against women in public institutions and the hidden curriculum that produced and reproduced the binary gender identities in schools (Kimura, 1999, 2005). In education the mixed-gender student roll, in particular, became the symbol of the movement. The 1999 adoption of the Basic Law for a Gender Equal Society further promoted such movements towards gender-equal education and society. In 2002 the Tokyo Metropolitan Board of Education, for instance, spearheaded the introduction of mixed-gender student rolls and other municipalities and prefectures quickly followed the move.

Once again, these progressive gains were partly promoted by business communities that were shifting away from the traditional, gendered human resource strategies (Kimura, 2005, p. 92; Ueno, 2006). Corporations began to see the traditional gender division in the workplace as an impediment to their global competitiveness and demanded the elimination of labor regulations that were designed to prevent women from competing with male employees in the name of "protection." In addition the workplace restructuring, along with the elimination of family wage, created many male employees who no longer make enough money to be the sole breadwinner. This forced many women to seek part-time employment to offset the declining income. These changes promoted the redefinition of traditional gender roles, rendering being a housewife a privilege limited to those who can afford to stay home. Many policies that address in one way or another gender equality issues were therefore promoted by the strange alliance between corporate sectors that sought to recruit more women in both high- and low-end labor markets on the one hand and grassroots feminist groups on the other that sought to challenge not only the gender discrimination but also the very capitalist system that perpetuates the patriarchal norm in public and private institutions.

The 1990s also witnessed another modest "progressive" gain in curricular policy, the MoE's adoption of child-centered, constructivist curricular orientation which progressive camps had demanded for years. The MoE's 1992 National Study Course for grades 1 to 9 introduced a constructivist curricular approach, repositioning teachers as "facilitators" for children's learning. Furthermore, the Ministry introduced many other changes that progressive camps had demanded for years. A five-day schooling week (a five-day work week) was introduced partially in 1992 and fully in 2002. Curricular content was significantly reduced in the 1992 and 2002 revisions to the national Study Course. The MoE also introduced the new assessment criteria, a shift from the absolute performance criteria (*sō tai hyō ka*) where fixed percentages of children are allocated to receive differentiated grades to the individual-based criteria (*zettai hyō ka*) where teachers assess how much each child has developed relative to his/her level at the previous report period. These curricular reforms, pursued under the slogan of *kosei* (individuality) and *yutori* (more latitude, more room for growth), were the agendas that the JTU had long demanded and thus undoubtedly reflected their interests.

However, the shift toward a constructivist pedagogical approach for instance derived also from corporate demands for developing students' problem-solving skills and independent and creative thinking deemed essential for Japan to shift towards post-Fordist, knowledge-intense economy. Hence, seemingly progressive gains in curricular reform were achieved through the "strange alliance" between progressive camps and neoliberal corporate sectors that see a constructivist, child-centered curriculum as appropriate for their ideologically conflicting goals (see Takayama, 2009b). Neoconservativism emerged in response to these series of changes both in education and society driven by the unusual partnership between progressive and neoliberal corporate sectors. Neoconservatives perceived these changes as undermining *the* national *his*tory, appropriate gender role, tradition, and patriotism.

Neoconservative Mobilization

The late 1990s marked the critical moment in the rightist political mobilization. In 1997 nationalist intellectuals, politicians, and religious leaders formed the largest far-right advocacy group, *Japan Conference* (*Nippon kaigi*), formed as a result of the merger between the two far-right groups: Society to Protect Japan (*Nihon wo mamorukai*) and People's Conference to Protect Japan (*Nihon wo mamoru kokumin kaigi*). The former consisted primarily of rightist religious organizations (the *Shintō* Shrine Association, *Seichō no ie*, and other religious organizations), while the latter had nationalistic intellectuals and former military personnel as the key constitutive members (Yamaguchi, 2006).[8] The organization aims to generate grassroots movements (*kokumin undō*) for the "renationalization" of the Constitution and the FLE, the national unity centered on the imperial family, the elimination of "masochistic" history teaching and textbooks and gender-free education, more patriotic and moral teaching, and a hard diplomatic stance on territorial disputes with South Korea and China and on North Korean civilian abduction issues (Japan Conference website).[9] It has grown to be the largest and the most influential right-wing advocacy group with local branches across the nation.

The organization has considerable political connection, as it has a sister organization, Diet Members' Committee of Japan Conference (*Nihon kaigi giren*), which is composed of approximately 230 members from both Houses of Representatives and Councilors.[10] Tarō Asō (Minister of Foreign Affairs in the Abe Cabinet) was the former chairperson and was replaced by Takeo

Hiranuma (former Economic, Trade and Industry Minister) (Japan Conference website). While 51 percent of the LDP diet members belong to this organization, 11 out of 18 Abe Cabinet members were part of the organization (Tawara, Uozumi, Sataka, & Yokota, 2006, pp. 85, 89). In addition, conservative ideologues, often in collaboration with LDP nationalists, established other "grassroots networks" all of which are closely aligned with Japan Conference. All these organizations claim themselves to represent grassroots conservativism and share remarkably similar views and almost identical endorsers. In fact, former Prime Minister Shinzō Abe (2006–2007) and his unofficial political strategists (Teruhisa Nakanishi and Hidetsugu Yagi) perceive grassroots conservatism as a new strategy for the LDP's political leadership (Tawara et al., 2006, pp. 49–50). Now that the LDP's traditional electoral base has been decimated by the neoliberal policy shift (the end of the interest-driven politics) (Pempel, 1998), the party has shifted towards the moral-based political mobilization, a change remarkably similar to that witnessed in the US Republican politics.

All these conservative "grassroots" organizations demand the revision to the war-renouncing Constitution and the FLE. The political mobilization to revise the FLE was closely linked with the increased demand to remove the Peace Clauses from the Constitution.[11] As discussed earlier, for many LDP right-wing politicians, the FLE and the Peace Constitution are the core of the MacArthur-led occupation strategy that attempted to "dismantle the institutions of enemy Japan" and to "render Japan incapable of thinking on its own and to be completely dependent upon others" (Nakasone, 1997, p. 9; Takahashi, 1995). In the late 1990s the constitutional revision assumed a renewed political significance, because corporate leaders became increasingly vocal about the amendment to remove the constitutional constraints on the Self Defense Force's military operations and thus to enable the nation to participate in the "international cooperation" and to become a "normal" nation (Watanabe, 2001). Conservatives perceive the FLE revision as a stepping-stone towards the total resettlement of the postwar regime, or "the end of the (US) occupation in a true sense" (Abe, Sakurai, & Yagi, 2004, p. 319).

The Neoconservative Backlash in Education

The aforementioned Japan Conference played a critical role in orchestrating the neoconservative mobilization in education which appeared in multiple, closely overlapping forms. First, the neoconservative backlash manifested in a series of political mobilizations to "renationalize" children. Since the late 1990s, there have been a variety of conservative attempts to infuse patriotism, "love for the nation" (*aikokushin*) in the mind of children. In August 1999 a national law was adopted that confirmed the legal status of *kimigayo*,[12] the national anthem and *hinomaru*, the national flag.[13] In 2002, the revised MoE's National Study Course included, as one of the objectives for the 6th grade, social studies cultivating a feeling to love the nation (*kuni wo aisurushinjō*). Since then, local boards of education at prefecture and municipal levels have resorted to this reference to enforce the use of the anthem and flag in schools.

Closely aligned with this is the nationalist history revisionist movement. The Japanese Society for History Textbook Reform (*Atarashii rekishi kyōkasho wo tsukuru kai*) was founded in 1997 by a group of intellectuals, historians, journalists, and educators who were concerned about the recent increase in the "masochistic" historical descriptions in school textbooks, and it soon became closely aligned with Japan Conference. The group argues that Japanese society and economy have started collapsing because of the "negativity of history education," calling for the creation of new history textbooks that enable children to be proud of being Japanese.[14] In their logic, the JTU and leftist teachers have controlled the textbook adoption processes and spread the "masochistic" history of the nation. As a result, argues the organization, the youth have developed indifference and disrespect to Japanese culture, history of their hometown, and their ancestors, and deride hard work and effort. The group's textbooks contain many mythological stories and descriptions of the glorified past, while eliminating from the history the description of wartime atrocities committed by the Japanese Imperial Army. They also provide a romanticized description of the Japanese citizens during the war as sacrificing their lives to the nation. In April 2000, the group's controversial textbooks passed the MoE's textbook screening after addressing the Ministry's 137 revision requests, creating intense opposition in and diplomatic strains with neighboring Asian nations such as China and South Korea (see Takayama, 2009c). The organization had 6964 members and 275 official supporters as of 1998 (Watanabe, 2001, p. 222) and has extended the nationwide network of grassroots local organizations (Oguma & Ueno, 2003).

Neoconservative politics came to dominate the curricular debate in the late 1990s. The intense national debate over the declining national achievement (1999–2005) reflected the neoconservative backlash against the constructivist curricular reform and school streamlining which culminated in the MoE's 2002 revision to the National Study Course, so-called *yutori* (low-pressure) curricular reform (announced in 1998). The reform introduced a 5-day school week and an Integrated Study Period (*sōgō gakushūno jikan*) and further decreased instructional hours and streamlined curricular content for the first nine years of compulsory education. According to the spokesperson of the reform, these measures had three chief objectives: (1) to shift the focus on to the development of children's ability to learn and think independently, (2) to de-emphasize rote memorization, and (3) to reduce pressure in children's lives (Terawaki, 2001).

Neoconservatives challenged these reform plans by borrowing US neoconservatives' crisis discourse of American education. They demanded "back to basics" and "zero tolerance," which they defined as the key to "successful" US education reform, and argued that the ongoing *yutori* curricular reform, which they perceived as the opposite of the American solutions, would put "the nation at risk" (Takayama, 2007). The neoconservative campaign for the termination of *yutori* reform gained legitimacy in the rising popular demands for law and order, discipline, and traditional authority in schools, and successfully generated the legitimacy crisis of the MoE's educational administration.

Gender politics is also central to the neoconservative reconstitution of children as a moralized subject. There has been an intense backlash against the progressive gain made in gender-sensitive education discussed earlier. LDP right-wing legislators and conservative intellectuals, many of whom are associated with Japan Conference, argue that under the name of "gender-free education," union teachers and feminist activists promote extreme sex education and teaching that rejects sex differences, demonizes marriage and family, and thus destroys the nation's cultural essence. Rearticulating gender-free education, feminism, and gender studies as "free-sex advocates" and "destroyers of the nation's culture," they demand the elimination of the term "gender" from any official documents and promote the distorted images of gender-sensitive approaches to teaching (see LDP, 2005; Nishio & Yagi, 2005; Yagi, 2002b; Yagi & Yamatani, 2002). Gender-free education, in their logic, moves Japan away from its glorified past when the economy was booming, children were diligent and willing to work for the good of the nation, and men and women knew their appropriate roles. The anti-gender-free discourse has gained legitimacy in the background of the massive production of men who can no longer become "real men" under the current corporate restructuring. The collapse of the postwar arrangement that sustained male workers' job security through the lifetime employment, family wage, and incremental salary scale placed many men in economic and social insecurity. Neoconservative discourse directs these men to blame feminist and gender-sensitive teaching for creating their economic and gender insecurities (Ida, 2006; Kaizuma, 2005; Ueno, 2006).

As the neoconservative backlash discourse gained more legitimacy in the public discourse, many municipalities that had adopted gender-free education just a few years earlier started withdrawing their support for gender equality initiatives in education. In April–July 2005, pressured by the LDP right wings, the MoE directed local school boards to refrain from extreme gender-sensitive teaching and explicitly sexual contents in sex education (Shinano Mainichi News, 2005). The MoE's 2005 textbook screening, published in March 2006, mandated that textbook publishers eliminate expressions such as "gender" and "gender-free" from the textbooks (*Asahi News*, March 30, 2006).[15]

These neoconservative political mobilizations, which are closely interconnected with each other through the overarching support network provided by Japan Conference, gained substantial popular support in the 2000s. Though initiated and promoted by established organizations and politicians, this neoconservative backlash movement was also driven by strong popular support from citizens who do not possess explicit conservative ideological underpinning. When the postwar cultural, economic, and political stabilities no longer exist, the language of populist nationalism provides powerful discursive tools with which people reestablish their sense of belonging and identity. The prolonged economic recession and insecurities, along with the postmodern condition of indeterminacy, has resulted in "the [people's] compulsion to find and invent new certainties for oneself and for others" (Beck, 1994, p. 14; Oguma, 2003b). The neoconservative calls for *the* national *his*tory as well as the traditional binary structure of human relations echoes with people's longing for a meta-narrative that provides them with a stable and singular identity. In this condition the neoconservative discourse works to direct people's frustrations to single out feminist and progressive educators as convenient scapegoats whose ideologically tainted teaching has supposedly resulted in the moral and economic decline of the nation. It is these political, economic and cultural instabilities at the turn of the century that make the borrowing of British crisis discourse particularly ideologically effective, the topic to which I now turn.

The Cultural Politics of Crisis Borrowing

In their attempt to legitimize the controversial FLE revision and other conservative agendas in education, conservative critics and politicians borrowed the crisis narrative of British education popularized by British New Right critics in the 1970s. They selectively appropriated the "examples from Britain," constructed a crisis-and-success melodrama of British education reform, and made it appear that Japanese schools were undergoing the same crisis as their British counterparts had undergone three decades earlier. In so doing, the Japanese conservatives appropriated the British New Right's "discourse of derision" to "debunk and displace not only specific words and meanings associated with" the postwar Japanese progressivism—democracy, pacifism, and egalitarianism—"but also those who speak these words" (Ball, 1990, p. 18).

The writings to be examined here are drawn primarily, but not exclusively, from a book entitled *Learning from Thatcher's reform: A path towards normalization of education* (*Sacchā kaikaku ni manabu: kyōiku seijōka eno michi*) (Nakanishi, 2005a). Published in 2005, the book is based on the study report compiled by a bipartisan group of legislators who visited Britain "to learn from Thatcher's reform." The book consists of a series of articles written by the LDP and the then largest opposition party Democratic Party of Japan (DPJ) legislators, namely: Keiji Furuya (LDP), Hakubun Shimomura (LDP, Chief Cabinet Secretary to Prime Minister Abe), Jin Matsubara (DPJ), Ikuo Kamei (LDP), and Eriko Yamtani (LDP, special advisor to Abe on education-related matters). Two influential LDP politicians, Takeo Hiranuma (LDP, the former Minister of Economic, Trade and Industry and the then chairperson of the Diet Members' Committee of Japan Conference) and Shōichi Nakagawa (the former Minister of Agriculture and the chairman of the LDP's Policy Research Council under Abe's leadership) write the introductions to the book, while Prime Minister Shinzō Abe joined a roundtable discussion with Furuya, Shimomura, and Yamtani, moderated by Yūzō Kabashima, the secretary general for Japan Conference. In fact, all of these contributors are closely affiliated with Japan Conference and actively involved in the neoconservative political mobilizations around the revisionist history textbooks, gender-free education bashing, the renationalization of the FLE, and *yutori* (low-pressure) education bashing.

Along with these powerful political figures' writings, I examine the writings of neoconservative intellectuals who are closely connected with these political figures and circulate a particular crisis narrative of British education. In particular, I focus on Terumasa Nakanishi and Hidetsugu Yagi who serve as the unofficial advisors for Abe's political leadership (see Tawara et al., 2006). Before engaging in the critical analysis of the conservatives' crisis discourse borrowing, however, I situate the analysis within the literature on educational borrowing and articulate the larger theoretical agenda that this analysis undertakes.

Rethinking Educational Borrowing

Though the phenomenon of educational borrowing has been a focus of theoretical discussion in the field of comparative and international education for some time (see Phillips, 1993, 1999; Phillips & Ochs, 2003; Steiner-Khamsi, 2000; Steiner-Khamsi, 2004), scholars in the field have made little attempt to situate educational borrowing within the legacy of Western cultural imperialism, which continues to create a hierarchical relationship between Western knowledge producers and "other" knowledge recipients (Alatas, 2003; Said, 1993). Hence, the theorization of educational borrowing advanced thus far has been inadequate in addressing the particular nature of borrowing from the perspective of non-Western "others." As a number of postcolonial theorists argue, the West's monopolistic control over the nature and the flows of knowledge remains in place, even decades after colonized territories achieved political independence and nationhood. Although the flow of influence is never one-sided and the powerful influence from the Western "center" is constantly mediated to generate hybridity in the cultural and racial identities of those in the peripheries (Appadurai 1996; Young, 1995), global cultural politics continue to perpetuate an unequal flow of cultural commodities, ideas, and discourses from the West to the rest of the world, affecting the cultural and racial identities of the marginalized populations, both within and outside the West (hooks, 1992; Smith, 1999). The West continues to be the chief source of cultural refinement, progress, and modernity, normalizing "other" people's ways of being and knowing according to the "global standard."

In the early part of the twentieth century, Japan was one of the world's imperial powers; and since the 1980s, it has been a global economic powerhouse. Nevertheless, the nation's economic prosperity has not translated into Japanese cultural hegemony (Alatas, 2003; Lie, 1996). The nation remains a relatively passive recipient of Western social scientific knowledge (Takayama, 2009a), and it continues to contend with its relative marginality as a non-Western "other" in the dominant Western Orientalizing cultural discourse (Ben-Ami, 1997; Lie, 1996; Moeran, 1989; Said, 1978). Japan's cultural marginality in global power dynamics has resulted in a complicated but still pervasive sense among Japanese of their intellectual inferiority against the West, keeping alive the Japanese traditional attitude popularized during the Meiji period (1868–1912) of "*Datsu-a nyū-yō*"— leaving feudal Asia and entering the modernized West.

Japan's postwar history of educational borrowing demonstrates its degree of dependence on the West, specifically on the United Kingdom and the United States, which Japan continues to perceive as purveyors of the greatest educational innovation and excellence. Japan's century-old tradition of "learning from the West" prevails among education scholars, policymakers, and bureaucrats who constantly assess the nation's schooling in comparison with the latest Western educational trends (Cummings, 1986; Ichikawa, 1984). Hence, in this continuing legacy of Western cultural dominance, the discursive construct "British education reform" has had considerable symbolic appeal in the Japanese domestic debate over education reform, often presented as the unquestioned "global standard" to which Japan must conform.

The postcolonial notion of ambivalence is useful in reconceptualizing educational borrowing from the perspective of non-Western "others." The term *ambivalence* here refers to the complex mix of attraction and repulsion that characterizes the colonial and postcolonial relationship. Western colonial power possesses powerful symbolic appeal for non-Western others, constituting the "universal" standard of human esthetics, cultural values, and social progress to which non-Western others are compelled to conform "not only as a matter of imposed will and domination, but by the power of inner compulsion and subjective conformation to the norm" (Hall in hooks, 1992, p. 3). Simultaneously, repulsive responses to Western ideas and discourses are a common nationalist reaction in non-Western nations. In what Robert Fox (1992) calls "affirmative Orientalism," non-Western cultural nationalism appropriates the Western Orientalist discourse and redefines the West as a cultural and social abnormality, or "the other" against which non-Western others assert their normality and superiority (Befu, 1993; Creighton, 1995). The borrowing of Western educational ideas and policies can thus generate a strong backlash from non-Western others who see the importation of Western ideas and discourses as encroaching undesirable influences that would "pollute" their cultural and spiritual "essence." This nationalistic response to the West occurs alongside their expressed desire to mimic the West. In sum, the discursive West as the quintessential "other" can simultaneously evoke in non-Western others both extremely positive and negative emotional responses. The phenomenon of educational borrowing in non-Western national contexts must be examined in light of this postcolonial cultural politics of ambivalence.

Because the symbolic registers "American education reform" and "British education reform" have enormous potential to generate strong reactions among people in non-Western nations, the characterization of educational concepts and policies as originating in and borrowed from the United Kingdom and the United States becomes an effective (and affective) political strategy, with politicians and policymakers accentuating their Western origins to achieve domestic political agendas. In the politics of education reform, the contradictory characterization of the West either as the "global standard" or as the "cultural pollutant" becomes the point of ideological struggles among multiple social groups. In the current cultural politics of Japanese education reform, such iconic keywords as "school voucher," "zero tolerance," "topic studies," "John Dewey," "back-to-basics," "child-centered teaching," and "A Nation at Risk," all of which are evoked either with American or with British education, have become a "multi-accentual" signifier (Hall, 1981), which can be rearticulated into multiple localized political discourses.

When these concepts are removed from the "home" discursive field and placed in an "other" national context, they are disarticulated from their particular political assumptions and meanings rooted in the "home" context and then made subject to the politics of disarticulation and rearticulation in the adapted context. Different social and political groups and individuals struggle to articulate these powerful symbolic registers into their own preferred discourses and, in turn, to constitute their own version of social reality as truth. In the recent education debate leading up to the revision of the FLE, the articulation of "British education reform" has derived largely from conservative politicians and intellectuals. The production and the dissemination of counter-hegemonic articulations of "British education reform" have occupied a marginal place in the public debate on education reform, allowing the dominant conservative articulation to acquire an uncontested truth status.

Japanese Neoconservatives' Borrowing of the "British Crisis"

Japanese neoconservatives have constructed a particular crisis melodrama that supposedly narrates the historical trajectory of British education reform. It frames the "crisis" thematically in economic, cultural, and academic terms and, temporally, in the 1960s and the 1970s, when—according to these critics—socialist ideology dominated British social and educational policies. They use "English illness" (*igirisu byō*), a term coined by Margaret Thatcher and by British New Right media and politicians, to describe the corrupted condition of British society at that time. Both the social welfare that post-war British governments instituted and these governments' nationalization of major industries appear on the Japanese conservatives' radar as the source of both Britain's culture of dependency and the decline of workers' productivity. According to Matsubara (2005), the British Labour governments collaborated with labor unions in promoting excessive egalitarianism, what he and other neoconservatives call "evil egalitarianism" (*akubyōdō*), which resulted in the decline of Britain's economic competitiveness. As a result, the United Kingdom, which had been the richest nation in the world in earlier decades, became economically deficient to the extent that it had to accept emergency financial assistance from the International Monetary Fund in 1976 (Matsubara, 2005, p. 25).

This crisis narrative features education as the culprit of the cultural and moral demise of British society. Drawing on the British New Right's discourse of derision (Ball, 1990), the narrative alleges that the dominance of progressive ideology in British schools caused the English illness. In particular, the account brands Britain's 1944 Education Act as the central villain of the crisis. To Nakanishi (2005b), the Act is the product of "the leftist liberal movement infused with socialism of the early 20th century" (p. 9). The narrative claims that the law assigned curricular authority to teachers and that, consequently, teachers' unions and the Labour Party dominated schools and local educational authorities and promoted unpatriotic leftist ideological indoctrination. The narrative derides, in particular, three pedagogical practices supposedly promoted under the 1944 Act: (1) "masochistic" history education, or anti-racist education, (2) child-centered pedagogy such as topic studies and experience-based learning, and (3) a lack of religious teaching.

In history teaching, the Japanese neoconservatives argue, ideologically biased teachers in Britain taught an "anti-British masochistic national historiography" (*hanei jigyaku shikan*), a history based on the Marxist theory of class conflict, which defined modern British history as the history of invasion and exploitation (Abe, 2006; Yagi, 2002a). To illustrate the masochistic history teaching at the time, Kabashima (2005) and Matsubara (2005) extensively discuss the history textbook *How racism came to Britain* (Institute of Race Relations, 1985) and show many illustrations from the textbook. They argue that this textbook represents the history curriculum under the 1944 Education Act which placed disproportionate emphasis on the British colonization in Asia, Africa, and Central America, on the slave trade, and on the British labor movement—an emphasis that encourages British children to feel ashamed of their British citizenship. Their description of the textbook misleads readers to believe that the textbook was used across the nation, when in fact it was used in a limited number of school districts (Tawara et al., 2006, p. 107).

Topic studies, or integrated and child-centered teaching, are another pedagogical practice that features prominently in this British crisis narrative. It describes these studies as less academically rigorous and less disciplined than the narrative's preferred modes of learning, such as rote memorization, spelling exercises, and drills, which lead to scholastic "cramming" (*tsumekomi kyōiku*). In the name of topic studies, maintains the narrative, Britain's school curriculum suffered erosion and fragmentation because each teacher used his or her discretion to select the preferred curricular content (Yagi, 2002a) and because these teachers placed disproportionate emphasis on children's spontaneity and individuality (Matsubara, 2005, p. 27). Adherents of this account declare that the topic-studies approach resulted in a massive number of British middle school graduates who could not perform basic reading, writing, and computation exercises (Abe, 2006, p. 204; Kabashima, 2005, p. 201; Ōmori, 2000). The narrative goes on to note several further negative outcomes: the child-centered pedagogical approach resulted in an increased incidence of student violence against teachers (Yagi, 2002a) and in high youth unemployment and low worker productivity (Ōmori, 2000; Shimomura, 2005).

Likewise, the narrative identifies ineffective religious education under the 1944 Education Act as another key culprit of the English illness. It claims that religious education was marginalized by British union teachers who rejected religious values and who promoted multicultural, antiracist education and value-relativism through John Dewey's progressive child-centered pedagogy (Kabashima, 2005, p. 217). As a consequence, Kabashima continues, British society faced "youths' spiritual desolation" as seen in a rise in crime and a decline in sexual morality (pp. 219–220). In sum, the narrative borrows the British New Right critique of public education in the 1970s, or the discourse of derision that "focused on the worst and the most problematic or contentious features of some aspects of government system" and "exaggerated these features through the use of ludicrous images, ridicule, and stereotypification" (Kenway, 1990, p. 201). Having attributed horrendous conditions to British education in the 1970s, the narrative transforms the scenario into a backdrop against which the account creates a dramatic success story of British school reform.

"Successful" British School Reform

The story of successful British school reform begins with the emergence of a "grassroots" movement, or what they call the "Education Black Paper Movement" (*kyōiku kokusho undō*), which allegedly ushered in the nationwide school-reform movement (Kabashima, 2005, p. 223; Yagi, 2002a, p. 2). According to Yagi (2002a), the movement was initiated by a group of education scholars, parents, and teachers who were concerned about "academic decline and school violence, progressive education, and enforced evil egalitarianism in public education" (p. 2). In order to bring the critical condition of schools to public attention and to generate more public support for the movement, explains Yagi, the group issued a series of publications that were known as "the Black Papers" and that continued from 1969 to 1977.[16] The climax of the narrative centers on Margaret Thatcher, who supposedly translated the movement's genuine goals into national education policies.

The Japanese neoconservatives' British school-reform melodrama identifies Thatcher's 1988 Education Act as pivotal in marking the end of the crisis and the beginning of school improvement. Kabashima focuses on three particular areas of change that resulted from the 1988 Education Act: history education, religious education, and academic standards. After the reform, continues Kabashima, history teaching became more balanced, with more attention given to the positive aspects of Britain's past. He shows contrasting treatments of Britain's colonial rule, slave trade, and monarchy in two textbooks. The pre-Act textbook is the aforementioned *How Racism Came to Britain*, and the post-Act textbook is *Britain 1750–1900* written by Walter Robson (1993). By selecting these two textbooks as representative of the general change in textbooks in the late 1980s, he concludes that the latter presents a more balanced description of the positives and the negatives of Britain's past.

In addition, Kabashima (2005) and Yamatani (2005) describe how Thatcher reestablished Christianity as the national religion by mandating that the school curriculum reflect the centrality of Christianity to British culture and tradition and that each school have a teacher who specializes in religious education. Thanks to this reestablishment of religious teaching in schools, Kabashima (2005) argues, cases of juvenile crime decreased by half—from over 200,000 in 1977 to 100,000 in 2002 (p. 221). Likewise, according to Kabashima (2005), Ōmori (2000), and Shimomura (2005), Thatcher's curricular centralization initiatives resulted in drastic academic improvements, as assessed through standardized test scores. Kabashima draws on the work *The betrayed generations: Standards in British schools, 1950–2000* by the noted conservative ideologue John Marks (2001) and uses his data on the General Certificate of Secondary Education's average test score and OECD's PISA 2000 to point out the "marvelous progress" that the British school system recently achieved, given that "British middle school students could not even spell out their names just thirty years ago" (Kabashima, 2005, p. 225).

Constructing the Historical Correspondence

While Japanese rightist politicians and intellectuals are ostensibly narrating the trajectory of British school reforms for Japanese readers, their description is in no way balanced. When placed back in the British discursive context, their narrative on British school reforms reveals its highly selective nature: the narrative draws exclusively on the dominant crisis-and-success narrative propagated by the New Right British critics of education such as John Marks, Margaret Thatcher, and Kenneth Baker (the Minister of Education for Margaret Thatcher). In so doing, it completely ignores alternative accounts that shed different light on Thatcher's education reform (see, e.g., Gewirtz, Ball, & Bowe, 1995; Tomlinson, 1994, 2005). The narrative is more than selective, however. It carefully crafts the British crisis melodrama to legitimize a given set of highly controversial education policies that had long been on the Japanese conservatives' political agenda. As discussed earlier, the crisis melodrama of British education identifies four key villains of the English illness: the 1944 Education Act, anti-racist ("masochistic" history) teaching, dysfunctional religious teaching, and child-centered pedagogical practices (topic studies and curricular integration). Japanese neoconservative observers carefully selected these specific factors to fabricate a set of "coincidental" correspondences: Britain's 1944 Education Act and the Japan's 1947 FLE; anti-racist history teaching in British schools and the "masochistic" history teaching in Japanese schools; dysfunctional religious teaching in British schools under the 1944 Act and the lack of religious and moral teaching in Japanese schools under the 1947 FLE; and topic studies or integrated and child-centered curriculum in Britain and the ongoing *yutori* curricular reform in Japan.

The comparison between the British 1944 Education Act and the Japanese 1947 FLE is the key discursive strategy by which these Japanese critics attempt to construct the parallel between, on the one hand, the English illness of the 1970s and, on the other hand, the Japanese counterpart of the 2000s. Nakanishi (2005b) and Yagi (2002a) claim that these two educational acts are identical in their ideological underpinning and that their consequences will hence be highly similar:

> The 1944 Education Act, which Thatcher set out to change, was born out of the leftist liberalism of the early twentieth century and mixed with socialist belief. It is American "progressivism," derived from the same liberal ideology, that brought the FLE to Japan during the occupation period. This is the fundamental reason for which many advanced nations faced similar educational crises and similar national declines in the latter half of the twentieth century.
>
> (Nakanishi, 2005b, p. 9)

By defining Britain's 1944 Education Act as the villain and the 1988 Act as the hero in the recent trajectory of British education reform and by comparing the former with the Japanese 1947 FLE, Japanese rightist critics attempt to naturalize the view that Japan must revise its counterpart to solve the much hyped "Japanese illness" (Matsubara, 2005, p. 24). Here, they rearticulate the FLE revision, the cornerstone of the LDP right wings' political agenda throughout the postwar history, to the discourse of "global standard" in education reform. The external reference to the British example thus helps give the conventional LDP right wings' agenda a renewed political legitimacy. It helps disarticulate this traditional conservative agenda from the highly contested history surrounding the revision and rearticulate it into the discourse of the "inevitability of globalization." Simultaneously, these conservative politicians and intellectuals attempt to erase the significant qualitative differences between the British Act and Japan's FLE. Unlike the former, which is purely an administrative law, the latter is known as the "educational constitution" created to promote in postwar Japanese schools the pacifist and democratic idealisms proclaimed in the Constitution.

Furthermore, their identification of anti-racist teaching as another cause of the English illness is no coincidence either. This coupling serves to legitimize the aforementioned revisionist-history-textbook movement led by Yagi's Japanese Society for History Textbook Reform and by rightist LDP politicians:

> Behind the English illness lies British youths who forgot their independent spirit and hard work. Without reinvigorating these youths, Britain could not have recovered from its illness. Confronted with this problem, Thatcher tried to reestablish history education so that the youths would learn about their predecessors who had worked hard for their nation and the world. Thatcher's educational belief is exactly what we need the most now for the further growth of our nation.
>
> (Nakagawa, 2005, p. 6)

Likewise, the Japanese neoconservatives' framing of Britain's topic studies as another key villain also speaks directly to a particular domestic agenda in Japan. Rightist politicians and intellectuals have been increasingly critical of the 2002 *yutori* reform, which they argue is based on Western child-centered ideology, the culprit of economic and moral decline in the United Kingdom and the United States in the 1970s (Abe, 2006; Wada, 1999). They extol Thatcher for having achieved success by rejecting the child-centered pedagogical approach akin to the *yutori* reform. The reference to Britain's "successful" school reform hence serves to legitimize otherwise highly contentious policy redirection, the replacement of the *yutori* reform with more traditional back-to-basics approaches to teaching.

The Japanese neoconservatives' construction of the crisis in British education reveals their ambivalence toward the West: the complex mix of attraction and repulsion that characterizes the colonial and postcolonial relationship. When they construct the Thatcherite-British education reform as the model best suited for Japan's emulation, they invoke the unquestioned superiority of the West—a West that has been the source of innovation, progress, and prosperity. And by invoking this "global standard," they try to depoliticize and deterritorialize their agendas, as if not pursuing them would put the nation at risk. On the other hand, in their rejection of the pacifist Constitution, the democratic FLE, and the *yutori* curricular reform, the rightist critics draw on a well-engrained repulsion to the West, which emerges not as a purveyor of progress but as a cultural pollutant, or a threat to Japan's cultural and moral essence. Therefore, the Japanese neoconservatives appropriate the contradictory symbolic images associated with the discursive West, born out of the continued legacy of Western cultural dominance, to articulate people's genuine feeling of insecurity in a time of political, economic, and social changes. This articulation harnesses the feeling of insecurity to bolster a conservative discourse of traditional values, patriotism, and discipline, from where the amendment to the FLE, renationalization of history teaching, gender-free education bashing, and the reintroduction of an authoritative pedagogical approach seem to be the only legitimate course of action.

Furthermore, this postcolonial ambivalence is clearly manifested in the particular way the Japanese rightists articulate the success of British education reform. Japanese far-right politicians and intellectuals insert Japanese cultural virtue into their construction of British *success*, emphasizing the fact that traditional Japanese education was the model for Thatcher's reform (Abe, 2006; Matsubara, 2005). Hence, the Japanese neoconservatives' borrowing of British education reform amounts to a retrieval of a lost past—of a Japanese education system unpolluted by the US-imposed postwar democracy and by the *yutori* reform. Their retrospective desire for this pristine cultural essence has found expression in their glorification of the Thatcherite-British education reform. The cultural politics of crisis borrowing played a key role in preparing the discursive ground for the politically charged FLE revision, the topic to which I now turn.

Deconstitutionalizing the FLE

Throughout Japan's postwar history, the FLE served as the final legal resort with which progressive activists challenged the state's subordination of education to capital's and nationalistic interests (Miyama & Oyama, 1970; Horio, 1988). The original 1947 FLE makes an explicit reference to the Constitution in its Preamble:

> Having established the Constitution of Japan, we have shown our resolution to contribute to the peace of the world and welfare of humanity by building a democratic and cultural state. The realization of this ideal shall depend fundamentally on the power of education.
>
> (FLE, as cited in Horio, 1988, p. 400)

This clause is central to the interpretation of the FLE as the constitution in education, marking its difference from other administrative educational acts that are placed under the FLE. It defines the mission of education as pursuing the pacifist and democratic idealism enshrined in the Constitution. The December 2006 legal amendment stripped this constitutional character from the FLE. The revised FLE adds to the Preamble "public spirit" and "inheritance of tradition," two concepts pursued by the right-wing LDP politicians throughout the postwar history, and more importantly it eliminates the last sentence of the Preamble: "The realization of this ideal shall depend fundamentally on the power of education," a change that critics claim disconnects the law from the Constitution (Narushima, 2006).

Indeed, the removal of the constitutional character from the FLE characterizes many other amendments. For instance, the original law contains Article X, which states that "Education shall not be subject to improper control, but it shall be directly responsible to the whole people" (Horio, 1988, p. 401). Though this clause does not specify whose "improper control," given that the law was created to prevent the state's improper control of education as witnessed during the Asia Pacific War, it clearly refers to the state's improper control, and has been interpreted thus in many legal cases (Munakata, 1975, pp. 75–76; see also Horio, 1988; Horio & Yamazumi, 1976). The revised FLE kept the phrase "Education shall not be subject to improper control," but placed it in a different discourse by replacing the subsequent sentence with a new phrase: "Education shall be put in practice in accordance with this and other laws." Here, the agent of the improper control is redefined as those who engage in teaching in violation of the revised FLE and related education laws, another long-term LDP agenda achieved in this revision. Since the new FLE proposes fostering patriotism as one of the goals of education, teachers who are opposed to teaching children to "love the nation" will be considered as exercising "improper control."

Instead of keeping state power in check, the revised FLE legalizes the imposition on children of a set of values, attitudes, and dispositions which the state deems necessary. By way of contrast, the original law proposed liberal-democratic and humanistic values as the goal of education:

> the full development of personality, striving for the rearing of the people, sound in mind and body, who shall love truth and justice, esteem individual value, respect labor and have a deep sense of responsibility, and be imbued with the independent spirit, as builders of a peaceful state and society.
>
> (1947 FLE Article I, as cited in Horio, 1988, p. 400)

The original law refrained from specifying particular values and dispositions that were to be fostered through education, other than those central to the liberal-democratic and pacifist principles of the nation. In clear contrast, the revised FLE, in Chapter I: Goals and Principles of Education (MoE, 2007), adds a number of attitudes and dispositions that should be fostered through education, making it reminiscent of the 1890 Imperial Rescript:

> Develop broad knowledge and culture, cultivate aesthetic sensitivity, morality, and healthy body
>
> (Article II, 1)

Develop individual potential, creativity, independent spirit, and work ethics

(Article, II, 2)

Develop appreciation for equality between men and women and an attitude that autonomously takes part in building society and contributing to its development on the basis of a public-oriented mind

(Article II, 3)

Nurture respect for life, appreciation of nature, and protection of environment

(Article II, 4)

Foster an attitude that respects tradition and culture and love of the national homeland that has fostered them, an attitude that respects other nations and contributes to the peace and development of international community.

(Article III, 5)

Furthermore, the new law adds a clause titled "home education" that emphasizes the parental responsibility for children's education (MoE, 2007): "Parents and other guardians have the primary responsibility for their children's education. They are to help them acquire habits necessary for living and develop independent spirit, and achieve balanced development of body and mind" (Article X). As will be further discussed below, these changes reflect neoliberal responsibilization, or neoliberal localism, which focuses its governing attention on what used to be deemed private: the self, family, and community. The renationalization of the FLE, though it has been the LDP's political agenda throughout the postwar history, assumes a renewed political significance in the ongoing neoliberal restructuring, the point that should become even clearer when I situate the FLE revision in the theoretical understanding of the state/education restructuring in the neoliberal times.

State/Education Restructuring in Neoliberal Times

The rightist revision of the FLE represents the intensification of the state's control over children's private selves, with a particular focus on children's subjectivity (*kokoro*). While one can interpret this as a manifestation of the LDP right wings' retrogressive desire to turn the clock back to the prewar imperial state, this common progressive critique does not help us understand the particular function of the same conservative agenda in the current dominance of neoliberal rationales in Japanese society. The intensification of state control over citizens' private selves is a phenomenon witnessed in many neoliberalized industrial nations. Neoliberalism demands that parts of the state be minimized through privatization and the elimination of social services. The underlying logic is that human well-being can best be advanced by liberating individual entrepreneurial freedoms and skills (Harvey, 2005). A neoliberal state embraces the notion of strong and enterprising individuals who take responsibility for their own actions and the resulting consequences, thus extolling the acceptance of personal responsibility as a practice of freedom, relief from state intervention (Duggan, 2003; Rose, 1999). Citizens of a nation no longer pool risk through state mechanisms. Instead individuals are to calculate and manage potential future risks regarding their own education, employment, and welfare.

Calling this new political rationality "responsibilization," Michelle Dean (1999) argues that this is an intensely moral activity, because morality is essentially about "mak[ing] oneself accountable for one's own actions" (Dean, 1999, p. 10). Neoliberal responsibilization, or "neoliberal localism" (Gough in Robertson & Dale, 2002, p. 463), focuses its governing attention on what used to be deemed private—the self, family, and community— in order to reconstitute their subjectivities as self-governing selves. The intense state intervention in children's subjectivity as seen in the FLE revision must be understood in this context of the new technology of the neoliberal state.

The neoliberalization of the state and social relations necessities the recentralization of state power to contain the capitalist state's insoluble contradictions. The capitalist state needs to strike a balance among the conflicting demands for capital accumulation and political legitimacy (Apple, 1995; Dale, 1989), serving as both "the guardian angel of the capitalist economic process" and "the chosen instrument for protecting society from the corrosive impact of that process" (Castles in Taylor, Rizvi, Lingard, & Henry, 1997, p. 30). During the postwar period, the state generated the people's consent to its capitalist rule through a developmentalist economic approach and a corporate-based social integration system (in Japan), or through consensus politics between capital and labor, the legalization of the latter's collective rights, and state-sponsored social welfare (in Western welfare states) (Gotō, 2002). In both cases, the state sustained people's consent to its complicity in capitalist rule by directly or indirectly intervening in the market and redistributing wealth. Now that the neoliberal state has abandoned these arrangements in favor of corporations' economic needs, it needs to compensate for its declining capacity to generate people's political consent. One strategy is to rely on more direct and intrusive forms of social control to produce subjects with dispositions and values appropriate to a neoliberal self-governing society (Gotō, 2002, p. 24).

Indeed, under the neoliberal state regime's aggressive pursuit for upward economic redistribution, education assumes increasing importance as one of the key mechanisms for "compensatory legitimation" (Weiler, 1983). When access to social services is increasingly determined by one's capacity to pay, the neoliberal state strategically maintains education as the symbol of meritocracy, so that people perceive that the classed consequences of neoliberal restructuring reflect individuals' achievements in schooling and therefore are morally and ethically acceptable. To this aim, the neoliberal state needs to protect education from marketization and privatization pressures to the extent that it still projects the ideals of "fair competition" and "equal educational opportunity."

This perspective is important in Japan where the centrality of education to the people's belief in meritocracy is particularly strong. The Japanese government has historically subsidized local municipalities to assure equal educational funding across the nation. This egalitarian funding, along with the national standardization of curriculum and the universal access to basic education, both achieved relatively early in the process of nation building, has resulted in general public consensus that people's social status is based on their educational background (*gakureki shakai*), that is, their effort and talent, rather than class or birth (Goodman, 2003; Kariya, 1995). Hence, if the Japanese state privatizes and deregulates education to the extent seen in other social services, and makes the availability of quality educational services dependent on one's capacity to pay, it will significantly undermine the various cultural "givens" (e.g., meritocracy and equal educational opportunity) that legitimize the neoliberal governance and its inevitable classed consequences.[17]

Furthermore, the accentuation of nationalistic and religious values in the FLE revision must be understood in terms of this compensatory legitimization. The neoliberal state's hyper-individualization of social relations, its attack against anything social, and increasing economic polarization have all contributed to today's pervasive sense of uncertainty and social disintegration (Yamada, 2004). What lies behind the recent rise of "grassroots nationalism" (Oguma, 1998; Oguma & Ueno, 2003) and "authoritarian populism" (Apple, 2006a) is the people's compulsion to seek stability in their identity and social location in these social and cultural fluctuations. In a manner that responds to such popular demands, the neoliberal state reinvigorates an imagined sense of community through the implementation of a "back-to-basics" approach to teaching, a core curriculum, and the teaching of a unified national history and tradition (Apple, 2006a; Coulby & Zambeta, 2005). All these measures project a clear sense of identities based on sets of hierarchical binaries: adult–child, teacher–student, male–female, and Western self–oriental other.

In sum, because of education's centrality to the neoliberal state's political legitimacy, education remains an area where the "countertrend to the denationalization of statehood" becomes particularly articulated (Jessop, 2000, pp. 63–65). The FLE revision reflects the Japanese neoliberal state's attempt to address its contradictory functions in the new global economy by radically reconfiguring the state/education relationship. This interpretation must be differentiated from the common progressive critique of the FLE revision as the LDP hawks' drive to "turn the clock backward."

The MoE Becoming the Right

The discussion thus far has described the FLE revision as closely aligned with the global trend of the neoliberal state/education restructuring and the neoconservative cultural politics that fundamentally alters the relationship between the state, civil society, and education. This global discussion however must be complicated by a focus on the domestic political struggles over the revision to avoid the perpetuation of the "globalization without a subject" thesis. Tracing the political motives of the MoE throughout the six-year deliberation of the FLE revision helps illuminate the Ministry's particular political agenda behind the revision, the Ministry's struggle for political legitimacy in a time of neoliberal attack against its bureaucratic administration of education.

When the conservative political mobilization towards the FLE amendment began in the late 1990s, the MoE was not initially keen on the agenda (Ichikawa, 2003; Kariya, 2006; Narushima, 2006; Sakurai, 2001). Ever since the end of postwar ideological contestation was announced at the historic 1995 reconciliation between the Ministry and the Japan Teachers Union, its long-time adversary, the Ministry had avoided becoming involved in explicitly ideological agendas so that it could concentrate on its new role as the "neutral" education administrator. Hence, when far-right LDP politicians mobilized towards the de-constitutionalization of the FLE in the late 1990s, the MoE initially kept its distance from this rightist political movement. Partly because of the MoE's unwillingness to take up the FLE amendment, then Prime Minister Mori, a long-time advocate for the amendment, proposed it at the National Commission on Educational Reform (NCER), a private advisory panel set up outside the MoE's jurisdiction.

When the council was initially established by his predecessor, Prime Minister Keizō Obuchi (1998–2000), who was replaced by Mori after his sudden death, the FLE revision was not specifically identified as one of the agendas intended for deliberation (Fujita, 2001; Obuchi, 2000). Upon taking office, Mori requested that the FLE amendment be deliberated at the council (Mori, 2000a, 2000b), and LDP politicians who participated in the deliberations as "observers" directed the council members to discuss the legal amendment (Namimoto, 2000). At this early stage, therefore, the political drive for the FLE amendment came mostly from the conservative LDP lawmakers and not from the MoE bureaucrats. In fact, key MoE bureaucrats who were in the forefront of the Ministry's education reform at the turn of the Millennium hardly mentioned the FLE revision as a pressing education policy concern (see, e.g., Terawaki, 2001; Tōyama, 2004).

This picture changed drastically after Prime Minister Junichirō Koizumi took office in April 2001 and aggressively pursued neoliberal fiscal and structural reforms towards a small and efficient state. Koizumi's Cabinet targeted the MoE as one of the primary state agencies needing to be restructured through devolution, liberalization, and privatization. As part of his comprehensive structural reform package, Koizumi pursued a so-called "trilogy of tax and fiscal measures" designed to reduce the state's fiscal deficits through privatization of public services and through increasing the fiscal autonomy of local governments. To pursue his agenda in a top-down manner, Koizumi formed two consultative councils, the Council on Economic and Fiscal Policy (CEFP) and the Council for Decentralization Reform (CDR), within his Cabinet Office. These bodies, whose members consisted primarily of corporate elites, neoliberal economists, the Minister of Finance, and the Minister of Internal Affairs and Communications, drove Koizumi's drastic neoliberal state restructuring.

For instance, Basic Policies 2002, drafted by the CEFP (2002), proposed the reduction of central state subsidies to local municipalities by several trillion yen, while Basic Policies 2004 (CEFP, 2004) set the goal for the subsidy reduction at 3.2 trillion yen by 2006. Koizumi then requested that a consortium of six mayors' and governors' associations discuss specific plans to achieve the 3.2 trillion yen subsidy cut. The consortium proposed in August 2004 that the MoE terminate its 1.3 trillion yen subsidization of compulsory education for local municipalities; this amount included 850 billion yen in subsidies for teachers' salaries in public junior high schools (Chijikai, 2004). Education Minister Nariaki Nakayama, along with other former Ministers, strongly opposed this fiscal decentralization proposal, warning that it would result in regional disparities in educational funding and in the quality of educational services (e.g., Kawamura, 2006; Nakayama, 2004; Tōyama, 2004).

Concurrently, the MoE was facing heavy neoliberal privatization pressure. In November 2004, the CDR (2004) submitted a policy recommendation to the Ministry calling for education reform that "places consumers of educational services (children and parents) as the leading actors in education reform" (p. 1). These education reform proposals were generated and deliberated at the CEFP and the CDR, both of which were outside the MoE's jurisdiction (Kariya, 2006; Tōyama, 2004). Koizumi's Cabinet often ignored policy proposals formulated by the Central Council of Education (*chūkyōshin*), the conventional deliberative body within the MoE, whose members are handpicked by the Ministry. Thus, since the turn of the Millennium, the MoE's legitimacy as the nation's sole educational administrator had been seriously challenged due to neoliberal political pressure to restructure and streamline the Ministry's educational administration.

Faced with the mounting neoliberal pressures, the MoE had to find a way to protect its administrative and financial prerogatives. The creation of the "the Basic Plan for Educational Promotion" (*Kyōiku shinkō kihon keikaku*) was one of the strategies that the Ministry adopted to protect its authority (Ichikawa, 2003; Ōuchi, 2003). In the 1990s, similar legislative attempts were successfully made to draw funding to specific governmental projects. For instance, the Basic Law for Science and Technology went into effect in November 1995, on the basis of which the Basic Plan for Science and Technology was created in March 2006. Similarly, the Basic Law for Gender-Equal Society went into effect in June 1999, on the basis of which the Basic Plan for Gender Equality was created in December 2000. According to Hirokazu Ōuchi (2003), once a basic law of this sort is established, the implementation of its basic plan does not necessitate the Diet's ratification, only the Cabinet's approval. This means that decision-making authority over the basic plan will rest squarely within a given ministry and its associated deliberative councils. Furthermore, once a basic law is enacted, the central government is mandated to provide sufficient funding to implement its related plan (Ōuchi, 2003). Hence, the creation of a basic law and a basic plan has become the ministries' key strategy for securing funding in a time of aggressive neoliberal cutting of state spending, and in a time of intense inter-ministry competition for funding. Following these legislative leads, the MoE attempted to create a similar initiative that would ensure educational funding, and that would enable the Ministry to retain its central role in educational decision-making and administration.

The proposal for the Basic Plan for Educational Promotion first emerged during the deliberation of the aforementioned 2000 NCER, where the FLE amendment was also deliberated for the first time at a governmental council since its 1947 creation. Initially, the creation of the Basic Plan and the FLE amendment were discussed as two separate agendas; the NCER's mid-term report, issued in September 2000 presented them as distinct issues in need of further discussion (Ōuchi, 2003, p. 109). As reported earlier, the MoE was initially uneasy about the explicitly ideological move to de-constitutionalize the FLE and was thus pursuing its own political agenda, the creation of the Basic Plan, at a remove from the far-right LDP politicians. However, in the

NCER's final report, issued in December of the same year, these two agendas were joined; the creation of the Basic Plan was integrated with the proposed amendment to the FLE along explicitly nationalistic lines (NCER, 2000). The final report proposed the inclusion of desirable dispositions and values (appreciation of tradition and culture, religious sensitivity, and patriotism) in the revised FLE, and went on to argue:

> the FLE must include not only educational philosophy to be pursued but also specify concrete plans. In this light, in order to dramatically improve the administrative and financial measures for education, the revised FLE, just like other basic laws, must include specific provisions pertaining to the Basic Plan for Educational Promotion.
>
> (NCER, 2000, p. 15)

Hence, during the course of the NCER deliberation, the MoE made a strategic move to align its political agenda with that of far-right LDP politicians.

It is more than revealing that the MoE chose to combine the creation of the Basic Plan with other explicitly nationalistic agendas, despite the fact that the former could have been achieved by simply changing the existing administrative laws, a move that would have been much less controversial than amending the FLE. Besides, the creation of the Basic Plan would have won support from progressive critics, who saw it as a necessary legislative attempt to secure more funding for education and to protect the egalitarian central funding system against neoliberal pressures, but who were opposed to the nationalistic FLE revision (e.g., Fujita, 2001, 2005; Ichikawa, 2003; Kariya, 2006). The problem, from the Ministry's perspective, was the lack of support within the Koizumi Cabinet, which was aggressively pursuing the state's fiscal and administrative streamlining and decentralization. The MoE's Basic Plan, which could have given the Ministry more authority over educational funding, ran counter to the central office's decentralization and cost-cutting efforts. Faced with the Cabinet's political inertia and mounting neoliberal pressure to devolve its administrative and fiscal prerogatives, the MoE increasingly came to see its tactical alliance with far-right LDP politicians as being necessary for the pushing through of its political agenda. Hence, the MoE "became the Right" by collaborating with powerful rightist LDP politicians who pursued the inclusion of nationalistic language in the revision, and who deemed it necessary to maintain the MoE's central administrative control over education to sustain national unity and social integration. In so doing, the MoE fundamentally redefined the nature of the FLE; the law was no longer the constitution of education, but was instead transformed into an administrative act that gives legal and fiscal backing to the MoE's new administrative role, and that legalizes intrusive state intervention in education for the purposes of moralizing, nationalizing, and responsibilizing children.

However, the NCER's final recommendation did not end the official deliberation on the FLE amendment. The MoE needed to prevent the NCER, established outside the Ministry's conventional policy-making process (that is, via the Central Council of Education, CCE), from finalizing the deliberation on the FLE amendment. Letting this happen could have significantly undermined the legitimacy of the MoE's education policy deliberation and decision-making mechanism. According to journalist Shigekazu Sakurai (2001), the MoE officials negotiated with the Mori Cabinet, and Mori agreed to refer the FLE amendment agenda to the MoE's Central Council of Education. In exchange, the Ministry agreed to write bills for other proposed, less controversial conservative educational interventions from the NCER, such as the introduction of service learning (*hōshi katsudō*), which Mori had strongly pushed. This allowed Mori to leave his post with a political accomplishment that reflected his conservative politics (Sakurai, 2001). Through this bargaining, the MoE gained the opportunity to have the FLE amendment deliberated once again, this time on its own turf. In November 2001, then Education Minister Atsuko Tōyama (2001–2003) requested that the CCE deliberate the FLE amendment. Her request letter to the CCE placed the Basic Plan for Educational Promotion ahead of the FLE (Tōyama, 2001), clearly reflecting the Ministry's original interests (Ichikawa, 2003).[18]

At the same time, the MoE needed to respond to the fiscal and administrative pressures for decentralization. In the then Education Minister's words, the Ministry was willing to "flexibly respond to the Koizumi Cabinet's structural reform, while protecting the institutional core essential for sustaining the current standard of education" (Tōyama, 2004, p. 110). The Ministry needed to achieve this goal without undermining its own administrative authority. The solution was to reconfigure its administrative control from input management towards output management. Since the late 1990s, the Ministry has drastically devolved its administrative authorities to the prefectures, local municipalities, and schools. For instance, the Ministry redefined the national curricular standard as the "minimum essentials" and introduced Integrated Study Hours, for which no curricular guideline was set for schools to follow (Terawaki, 2001). The Ministry also introduced the block-grant system in its distribution of national educational subsidies in order to increase local fiscal autonomy.[19] These administrative and fiscal decentralization moves were accompanied by the MoE's refocusing its administrative authority in the areas of goal-setting, testing, auditing, and evaluation (Takayama, 2008a). By allowing schools and school boards to operate "freely" to achieve the goals and benchmarks set by the Ministry, the Ministry sought a renewed political legitimacy as the "evaluative state," the marked shift of educational governance towards "steering at a distance" (Ball, 1997).

The shift towards the evaluative state was clearly reflected in the CCE's final report on the FLE amendment, entitled "The FLE Appropriate in the New Era and the Basic Plan for Educational Promotion" (CCE, 2003). The report explains the objective of the Basic Plan for Educational Promotion, which is now included with the amendments to the FLE:

> To promote comprehensive and systematic policy changes in education, the state is responsible for laying out the fundamental policy direction, concrete policies to be considered, and other important matters with regard to education and for reporting these to the national diet and publicly announcing them.
>
> (CCE, 2003)

The Basic Plan also requires the MoE to draw up a five-year plan and to set up numerical goals to improve the quality of education. The new FLE also stipulates that local municipalities are responsible for drafting their own education policies in close accordance with the goals set by the central government (CCE, 2003). These additions indicate the Ministry's shift towards the output management model of educational administration (Kariya, 2006). This governing-at-a-distance mode allows the Ministry to act as "a neutral, honest broker" whose roles are simply to set the benchmarks and collect and disseminate information about each school's performance (Clarke & Newman, 1997). The new control mechanism thus allows the Ministry to export its legitimacy crisis downward to local schools and districts, making it seem as if it were entirely each school's responsibility to educate children, not the state's. Furthermore, by marking its central role in educational goal-setting and output management in the revised law, the MoE preempted the aggressive neoliberal attempt to decentralize and privatize much of its educational administration (Natsushima, 2006). In sum, hidden behind the politically charged debate over the inclusion of the nationalistic language in the amendment was the MoE's strategic move to tighten its administrative authority and to secure funding sources for its administration, while creating the legal foundation for its institutional shift towards the outcome-based educational governance.

The New Beginning of Progressive Politics

As the postwar history of Japanese progressive struggles testifies, the rise of conservative movements generates the revitalized progressive counter-movement that often leads to more progressive gains (Kyōiku undōshi kenkyūkai, 1976; Ōtsuki, 1982, p. 26). As will be discussed later, the deconstitutionalization of the FLE has indeed resulted in the looming progressive educational movement which continues on even after the "coup." The strategic discussion below seeks to expand the progressive possibilities, illuminating possible spaces and tactics for progressive political gains.

In considering counter-hegemonic tactics, progressives must begin with a serious recognition of "good sense" in the rightist restructuring (Apple, 2006a). People are not simply duped but endorse neoliberal/neoconservative attack against the postwar democratic settlement because they see elements of good sense in these reform proposals. Neoconservatives achieved substantial popular support for the "gender-free" education bashing, the nationalistic history textbook movement, and the revision of the FLE by articulating these reforms in a manner that addressed people's anxieties, fears, and future aspirations. Neoconservative reform proposals generated people's support, partly because they offered people a clearer sense of belongingness, identity, and social location in a time of radical social transformation. Likewise, neoliberal challenge against the state bureaucracy encompasses elements of good sense. In a nation like Japan where progressive struggles have historically centered on the freedom from the state's bureaucratic control over curriculum, teaching, and evaluation, the neoliberal rejection of the state control in input areas of education is immensely "liberating," resonating with people's genuine frustration about the inflexibility and unresponsiveness of public education. The Right has been successful in understanding the changing social conditions, shaping people's perceptions of their needs, and then articulating their proposals in a manner to fulfill the perceptions (Fraser, 1989).

The task for progressives is then not to immediately dismiss people's support for patriotic teaching, moral education, expanded school choice, and national standardized testing as indicating that they are manipulated by the dominant groups but to understand how each of these proposals rearticulate and partially address their needs. In so doing, progressives must learn to articulate more progressively oriented agendas in a way to represent people's voices and concerns that the Right has been so successful in responding to thus far.

The fact that many of the rightist reform proposals contain good sense speaks to the possibility for progressives to form tactical alliances with groups that usually have agendas contrary to progressive causes (Apple, 2006a). Tactical alliances can be made especially where tensions arise within the current conservative movement. I discussed how neoconservatives are weary of the social disintegrating effects of neoliberal economic and social changes that they fear would divorce people from the traditional cultural norms, families, communities, and the nation. The 1990s curricular reform, primarily driven by corporate demands for streamlining public education and constructivist curricular mode, tended to prioritize students' *kosei* (individuality) *and yutori* (more room for growth), while deemphasizing their dedication and loyalty to their families, communities, and the nation. I also identified the tension between neoliberal Prime Minister's Central Office and the MoE bureaucrats as one of the key factors behind the FLE revision. The task for progressives is then to identify these tensions within the conservative bloc and to explore ways to take advantage of these cracks to advance more progressive agendas (Apple, 2006a).

Progressives can form tactical alliances with some elements of neo-conservatives. While disagreeing with the neoconservative support for explicitly nationalistic, paternalistic education reform agendas, progressives can still work with them and propose measures that address their fears and anxieties in a more progressive manner. For instance, just as progressives do, some segments of neoconservatives strongly oppose the quasi-market approach to education that they fear will further disconnect children and schools from local communities. Hence, progressives can use some of the neoconservative themes to direct their anxieties against quasi-market school choice proposals, while proposing initiatives that strengthen the tie between community and schools. Progressives must also work with those who currently support conservatives' attack against gender-equality initiatives in education. As discussed earlier, many men support the feminist bashing movement, because they perceive the gender-equality reform both in education and employment as the cause of their economic and social marginalization. Feminists and progressives must fully understand their frustration and anxiety and redirect them against the very corporate restructuring that has absolved itself of the social responsibility for providing secure employment for both men and women (Kaizuma, 2005, pp. 47–48).

Likewise, progressives can form tactical alliances with some elements of neoliberals, as well. While opposing the MoE's shift towards the standardized-test-based accountability system and less regulated school choice that the neoliberal wing strongly endorses, progressives can still work with the neoliberal counterpart to promote more administrative decentralization in education. As I discussed earlier, it was partly due to the corporate pressure that many of the progressive gains were made in the MoE's curricular and administrative policies in the 1990s. One of such gains was the creation of the Integrated Learning Hours during which teachers enjoy full autonomy over curriculum and textbooks. Progressive teachers have appropriated this space for counter-hegemonic teaching practice (see Nagao, 2002). Progressives can also tap into the neoliberal pursuit of a market approach in education, though this requires much more careful political work. As Isao Kurosaki (2003) argues, in an increasingly pluralistic society where divergent values and interests are celebrated, some form of differentiation scheme through market approaches is more likely to stay.

Thus, instead of rejecting school choice programs that are increasingly popular among the public, progressives need to cooperate with some elements of neoliberals to promote more choice in public education and challenge the MoE's administrative control. While pursuing this, progressives must make sure that school choice is adequately controlled. Here, progressives can work with neoconservatives to assure that school choice does not go all the way to the free market approach. The task for progressives is to mediate the conflicting interests of neoliberals and neoconservatives and use them to shift the debate from "whether or not choice" to "what kind of choice" can serve the progressive interests of protecting school–community connections and providing adequate degree of choice for those who need it due to various educational needs.

The fissure between the MoE and the neoliberal Central Office also provides space for progressives' creative political work. This chapter has shown how the MoE appropriated the rising neoconservative force to counter the neoliberal demands for fiscal and administrative decentralization. The Ministry made this tactical alliance despite the likelihood of involving itself in unwanted ideological conflicts. Here, the key word is "tactical," indicating that the MoE would have possibly made a different alliance, had there been a strong presence of an alternative, progressive discourse demanding more educational funding and the MoE's central administrative role in public education. In fact, in the debate over the termination of the national education subsidy system [*gimu kyōikuhi kokko futankin seido*], an agenda that neoliberals fiercely pushed in the early 2000s, the MoE made an unprecedented alliance with progressive scholars to protect its fiscal lifeline. In its desperate defense of the national educational subsidy system through which the Ministry has historically controlled local school districts, the MoE relied upon progressive scholars to counter the neoliberal attack. Furthermore, in the same debate, the MoE appropriated the traditional progressive discourse to appeal to the public for the preservation of its funding system, accentuating the Ministry's redistributive and egalitarian role (see Nakayama, 2004), the notion that is rarely used by the increasingly neoliberalized Japanese state. This incident shows how the aggressive neoliberal restructuring demands paradoxically forced the Ministry to assert its redistributive function in its defense, a phenomenon rather unique to centrally controlled education systems such as in Japan. Under the neoliberal onslaught on public institutions, the Ministry's institutional needs can be aligned with traditional progressive demands for equal educational opportunities and egalitarian school funding.

In addition, as discussed earlier, the MoE's insistence on equal educational funding results from the state's necessity to address its inherent contradictions that are increasingly difficult to manage under the neoliberal regime. The neoliberal state cannot afford to be too aggressive in streamlining and privatizing public education to the extent that the availability of quality education depends on one's capacity to pay. The formal institutional commitment to equality in education needs to be preserved so that the state can perpetuate its core cultural and institutional assumption, the ideology of meritocracy. This has made education one of the few social policy areas where the state's redistributive function remains a legitimate policy concern. All of these mean that education can occupy a central place in progressive politics from where a social-democratic vision of society continues to be articulated, revitalized, and expanded to other social and economic fields. Progressives must recognize the MoE's desperate needs to sustain its legitimacy under the neoliberal pressures and utilize them towards more progressive ends. For this unusual collaboration to materialize, the traditional political paradigm, which pits the MoE against the progressive political causes, must be reconsidered.

International Alliance Making

One of the limitations of the recent literature on progressives' strategic alliance with conservative groups is that the discussion is often limited within the framework of a nation state. For instance, Apple's (2006a) call for progressives' tactical alliance does not address the possibility of cross-national alliance for progressive causes. Learning from other nations about consequences of neoliberal/neoconservative changes and progressive tactics to counter them is important (Apple, 2006a, p. 247). However, more effort must be made to move beyond mere learning from other nations, when the politics of education within a nation state is increasingly shaped by the larger international relations and regional geopolitics (see Takayama, 2009c). As detailed below, the rising neoconservative politics in and outside Japanese education has created tensions in the nation's diplomatic relationship with the United States and neighboring Asian nations, undermining Japanese capital's overseas profit-making. This indicates that the alliance-making that cuts across national boundaries can be effective in challenging the conservative politics in Japanese education.

Recent fissures within the Japanese Right have amply shown the potential effectiveness of these tactics. In 1982, when the conservative LDP right-wings pushed the MoE to tighten its textbook screening to reflect their nationalistic agenda in history textbooks, South Korean and Chinese governments and the citizens generated considerable political pressure that eventually forced the MoE to revise the underplaying of its past aggression in the approved history and social studies textbooks. Subsequently, the international pressures forced the Ministry to create a new textbook screening criteria: the so-called "near neighbors clause" (*kinrin shokoku jōkō*)—mandating that textbook passages that deal with the events of modern and contemporary history involving Japan and neighboring Asian countries give due consideration to the need for international understanding and harmony. The criteria played a key role in preventing the LDP far-rights from further pushing nationalistic agenda in the textbook screening (Kitazawa, 2001).[20]

In the early 1990s, international collaborations between Japanese and South Korean grassroots organizations successfully brought sudden media attention to "comfort women" whose voices had been silenced by the respective governments (Kim, 1997). It eventually forced the Japanese government to officially apologize to these women and to set up a private fund to compensate for their wartime suffering. This also contributed to the MoE's approval of textbook references to these women in the late 1990s. These progressive gains in the nation's textbooks were promoted by Japanese multinational corporations' demands to "clean" the past along with various—progressive (in Japan) and progressive and nationalistic (in China and South Korea)—social movements that cut across national boundaries (Takayama, 2009c).

More recently, Prime Minister Koizumi's annual visits to the controversial *Yasukuni* Shrine caused Asian neighbors' strong protest.[21] With China as one of the major destinations for many Japanese multinational corporations' plant relocations and one of the largest markets for their commodities, they quickly expressed concerns over his visits. Faced with the discontinuation of diplomatic exchanges and people's boycotting of Japanese products in China, the head of the Japan Association of Business Executives issued a statement criticizing the Prime Minister for visiting the shrine, which immediately faced the ultra-nationalist accusation for being unpatriotic. These examples demonstrate how progressive international alliances can take advantage of the fissure between far-right nationalists and multinational corporations to pursue progressive agenda in education. Japanese progressives must utilize business sectors' increasing frustration with the rising ultra-nationalism within the LDP and collaborate with Chinese and South Korean grassroots organizations to prevent the glorification of the past in education.

In addition to international alliances with grassroots movements in neighboring Asian nations, Japanese progressives must also collaborate with

US-based social movements as well. As this chapter has amply shown, the neoconservative glorification of Japan's past necessarily involves the denigration of the United States. The LDP far-right legislators, the revisionist history textbook group led by Yagi, and the *Yasukuni* Shrine all promote a historical narrative that positions the United States as the villain. In their mind, the US's postwar occupation policy towards Japan destroyed the essence of national tradition and spiritual foundation and emasculated the nation through the "imposition" of democracy, the Peace Constitution, and the FLE. They argue that the United States deprived the Japanese of national pride through the inculcation of war guilt during the occupation period, imposing the view that Japan invaded neighboring Asian nations rather than liberating them from Western imperial oppressors (see, e.g., Takahashi, 1995). The neoconservative historical perspective questions the legitimacy of the US-led postwar world order, casting doubts on the validity of the US-led International Military Tribunal for the Far East and the US occupation's demilitarization policies towards Japan.

American neoconservatives were the first to question the ultra-nationalistic and anti-American historical narrative of Koizumi's and Abe's Cabinets (see Boot, 2003; Fukuyama, 2007). In a manner that builds upon these neoconservative critics' accusations, in February 2007, a bipartisan group of US lawmakers led by Democratic Representative Mike Honda of California submitted a resolution to the US House of Representatives denouncing Japan for enslaving foreign women for enforced sexual services during the wartime, and the resolution passed through the House of Representatives on July 30, 2007.[22]

These accusations and diplomatic pressure from the US government intensified the existing tension within Japanese conservatives between pragmatic conservatives and traditional nationalists (Tawara et al., 2006; see also Watanabe, 2001, pp. 233–235). While the former, who considered the US–Japan bilateral relationship as central to Japan's national interests, demanded the immediate elimination of the controversial exhibitions from the *Yasukuni* Shrine's war museum and the similar nationalistic, anti-American historiography from the revisionist history textbooks, the latter accused the former for cooperating with the US interests (Tanaka, 2007). In response to the US accusation, Masahiko Okazaki, one of the founders of the revisionist textbook group and the editor for the revised edition of the group's original history textbook, eliminated all the anti-American description (Okazaki, 2006). This action created serious tensions within the group and, combined with the extremely low adoption rate of the group's textbooks by local school districts,[23] it resulted in the subsequent break-up of the movement (Tawara et al., 2006, p. 26 & pp. 43–44). While these conservatives maintained their united front when demanding the elimination of textbook references to Japan's wartime aggressions, they sharply disagreed over the historical narrative that demonizes the US.

This series of events demonstrates two important lessons for progressive movements. First, it shows how the rising rightist politics could threaten the US–Japan diplomatic relationship and result in the internal tension within the Right. Second, it shows how an incident of this nature could open up possibilities for international alliances between Japan-based progressive organizations and US-based progressive groups and even US-based neo-conservative social movements. In the post-postwar politics where the internal tension within the Right is more intensified than ever, it is crucial for Japanese progressives to think heretically and explore ways to form both domestic and international alliances with groups of various ideological underpinnings.

Summary

This chapter has focused on one of the most significant events in the postwar history of Japanese education, the conservative revision of the Fundamental Law of Education. The mobilization to revise the law was part of the larger neoconservative politics that emerged in response to the economic restructuring and the associated social and cultural instabilities at the turn of the century. It was in this context of flux that cultural politics of crisis borrowing powerfully worked to shift people's common sense about the FLE and the role of the state in education. In the emerging neoliberal risk society, where people's lives are increasingly exposed to unpredictable factors, and in a partly postmodern society, where traditional values, authority structures, and morality are constantly questioned, rightist politicians and intellectuals creatively appropriated the people's attraction and repulsion in relation to the discursive West to reconstitute their common sense about Japanese education's current condition and its future course. They played on these ambivalent tendencies in order to harness Japanese people's genuine feelings in support of the conservative discourse of tradition, order, patriotism, and discipline.

My analysis of the crisis borrowing had a theoretical agenda as well, one directly related to how critical educational researchers should think about the issue of borrowing in more complex ways. By using material from both postcolonial understandings and from cultural studies I attempted to illustrate the cultural politics over "British education reform" as currently played out in the Japanese discussion of education reform. The still-vibrant legacy of Western imperialism and colonialism endows "British education reform" with considerable symbolic power that Japanese rightist politicians and intellectuals re-direct toward a de-territorialization of their contentious domestic political agendas. They appropriate the discursive West both to legitimize their calls for learning from British school reform and to de-legitimize the FLE's democratic and pacifist idealism. Hence, this Japanese case has shown that, in a wider context, the cultural constructs "the West," "the United States," and "the United Kingdom" constitute a powerful discursive tool with which dominant political forces in non-Western nations (1) rearticulate their domestic political agendas and (2) base them on the "inevitability of globalization." The analysis has shown the importance of re-conceptualizing the politics of educational borrowing in a way that takes full account of the continuing effects of Western cultural imperialism in non-Western national contexts, a point that has been underemphasized in the hitherto-privileged conceptualization of educational borrowing.

Then, the chapter focused on the actual content of the revision and the MoE's political interests behind the ideologically charged revision. The revision reflected not only traditional conservative agendas, but, more importantly, neoliberal localism and responsibilization, the state's attempt to produce self-governing subjects appropriate in the hyper-individualized social relations. The FLE amendment also reflects the state's attempt to reinvent an imagined sense of national community to contain the dis-integrating effects of neoliberal social changes. Thus, the FLE revision must not simply be understood as the manifestation of retrogressive conservative politics that the right-wing LDP politicians had pursued throughout the postwar history. The chapter demonstrated that the recent articulation of the half-century-old conservative agenda assumes a renewed political significance in the larger neoliberal restructuring of the state–civil society relationship.

Having situated the FLE amendment within the larger global context of neoliberal/neoconservative educational restructuring, I then complicated this picture by illuminating the complex domestic politics that drove the constitutional revision, with a particular focus on the MoE's political agency. I demonstrated how the MoE made a strategic move to appropriate the powerful neoconservative force for the purposes of protecting itself against neoliberal decentralization and marketization and of establishing itself as the evaluative state agency. This chapter thus shed light on the complex domestic political processes implicated in the alignment of Japanese educa-tion with the global trend towards neoliberal/neoconservative governance in education. The study of globalization in education must examine the global "external" pressures that generate policy convergence, while at the same time analyzing their dialectic connections with the domestic political struggles hidden behind the seemingly "automatic" shift towards a "global standard." In the case of Japanese education characterized by the strong state control, the MoE's political interests played a crucial role in shaping the particular articulations of the neoliberal/neoconservative politics in the ongoing educational restructuring. Lastly, the chapter discussed the spaces for progressive interruption. Though progressives are largely marginalized in the post-postwar politics, this does not mean that they have no possibility for political gains. I identified the tensions within the conservative bloc that can be plied open for progressive gains and demonstrated several ways in which various alliances—domestic, international, and "unusual"—can be formed to challenge the conservative turn in Japanese education.

The creative tactical work and international collaboration explored in this chapter must be pursued along with attempts to generate domestic social movement around education reform (Anyon, 2005; Apple, 2006a). In the current rightist turn both in and outside education, the possibility of progressive social movement is looming larger, with the rise of people's frustration about the ongoing restructuring of labor markets, social policies, education, and Japan's ongoing support for the US-led "war on terrorism" (Mōri, 2003). These changes have resulted in the increasing awareness of collective actions among youth and young adults who bear the harshest consequences of the upward economic redistribution. Likewise, the recent nationalist turn in politics has encouraged nonpartisan, ordinary citizens to join progressive grassroots organizations.

Many progressive grassroots organizations sprang up in opposition to the recent right turn in Japanese politics. Just to name a few, established in June 2004, the Article 9 Association (*Kyūjō no kai*) calls for the protection of the war-renouncing Article 9 of the Constitution.[24] Led by "old liberalists" (Nobel Prize Laureate in Literature Kenzaburo Ōe, novelist Hisashi Inoue, and philosopher Shunsuke Tsurumi, etc.), the association appealed to older generations and successfully extended its support network across the nation. In early 2004, a group of citizens decided to collect petitions against Tokyo Governor Shintarō Ishihara's enforcement of the national anthem and flag in public schools' entrances and graduation ceremonies.[25] The citizens' local initiative eventually led to the formation of Freedom Wind Network (*Jiyū no kaze netto wāku*) which organized a series of protest events against the Tokyo governor and other rightist political leaders.[26] In April 2004, four progressive scholars founded the National Association "Stop the Dangerous Revision to the Fundamental Law of Education." The organization's "sound parades," which integrated popular music and DJ performance in street demonstrations, successfully mobilized a large number of youth and young adults.[27] In addition, many other national and local organizations were created across the nation to oppose the LDP's total disregard for people's pacifist and democratic beliefs.

All these organizations came together to form a loose coalition in resisting the FLE revision. The internet-based petition to oppose the destruction of the educational constitution elicited the endorsement of 175 organizations that diverged in their specific interests. Local branches of labor unions, women's groups, teachers' unions, antiwar groups, various religious (Catholic, Baptist, Christian, and Buddhist) organizations, oppressed groups (*Buraku*, ethnic Korean, and indigenous *Ainu*)[28], human rights organizations, YMCA, and many other citizens' groups joined to challenge the LDP right wings' attempt to "undo the postwar regime."[29]

Therefore, as was seen in the rise of progressive educational struggles in the past, the left became revitalized as an ironic consequence of the rightist destruction of the educational constitution. It allowed for the formation of a de-centered unity (Apple, 2006a, p. 81) where groups of multiple interests join together to challenge the neoliberal/neoconservative politics in education as well as in wider society. Though the cornerstone of postwar progressive struggles no longer exists, the democratic and pacifist spirit is still alive. Many grassroots organizations created primarily to oppose the FLE revision continue to provide progressive spaces for different political actions. These local and national organizations must strengthen the existing progressive alliances to prevent the forthcoming regressive changes in education. At the same time, they must explore ways to take advantage of the tensions within the Right and form tactical alliances with domestic conservative groups and international coalitions with progressive and non-progressive organizations outside Japan.

Notes

1   This chapter draws partly on two published articles (see Takayama, 2008b; Takayama & Apple, 2008). I would like to thank all the contributors to this book for their helpful comments on the early draft of this chapter.

2   Dale and Robertson use this expression to discuss New Zealand education. The thesis proposed here challenges the existing English language literature on the recent Japanese education reform that perceives it as an exception to the global restructuring movements (see Takayama, 2008a, 2009b).

3   According to the Ministry of Health, Labor and Welfare's report (2006), the unemployment rate for ages 15–24 was 9.9 percent for men and 7.4 percent for women in 2005.

4   The percentage of irregular employment hovered around 20–25 percent during the 1990s and 26–33 percent in the 2000s. In 1984, when the Ministry began collecting this data, it was 15.3 percent (Ministry of Health, Labor and Welfare, 2006).

5   Indeed, Japan was one of the most egalitarian societies among the OECD nations for most of the postwar years, and Japan's poor have been relatively less poor than in most other industrial nations (Pempel, 1998, pp. 8–9).

6   "Comfort women" euphemistically refers to the enslaved women who were forced to sexually serve the Japanese military. Between 1932 and 1945, thousands of women, mostly from China, Korea, and the Philippines, were rounded up and imprisoned in so-called "comfort stations" (*ianjo*)—brothels—where they were repeatedly raped and abused by Japanese military personnel (Tanaka, 2002). The subsequent governments refuse to acknowledge the military involvement in the operation of comfort stations, arguing that they were managed by civilian brothel owners and that the women were recruited by private procurers.

7   Igarashi (2000) argues that the postwar foundational narrative was constructed by the complicity between the US-led occupation whose geopolitical interest was in keeping Japan

as the key strategic post over Asia on one hand and Japanese LDP conservatives on the other. The narrative cast Japan's defeat as a drama of "rescue and conversion" (p. 43): the US rescued Japan from the menace of its militarists, and Japan was converted into a peaceful, democratic country under the US hegemony. It articulated Japan's war experience solely as a conflict with the US and thus concealed Japan's memories of colonial ambition in the neighboring Asian nations (see also Field, 1997).

8　The considerable presence of far-right religious organizations in Japan Conference and the organization's close ties to powerful LDP legislators indicate the increasing political significance of religion in Japanese conservative politics. This resulted from the decline of partisanship in Japanese politics. While in the 1960s fewer than 10 percent of voters identified themselves as independent, the figure was up to 38 percent by the 1993 election, and 50 percent in January 1995 (Pempel, 1998, p. 159). Besides, due to the increasing neoliberal turn in the ruling LDP, the party has lost steady electoral support from agricultural and small business sectors who had traditionally endorsed the LDP candidates. In this context of political fluidity, religious organizations have become the most reliable and thus the most sought-after political constituencies in the post-postwar politics (Takenobu, 2005, pp. 28–29).

9　http://www.nipponkaigi.org/reidai02/About%20Us/Profile.htm.

10　Two former prime ministers, Keizō Obuchi and Yoshirō Mori were the founding members of this organization (Tawara et al., 2006. p. 69).

11　Article 9 of the Constitution, known as the peace clause, stipulates that the Japanese people "forever renounce war as a sovereign right of the nation and the threat or use of force as means of settling international disputes."

12　Because of the relic of the song that celebrates the long-lasting reign by the emperor, *kimigayo* is unofficially translated as "His Majesty's Reign." The idea of the "emperor's reign" of course contradicts the Constitution that situates the emperor merely as a symbol with no political authority.

13　At the time, Keizō Obuchi (1998–2000), the then Prime Minister, Yoshihito Arima, the then Education Minister, and Tsutomu Nonaka, the then Secretary General to the Obuchi Cabinet, announced that the law would not change the status of *hinomaru* and *kimigayo* in schools (Takahashi, 2004, p. 159). Once they were legalized, however, they were made mandatory by municipalities in school ceremonies.

14　The homepage of the organization's Tokyo Chapter: http://tukuru-kai.hp.infoseek.co.jp/NewFiles/nazeima.html.

15　All the textbooks to be used in Japanese schools have to be approved by Ministry-appointed examiners. They must be written in a manner that strictly follows the Ministry's national Study Course.

16　For British scholars' critiques of the Black Papers, see Ball (1990), Dale (1989), and Wright (1977). Yagi edited a Japanese book entitled "Education Black Papers" (*kyōiku kokusho*) (Yagi, 2002) wherein articles by conservative intellectuals discuss ideologically tainted teaching in Japanese schools. Comparing his book with the British Black Papers, he urges for grassroots conservative political mobilization for the "normalization" of Japanese public education.

17　In fact, the Japanese state recently decided to maintain the national educational subsidy system, despite aggressive pressure from neoliberals to demolish it. Though other educational changes strongly reflect capital's financial and labor needs and have already significantly altered the egalitarian principles of Japanese education, the state could not afford to lose the central funding system, the most crucial element of Japanese education's egalitarianism (Fujita, 2005).

18　In March 2003, the CCE issued the final report that recommended specific agendas to be included in the revised FLE, but these closely resembled those already proposed in the NCER report. In fact, as one of the CCE members noted, the CCE's deliberations and the public hearings had no effect on the final recommendations, which had been pre-established by Ministry officials (Ichikawa, 2003). Hence, the CCE deliberation simply served to re-legitimize the Ministry's conventional policy-making process.

19　This was a desperate attempt on the part of the Ministry to protect the national subsidy system, the elimination of which other powerful ministries and neoliberals demanded, while conceding to the pressure for decentralization.

20　It was in response to this progressive gain in textbook issues that nationalistic revisionist movements, including the controversial history textbook group led by Yagi, emerged in the late 1990s (Kitazawa, 2001).

21 The shrine is dedicated to the spirits of soldiers and others who died fighting on behalf of the Emperor of Japan. In 1978, fourteen major war criminals of the Asia Pacific War were also enshrined there, hence making state officials' visits to the shrine highly controversial. Koizumi's annual visits during his tenure generated considerable protest from China, North and South Korea, and Taiwan. The war museum adjacent to the shrine has many exhibitions justifying Japan's action during the Asia Pacific War.

22 Japanese grassroots organizations working for the surviving comfort women welcomed the US resolution that would add more diplomatic pressure on the Japanese government to recognize the past issue (Kamiya, 2007).

23 In the spring of 2002, the market share of the group's history textbook was approximately 0.04%. Intense local pressure by grassroots progressive groups effectively prevented school districts from adopting the textbook (Nozaki, 2002, p. 619). In 2005, the market share for its history and social studies textbooks were 0.39% and 0.19% respectively, considerably lower than their targeted 10% market share (Tawara et al., 2006).

24 http://www.9-jo.jp/index.html.

25 The Tokyo Metropolitan Board of Education issued a notice in October 2003 to public school principals, telling them to order all teachers to stand and sing the anthem at graduation and entrance ceremonies. In spring 2004, 248 teachers were punished for disobeying the orders at ceremonies, and of them, approximately 200 refused to stand at graduation ceremonies (Arita, 2005).

26 http://comcom.jca.apc.org/freedom/index.html.

27 http://www.kyokiren.net/.

28 Ethnic Koreans are the largest minority in Japan. *Buraku(min)* are the descendants of premodern social outcasts, and *Ainu* are Japan's indigenous people who primarily reside in the northern part of Japan.

29 http://www.geocities.jp/edsigns2005/.

References

Abe, S. (2006). *Utsukushii kunihe* (Toward beautiful nation). Tokyo: Bungei shunjū.

Abe, S., Sakurai, Y., & Yagi, H. (2004). Imakoso jubaku kenpō to hyōrū rekishi kara ketsubetsu wo (Time to leave the haunted Constitution and historical drifting). In Seiron Henshūbu (Ed.), *Seiron kessaku sen: Kenpō no ronten.* Tokyo: Sankei Shinbunsha.

Alatas, S. F. (2003). Academic dependency and the global division of labour in the social sciences. *Current Sociology,* 51(6), 599–613.

Anyon, J. (2005). *Radical possibilities: Public policy, urban education, and a new social movement.* New York: Routledge.

Appadurai, A. (1996). *Modernity at large: Cultural dimensions of globalization.* Minneapolis: University of Minnesota Press.

Apple, M. W. (1995). *Education and power* (2nd ed.). New York: Routledge.

Apple, M. W. (2006a). *Educating the "right" way: Markets, standards, God, and inequality* (2nd ed.) New York: Routledge.

Apple, M. W. (2006b). Rhetoric and reality in critical educational studies in the United States. *British Journal of Sociology of Education,* 27(5), 679–687.

Arita, E. (2005). 52 teachers penalized for anthem snub: Tokyo doles out warnings and pay cuts for disobeying order to stand and sing. *The Japan Times,* April 1. Retrieved from http://search.japantimes.co.jp/member/member.html?nn20050401a3.htm.

Otoko to onnna hyōgen yurimodoshi (Bringing back "men and women" expressions). (2005, April 6). *Asahi News,* p. 30.

Kenshō tsukurukai kyōkasho (Examining controversial group's textbooks). (2005, April 6). *Asahi News,* p. 15.

Kieta jendāfurī (Gender-free disappears). (2006, March 30). *Asahi News,* p. 38.

Ball, S. J. (1990). *Politics and policy making in education: Explorations in policy sociology.* London: Routledge.

Ball, S. J. (1997). Policy sociology and critical social research. *British Educational Research Journal,* 23(3), 257–275.

Beck, U. (1994). The reinvention of politics. In U. Beck, A. Giddens, and S. Lash (Eds.), *Reflexive Modernization.* Cambridge: Polity Press.

Befu, H. (1993). Nationalism and nihonjinron. In H. Befu (Ed.), *Cultural nationalism in East Asia: Representation and identity.* Berkeley, CA: The Institute of East Asian Studies, University of California-Berkeley.

Ben-Ami, D. (1997). Is Japan different? In P. Hammond (Ed.), *Cultural difference, media memories: Anglo-American images of Japan.* London: Cassell.

Boot, M. (2003). Japan's memory lapses. Retrieved from http://www.cfr.org/publication/6565/japans_memory_lapses.html.

Brown, P. & Lauder, H. (2001). *Capitalism and social progress: The future of society in a global economy.* Basingstoke, Hampshire and New York: Palgrave.

Central Council of Education. (2003). *Atarashii jidai ni fusawashii kyōiku kihonhō to kyōiku shinkō kihon keikaku no arikata ni tsuite* (The FLE appropriate in the new era and the basic plan for educational promotion). Retrieved December 10, 2005, from http://www.mext.go.jp/b_menu/shingi/chukyo/chukyo0/toushin/030301.htm

Chijikai. (2004). *Kokko hojo futankin ni kansuru kaikakuan no gaiyō* (Summary of reform proposal for national subsidy system). Retrieved June 15, 2005, from http://www.nga.gr.jp/chijikai_link/2004_8_x03.pdf.

Clarke, J. & Newman, J. (1997). *The managerial state: Power, politics and ideology in the remaking of social welfare.* London: Sage.

Coulby, D. & Zambeta, E. (Eds.). (2005). *Globalization and nationalism in education.* London: RoutledgeFalmer.

Council for Decentralization Reform. (2004). *Monbukagakushō no gimukyōikukaikaku nikannsuru kinkyūteigen* (Emergency proposal regarding MEXT's compulsory education reform). Retrieved December 5, 2005, from http://www.kisei-kaikaku.go.jp/minutes/meeting/2004/08/meeting04_08_01.pdf.

Council on Economic and Fiscal Policy. (2002). *Basic policies for economic and fiscal policy management and structural reform 2002.* Retrieved December 5, 2005, from http://www.keizai-shimon.go.jp/english/publication/pdf/0621item2-e.

Council on Economic and Fiscal Policy. (2004). *Basic policies for economic and fiscal policy management and structural reform 2004.* Retrieved December 5, 2005, from http://www.keizai-shimon.go.jp/english/publication/pdf/040604basic_policies.pdf.

Creighton, M. (1995). Imaging the other in Japanese advertising campaigns. In J. Carrier (Ed.), *Occidentalism: Images of the West* (pp. 135–160). New York: Clarendon Press.

Cummings, W. K. (1980). *Education and equality in Japan.* Princeton, NJ: Princeton University Press.

Cummings, W. K. (1986). Japanese images of American education. In W. Cummings, E. Beauchamp, S. Ichikawa, V. Kobayashi, & M. Ushiogi (Eds.), *Educational policies in crisis* (pp. 275–292). New York: Praeger.

Dale, R. (1989). *The state and education policy.* Toronto: OISE Press.

Dale, R. & Robertson, S. (1997). Resisting the nation, reshaping the state: Globalization effects on education policy in New Zealand. In M. Olssen & K. M. Matthews (Eds.), *Education policy in New Zealand: The 1990s and beyond* (pp. 209–227). Wellington, New Zealang: Dunmore Press.

Dale, R. & Robertson, S. (2002). The varying effects of regional organizations as subjects of globalization of education. *Comparative Education Review, 46*(1), 10–36.

Dean, M. (1999). *Governmentality: Power and rule in modern society.* London and Thousand Oaks, CA: Sage.

Dower, J. W. (1999). *Embracing defeat: Japan in the wake of World War II* (1st ed.). New York: Norton/New Press.

Duggan, L. (2003). *The twilight of equality?: Neoliberalism, cultural politics, and the attack on democracy* (1st ed.). Boston: Beacon Press.

Field, N. (1997). War and apology: Japan, Asia, the fiftieth, and after. *Positions, 5*(3), 1–49.

Fox, R. G. (1992). East of Said. In M. Sprinker (Ed.), *Edward Said: A critical reader* (pp. 144–156). Oxford: Blackwell.

Fraser, N. (1989). *Unruly practices: Power, discourse, and gender in contemporary social theory.* Minneapolis: University of Minnesota Press.

Fujioka, S., Nakano, H., Nakauchi, T., & Takeuchi, T. (1987). *Nihon kyōiku no sengoshi* (Postwar history of Japanese education). Tokyo: Sanseidō.

Fujita, H. (2001). *Shinjidai no kyōiku wo dou kōsōsuruka* (How do we imagine education in the new era?). Tokyo: Iwanami shoten.

Fujita, H. (2005). *Gimukyōiku wo toinaosu* (Rethinking compulsory education). Tokyo: Chikuma shobō.
Fukuyama, F. (2007). The trouble with Japanese nationalism. Retrieved August 10, 2007, from http://www.project-syndicate.org/commentary/fukuyama2.
Gewirtz, S., Ball, S. J., & Bowe, R. (1995). *Markets, choice, and equity in education.* Buckingham and Philadelphia, PA: Open University Press.
Goodman, R. (2003). The why, what and how of educational reform in Japan. In R. Goodman & D. Phillips (Eds.), *Can the Japanese change their education system?* (pp. 7–30). Oxford: Symposium Books.
Gotō, M. (2002). *Shūshukusuru nihongata taishūshakai* (Shrinking Japanese mass society). Tokyo: Aoki shoten.
Hall, S. (1981). Notes on deconstructing "the Popular." In R. Samuel (Ed.), *People's history and socialist theory* (pp. 227–240). London: Routledge & Kegan Paul.
Harvey, D. (2005). *A brief history of neoliberalism.* Oxford: Oxford University Press.
Hasegawa, Y. (2006). Takaga meibo saredo meibo (Just a roll but more than a roll). In Sōfūsha (Ed.), *Bakku rasshu! Naze jendāfūrī wa tatakaretanoka* (Backlash! Why gender free was attacked) (pp. 340–356). Tokyo: Sōfūsha.
Henry, M., Knight, J., Lingard, R., & Taylor, S. (1990). *Understanding schooling.* Sydney: Routledge.
hooks, b. (1992). *Race and representation.* Boston: South End Press.
Horio, T. (1988). *Educational thought and ideology in modern Japan: State authority and intellectual freedom.* Tokyo: University of Tokyo Press.
Horio, T. & Yamazumi, M. (1976). *Kyōiku rinen: Sengo nihon no kyōiku kaikaku 2* (Educational principle: Postwar Japanese education reform 2). Tokyō Daigaku Shuppan Kai.
Ichikawa, S. (1984). Japan. In J. R. Hough (Ed.), *Educational policy: An international survey* (pp. 100–135). New York: St. Martin's Press.
Ichikawa, S. (2003). *Kyōiku kihonhō wo kangaeru: Hūritsu de kokoro wo rissu bekika* (Considering the FLE: should we control mind?). Tokyo: Kyōiku kaihatsu kenkyūjo.
Ida, H. (2006). Bakku rasshu no haikei wo saguru (Examining the background of the backlash). In Nihon josei gakkai jendā kenkyūkai (Ed.), *Danjo kyōdō sanga/jendā furī basshingu* (Bashing against gender-free society and gender free) (pp. 176–186). Tokyo: Akashi shoten.
Igarashi, Y. (2000). *Bodies of memory: Narratives of war in postwar Japanese culture, 1945–1970.* Princeton, NJ: Princeton University Press.
Institute of Race Relations. (1985). *How racism came to Britain.* London: Institute of Race Relations.
Japan Times. (2006). Molding children by design (Editorial). (2006, December 18). *Japan Times.* Retrieved December 18, 2006, from http://www.japantimes.co.jp/.
Jessop, B. (2000). Restructuring the welfare state, re-orienting welfare strategies, re-visioning welfare society. In B. Greve (Ed.), *What constitutes a good society?* New York: St. Martin's Press.
Kabashima, Y. (2005). Kyōiku kihonhō kaisei kara hajimatta igirisu kyōiku kaikaku (British education reform initiated from the revision to the FLE). In T. Nakanishi (Ed.), *Sacchō kaikaku ni manabu.* Tokyo: PHP Shuppan.
Kaizuma, K. (2005). Taikō bunka toshiteno han feminachi (Anti-feminism as culture of resistance). In R. Kimura (Ed.), *Jendā toraburu: Basshingu genshō wo kenshōsuru* (Gender trouble: Examining the bashing phenomenon) (pp. 19–34). Tokyo: Hakutakusha.
Kamiya, S. (2007). Supporters laud U.S. motion on 'comfort women' as first step. *Japan Times,* June 28. Retrieved June 28, 2007, from http://www.japantimes.co.jp/.
Kariya, T. (1995). *Taishō kyōiku shakai no yukue* (The future of mass education society). Tokyo: Chōkō shinsho.
Kariya, T. (2001). *Kaisōka nihon to kyōiku kiki* (Stratification of Japan and crisis in education). Tokyo: Yūshindō.
Kariya, T. (2006). Dakiawase kaisei ni dou taisho suruka (How to deal with the comprised amendment to the FLE). *Sekai,* July, 100–107.
Kariya, T. et al. (2002). *Chōsa hōkoku gakuryoku teika no jittai* (Study report: Reality of academic decline). Tokyo: Iwanami shoten.
Kawamura, T. (2006). Kawamura moto monkashō, saigomade umaranakatta gyappu (Former Education Minister Kawamura, the gap that could not be buried). *Asahi News* (International Edition), September 17, p. 17.
Kenway, J. (1990). Education and the Right's discursive politics: Private versus state schooling. In S. J. Ball (Ed.), *Foucault and education* (pp. 167–206). London: Routledge.

Kim, S. H. (1997). History and memory: The "comfort women" controversy. *Positions*, 5(3), 73–106.

Kimura, R. (1999). *Gakkōbunka to jendā* (School culture and gender). Tokyo: Keisōshobō.

Kimura, R. (2005). Kyōiku ni okeru jendā no shiten no hitsuyōsei (Need for a gender perspective in education). In R. Kimura (Ed.), *Jendā toraburu: Basshingu genshō wo kenshōsuru* (Gender trouble: Examining the bashing phenomenon) (pp. 75–94). Tokyo: Hakutakusha.

Kitazawa, T. (2001). Textbook history repeats itself. *Japan Quarterly*, 48(3), 51–57.

Kurosaki, I. (2003). Public education in a pluralistic society: The establishment of a new public school system and its public educational implications. In I. Kurosaki (Ed.), *Tagenka shakai no kōkyōiku* (Public education in diverse society) (pp. 131–146). Tokyo: Dōjidai sha.

Kyōiku undōshi kenkyūkai. (Ed.). (1976). *Kokumin no kyōikuken to kyōiku undō* (Citizens' rights to education and education movement). Tokyo: Sōdo bunka.

Liberal Democratic Party. (2005). Danjo kyōdō sanga kihon keikaku kaitei ni atatte no yōbōsho (Request upon the revision of the Basic Law for Gender Equal Society). Retrieved from http://www.jimin.jp/jimin/seisaku/2005/pdf/seisaku-017.pdf.

Lie, J. (1996). Sociology of contemporary Japan, trend report. *Current Sociology*, 44(1), 1–101.

Machimura, N. (2001). Monbukagakudaijin ga teiansuru "jiyū to kiritsu" (Freedom and discipline, Education Minister's proposal). In Bungei shunju (Ed.), *Kyōiku no ronten* (pp. 133–149). Tokyo: Bungei shunjū.

Marks, J. (2001). *Betrayed Generations: Standards in British Schools, 1950–2000*. London: Centre for Policy Studies.

Matsubara, J. (2005). Sacchō shushō wa ikani kyōiku kaikaku wo dankō shitanoka (How Prime Minister Thatcher pursued education reform). In T. Nakanishi (Ed.), *Sacchō kaikaku ni manabu*. Tokyo: PHP Shuppan.

Ministry of Education. (2003). Atarashii jidaini fusawashii kyōiku kihonhō to kyōiku shinkō kihonkeikaku no arikata ni tsuite (Fundamental Law of Education and Basic Plan for Educational Promotion appropriate for new era). Retrieved May 20, 2004, from http://www.MOE.go.jp/b_menu/shingi/chukyo/chukyo0/gijiroku/001/030302ab.htm.

Ministry of Education. (2007). *Kaisei zengo no kyōiku kihonhō no hikaku* (Comparison between the original and revised FLEs). Retrieved January 30, 2007, from http://www.MOE.go.jp/b_menu/kihon/about/index.htm.

Ministry of Health, Labor and Welfare. (2006). *Hakusho: Rōdōkeizai no bunseki* (White paper: Analysis of labor economy). Retrieved from http://www.mhlw.go.jp/wp/hakusyo/roudou/06/index.html.

Miyama, M. & Oyama, H. (1970). *Kyōkasho saiban to kokumin kyōiku undō* (Educational lawsuit and citizens' educational movement). Tokyo: Rōdō junpōsha.

Moeran, B. (1989). *Language and popular culture in Japan*. Manchester: Manchester University Press.

Mori, Y. (2000a). Kyōiku kokuminkaigi no dainikai kaigō, naikaku sōridaijin aisatsu (The second NCER meeting, Prime Minister's opening remarks, April 14). Retrieved March 20, 2005, from http://www.kantei.go.jp/jp/kyouiku/dai2/souri.html.

Mori, Y. (2000b). Naikaku sōridaijin aisatsu (Prime Minister's opening remarks, May 11). Retrieved March 20, 2005, from http://www.kantei.go.jp/jp/kyouiku/dai4/511souri.html.

Mori, Y. (2006). Kihan oshiekomi, shakai wo kaetai (Changing society, teaching discipline). *Asahi News*, May 1, p. 17.

Mōri, Y. (2003). *Bunka=seiji* (Culture=politics: New cultural-political movements in the age of globalization). Tokyo: Getsuyōsha.

Munakata, S. (1975). *Munakata seiya kyōikugaku chosakushū, dai yon kan* (Collection of Seiya Munakata's writing on education, Vol. 4). Tokyo: Aoki shoten.

Nagao, A. (2002). *Karikyuramu zukuri to gakuryoku hyōka* (Curriculum development, scholastic achievement, and assessment). Tokyo: Meijitosho.

Nakagawa, S. (2005). Hakkan ni yosete (Forward). In T. Nakanishi (Ed.), *Sacchō kaikaku ni manabu*. Tokyo: PHP Shuppan.

Nakanishi, T. (2001). *Ima hontō no kikiga hajimatta* (Beginning of the real national crisis). Tokyo: Shūeisha.

Nakanishi, T. (2005a). *Sacchā kaikaku ni manabu: Kyōiku seijōka eno michi* (Learning from Thatcher's reform: A path towards normalization of education). Tokyo: PHP Shuppan.

Nakanishi, T. (2005b). Kanshū no kotoba (Words from the Editor). In T. Nakanishi (Ed.), *Sacchā kaikaku ni manabu*. Tokyo: PHP Shuppan.

Nakasone, Y. (1997). Rethinking the constitution (1): Make it a Japanese document. *Japan Quarterly*, 44(3), 4–9.

Nakayama, N. (2004). *Yomigaere Nihon* (Revive Japan) (Tokyo, MOE). Retrieved December 10, 2004, from http://www.MOE.go.jp/b_menu/shingi/chukyo/chukyo3/siryo/004/04120701/001/001.pdf.

Namimoto, K. (2000). Kyōiku kaikaku kokumin kaigi no seitōsei wo tou (Questioning the legitimacy of the NCER). *Sekai*, November, 69–77.

Narushima, T. (2006). Kyōiku kihonhōan tuijō hihan (Article by article critique of the FLE amendment proposal). *Sekai*, July, 108–118.

National Council for Education Reform. (2000). *Kyōiku kaikaku kokumin kaigi hōkokusho: Kyōiku wo kaeru 17 no teian* (NCER report: 17 proposals to change education). Tokyo: NCER.

Natsushima, Y. (2006). Jimint_ bunky_zoku wa dakyō shiteinai (The JDP Bunkyo-zoku did not compromise). *Sekai*, July, 119–125.

Ninomiya, A. (1999). *Gendai shihonshugi to shinjiyūshugi no bōsō* (Contemporary capitalism and neoliberalism). Tokyo: Shinnihon Shuppansha.

Nishihara, H. (2003). *Gakkō ga aikokushin wo oshieru toki* (When schools teach patriotism). Tokyo: Nihon hyōronsha.

Nishihara, H. & Ogi, N. (2006). Korewa kyōiku no kudetā da (This is a coup in education). *Sekai*, July, 89–99.

Nishio, K. & Yagi, H. (2005). *Shin kokumin no yudan* (New people's carelessness). Tokyo: PHP Kenkyūjō.

Nozaki, Y. (2002.) Japanese politics and the history textbook controversy, 1982–2001. *International Journal of Educational Research*, 37, 603–622.

Obuchi, K. (2000). Kyōiku kokuminkaigi no daiikkai kaigō, naikaku sōridaijin aisatsu (The first NCER meeting, Prime Minister's opening remarks, March 27). Retrieved March 20, 2005, from http://www.kantei.go.jp/jp/kyouiku/dai1/souri.html.

OECD. (2006). Economic survey of Japan 2006. Retrieved June 15, 2007, from http://www.oecd.org/document/55/0,3343,en_33873108_33873539_37127031_1_1_1_1,00.html.

Oguma, E. (1998). Hidari wo kihi suru popurizumu (Populist evasion of Left), *Sekai*, December, 94–105.

Oguma, E. (2003a). *Minshu to aikoku* (Democracy and patriotism). Tokyo: Shinyōsha.

Oguma, E. (2003b). "Tsuyoinihon o" no fūchō naze: "Fuan" ga michibiku nashonarizumu (Why "Strong Japan:" "Anxiety" leads to nationalism). *Asahi News*, September 9, p. 13.

Oguma, E. & Ueno, Y. (2003). *Iyashi no nashonarizumu: Kusanone hoshushugi no jisshō kenkyū* (Consoling nationalism: Empirical studies on grassroots conservative movement). Tokyo: Keiō University Press.

Ōmori, F. (2000). *"Yutori kyōiku" bōkokuron* (Theory of "*yutori* education" and of national demise), Tokyo: PHP Shuppan.

Ōtsuki, T. (1982). *Sengo minkan kyōiku undō shi* (Postwar history of the people's education movement). Tokyo: Ayumi Shuppan.

Ōuchi, H. (2003). *Kyōiku kihonhōkaiseiron hihan* (Criticizing the revision of education fundamental law). Tokyo: Gendai Shokan.

Pempel, T. J. (1998). *Regime shift: Comparative dynamics of the Japanese political economy*. Ithaca, NY: Cornell University Press.

Phillips, D. (1993). Borrowing Educational Policy. In D. Finegold, L, McFarland, & W. Richardson (1993). *Something borrowed, something learned?: The transatlantic market in education and training reform*. Washington, DC: Brookings Institution.

Phillips, D. (1999). On borrowing. In R. Alexander et al. (Eds.), *Learning from Comparing: New directions in comparative educational research*. Wallingford: Symposium Books.

Phillips, D. & Ochs, K. (2003). Processes of policy borrowing in education: Some explanatory and analytical devices, *Comparative Education*, 39(4), 451–461.

Robertson, S. & Dale, R. (2002). Local state of emergency: The contradictions of neoliberal governance in education in New Zealand. *British Journal of Sociology of Education*, 23(3), 463–482.

Robson, W. (1993). *Britain 1750–1900*. Oxford: Oxford University Press.

Rose, N. S. (1999). *Powers of freedom: Reframing political thought*. Cambridge and New York: Cambridge University Press.

Said, E. W. (1978). *Orientalism*. New York: Pantheon Books.

Said, E. W. (1993). *Culture and Imperialism.* New York: Random House.

Sakurai, Y. (2001). Seiji rikigaku de susumu kyōiku kihonhō rongi (Politics-driven debate over the FLE revision). *Sekai,* April, 115–119.

Sanuki, H. (2002). *Igirisu no kyōiku kaikaku to nihon* (British education reform and Japan). Tokyo: Kōbunken.

Sanuki, K. (2003). *Shinjiyūshugi to kyōikukaikaku* (Neoliberalism and education reform). Tokyo: Shunpōsha.

Sato, T. (2001). Is Japan a 'classless' society? *Japan Quarterly,* 48(2), 25–30.

Shimomura, H. (2005). Kokka senryaku toshiteno kyōiku (Education as a National Strategy). In T. Nakanishi (Ed.), *Sacchā kaikaku ni manabu.* Tokyo: PHP Shuppan.

Shinano Mainichi News. (2005). Seikyōiku hikaeru ugoki, shushō no "ikisugi" ninshiki ukete (Move to refrain from sex education, reflecting Prime Minister's recognition of "extreme"). *Shinano Mainichi News,* December 13. Retrieved December 13, 2005, from http://www.shinmai.co.jp/news/20051213/mm051213sha4022.htm.

Smith, L. T. (1999). *Decolonizing methodologies: Research and indigenous peoples.* New York: Zed Books, University of Otago Press.

Steiner-Khamsi, G. (2000). Transferring education, displacing reforms. In J. Schriewer (Ed.), *Discourse formation in comparative education* (pp. 155–187). New York: Peter Lang.

Steiner-Khamsi, G. (2004). *The global politics of educational borrowing and lending.* New York: Teachers College Press.

Takahashi, S. (1995). *Kenshō sengo kyōiku* (Critique of postwar education). Tokyo: Hiroike Shuppan.

Takahashi, T. (2003). *Kokoro to sensō* (War and mind). Tokyo: Shōbunsha.

Takahashi, T. (2004). *Kyōiku to kokka* (Education and the state). Tokyo: Kōdansha.

Takayama, K. (2007). A nation at risk crosses the Pacific: Transnational borrowing of the US crisis discourse in the debate on education reform in Japan. *Comparative Education Review,* 51, 423–446.

Takayama, K. (2008a). Beyond Orientalism in comparative education: Challenging the binary opposition between Japanese and American education. *Asia Pacific Journal of Education* 28(1): 19–34.

Takayama, K. (2008b). Japan's Ministry of Education "becoming the right:" Neoliberal restructuring and the Ministry's struggles for political legitimacy. *Globalisation, Societies, and Education,* 6(2): 131–146.

Takayama, K. (2009a). Progressive struggle and critical education scholarship in Japan: Toward democratization of critical education studies. In M. W. Apple, W. Au, and L. Gandin (Eds.), *International handbook for critical education* (pp. 354–367). New York: Routledge.

Takayama, K. (2009b). Is Japanese education the "exception"?: Examining the situated articulation of neoliberalism through the analysis of policy keywords. *Asia Pacific Journal of Education,* 29(2): 125–142.

Takayama, K. (2009c). Globalizing critical studies of "official" knowledge: Lessons from the Japanese history textbook controversy over "comfort women." *British Journal of Sociology of Education,* 30(5): 577–589.

Takayama, K. & Apple, M. W. (2008). The cultural politics of borrowing: Japan, Britain, and the narrative of educational crisis. *British Journal of Sociology of Education,* 29(3), 289–301.

Takenobu, M. (2005). Yappari kowai? jendā furī basshingu (Scary? Gender-free bashing). In R. Kimura (Ed.), *Jendā toraburu: Basshingu genshō wo kenshōsuru* (Gender trouble: Examining the bashing phenomenon) (pp. 19–34). Tokyo: Hakutakusha.

Tanaka, S. (2007). *Nichibeidōmei wo yurugasu ianfu mondai* (Comfort women issue shaking the US–Japan alliance). April 3, retrieved May 18, 2007, from http://www.tanakanews.com/070403JPUS.htm.

Tanaka, Y. (2002). *Japan's comfort women: Sexual slavery and prostitution during World War II and the US occupation.* New York: Routledge.

Tawara, Y., Uozumi, A., Sataka, M., & Yokota, H. (2006). *Abe Shinzō no honshō* (Shinzō Abe's true character). Tokyo: Shūkan kinyōbi.

Taylor, S., Rizvi, F., Lingard, B., & Henry, M. (1997). *Educational policy and the politics of change.* London: Routledge.

Terawaki, K. (2001). *21 seiki no gakkō: Yutori kyōiku no honshitsu wa koreda* (School for the 21st century: This is the essence of Yutori education). Tokyo: Shinchōsha.

Tomlinson, S. (Ed.). (1994). *Educational reform and its consequences.* London, IPPR/Rivers Oram Press.

Tomlinson, S. (2005). *Education in a post-welfare society* (2nd ed.). Maidenhead: Open University Press.

Tōyama, A. (2001). *Kyōiku shinkō kihon keikaku no sakutei to kyōiku kihonhō no arikata ni tsuite* (Deliberation request regarding Basic Plan for Educational Promotion and the FLE). Retrieved August 14, 2006, from http://www.mext.go.jp/b_menu/shingi/chukyo/chukyo0/index.htm.

Tōyama, A. (2004). *Kōkawaru gakkō kōkawaru daigaku* (This is how school will change. This is how university will change). Tokyo: Kōdansha.

Ueno, C. (2006). Fuanna otoko tachi no kimyōna rentai (Unusual alliance among anxious men). In Sōfūsha (Ed.), *Bakku rasshu! Naze jendāfūrī wa tatakaretanoka* (Backlash! Why gender free was attacked) (pp. 378–439). Tokyo: Sōfūsha.

Wada, H. (1999). *Gakuryoku hōkai: "Yutori kyōiku" ga kodomo wo damenisuru* (Collapse of academic achievement: *Yutori* education will ruin our children). Tokyo: PHP shuppan.

Watanabe, O. (2001). *Nihon no taikokuka to neo nashonarizumu no keisei* (Japan's expansionism and the formation of neo-nationalism). Tokyo: Sakurai shoten.

Weiler, H. N. (1983). Legalization, expertise, and participation: Strategies of compensatory legitimation in educational policy, *Comparative Education Review,* 27(2), 259–277.

Whitty, G. (2002). *Making sense of education policy: Studies in the sociology and politics of education.* London: Sage.

Whitty, G., Power, S., & Halpin, D. (1998). *Devolution and choice in education: The school, the state, and the market.* Buckingham and Bristol, PA: Open University Press.

Wright, N. (1977). *Progress in education: A review of schooling in England and Wales.* London: Croom Helm.

Yagi, H. (Ed.). (2002). *Kyōiku kokusho* (Education black papers). Tokyo: PHP Kenkyūjo.

Yagi, H. (2002a). Monbushō wa yutori kyōiku no haiboku wo mitomeyo (Ministry of Education must admit its failure with *yutori* education). In H. Yagi (Ed.), *Kyōiku kokusho* (Educational black books) (pp. 91–93). Tokyo: PHP Kenkyūjo.

Yagi, H. (2002b). Danjō kyōshū kateika dewa konna kotoga oshierareteiru (This is what is taught in co-ed home economics). In H. Yagi (Ed.), *Kyōiku kokusho* (Educational black books) (pp. 162–199). Tokyo: PHP Kenkyūjo.

Yagi, H. and Yamatani, E. (2002). Seisa kaishō kyōiku ni igiari (Questioning gender-free education). In H. Yagi (Ed.), *Kyōiku kokusho* (Educational black books) (pp. 200–240). Tokyo: PHP Kenkyūjo.

Yamada, M. (2004). *Kibō kakusa shakai* (Hope disparity society). Tokyo: Chikuma shobō.

Yamaguchi, T. (2006). Jendā furīronsō to feminizumu undō no ushinawareta jūnen (Gender-free and feminist movements' lost ten years). In Sōfūsha (Ed.), *Bakku rasshu! Naze jendāfūrī wa tatakaretanoka* (Backlash! Why gender free was attacked) (pp. 378–439). Tokyo: Sōfūsha.

Yamatani, E. (2005). Shūkyō kyōiku no jūjitsu to kazoku kyōka no kokoromi (Enrichment of religious education and reinforcement of family values). In T. Nakanishi (Ed.), *Sacchā kaikaku ni manabu.* Tokyo: PHP Shuppan.

Yomiuri News. (2007, March 2). Hiseiki *koyō ga 33% ni, shūnū 199manenika ga kahansūni* (Non-regular employment hits 33%. Majority making less than 1.99 million yen). Retrieved March 2, 2007, from http://www.yomiuri.co.jp/politics/news/20070302i204.htm.

Young, R. (1995). *Colonial desire: Hybridity in theory, culture and race.* New York: Routledge.

CHAPTER 4

Israel/Palestine, Unequal Power, and Movements for Democratic Education*

ASSAF MESHULAM AND MICHAEL W. APPLE

Introduction

The idea that public education systems and their policies are the products of social conflicts and compromises raises a series of questions: Why and what kinds of tensions exist? Who is in conflict and over what? And why and how are compromises reached? These questions about the way that schools work and their relations with society, or the more direct and open questions of what schools do and who benefits (Apple & Weis, 1983), are part of a broad field that tries to make sense of the relationship between education and differential power in society. Critical educational theories have grappled with these and other issues, offering a variety of answers over the years. And as new theories have developed, the solutions have become more complex and nuanced, as a multiplicity of (sometimes contradictory) dynamics, factors, powers, and players, local and global, have been added to the equation.

Central to all these evolving responses, however, has been the understanding that the public education system lies at the heart of economic, cultural, and political struggles over (shifting) consciousness, (fluid) social identities, and the (unequal) distribution of social positions (Wong, 2002)—struggles in which many players take part: social groups and movements consisting of multiple communities, cultural and educational institutions, dominant groups, and, of course, the state. The complexity of the relations amongst these players can be unraveled by looking at how the various theories have evolved out of, departed from, and/or augmented their predecessors, what new knowledge and insights have been added from theory to theory, and the different understandings of the connection between schools, the state, social conflicts, and differential power in society.

This chapter explores these dynamics and interrelations in light of the theoretical developments in the analysis of education, the state, and cultural hegemony, through the specific case of the Israeli public education system. We will show how the incorporation of four components or insights into the analysis of the school as a site of struggle and compromise has shed light on how it is not only a producer and reproducer of power relations in society, but also an active autonomous agent and mediator in these struggles and their results: the addition of the cultural and political spheres, alongside the economic sphere, in the analysis of hegemonization and the role of the school, with multiple dynamics, such as race and gender, joining class; a new conception of the role of the state in these processes and struggles and its relationship with public education; the insight that a two-way reciprocal, not top-down, relationship exists between dominant and dominated groups and, similarly, between the state and schools; and, finally, Wong's (2002) elaboration of the functioning of cultural hegemony, showing that different regimes use different (or multiple) hegemonizing strategies, which, in turn, lead to different outcomes.

This is most compellingly illustrated by the Israeli case. We look at the special circumstances of Israel's state formation, the tensions and compromises out of which and into which it was born, and the hegemonic culture and ideology that have dominated its society and guided its public education. This is followed by an analysis of binarism and duality in the national public education of Israel's "Mizrahi"[1] ("Oriental" or "Eastern" literally translated) Jewish citizens, who originated from Arab and Muslim countries, and its Palestinian (mainly Muslim) citizens. In this context, we look at the emergence of opposition to the cultural hegemonization and the state's strategic responses to these struggles and their outcomes. Another layer is added to the dynamics of cultural hegemony and the school's role, taking a postcolonial perspective of the interaction between the cultural subordinator and subordinated in the domination process of cultural hegemonization.

Finally, we look at three specific instances of concrete Israeli educational projects that have challenged the cultural hegemony in Israel in different ways and with different results and degrees of success. Ironically, the three schools considered, all of which were established over the last two decades, are a product both of the old reality that the original counter-hegemonic social movements failed to tangibly change and of the new realities born of globalization. They thus provide a glimpse into the complexities, pitfalls, and promise of making a lasting impact on hegemonic dominance of society, particularly in this new era. Moreover, taking a postcolonial view of the Israeli case raises the question of the potential of conceptions of hybridity and fluidity of identity and cultural formation to explain and express the impacts and outcomes of cultural subordination. We ask whether a postcolonial understanding of cultural hegemonization in the Israeli context can offer general insight into the school as both a site of conflict and compromise. We think it can.

It is first crucial, however, to clearly lay out the theoretical underpinnings and expansion of the neo-Gramscian approach in critical education studies and the contribution of new theories of the state and state formation to this development.

Critical Education Studies

In the 1970s, a more subtle approach in critical education studies emerged with regard to the questions of what schools do and who benefits from what they do, expanding on the relatively flat and unidimensional version of Marxist analysis that was current at that time. The dominant perspective presented a reductive understanding of schools as purely a reflection of economic power relations, articulated by Bowles and Gintis (1976) as the *correspondence principle,* which frames schools as selectively preparing students for the job market, for "well" socialization that fits the hierarchical structure of modern corporations. This approach, in regarding schools as simply reproducing asymmetrical power relations by responding to the needs of the division of labor, failed to take into account culture as a relevant component in the relationship between dominant and subordinated groups, relegating it to the level of superstructure. Moreover, no attention was paid to the content of knowledge taught in schools, or, more generally, to what really happens *inside* these institutions, nor was the state considered a relevant player, with its own autonomous agenda, in the struggles over education policies.

Scholars in Europe and the US, influenced by the work of Antonio Gramsci (1971), began to rethink both what happens in schools and the structure of domination that emerges out of them. Gramsci's innovative notion of hegemony explained how control of culture relates to reproduction of asymmetrical power relations. This control is achieved not by coercion but by gaining the (not always clear-cut[2]) "active consent" of the ruled through a continuous process in which their culture is incorporated and reshaped so as to advance the interests of the ruling groups. In line with this understanding, scholars (Apple, 1979/2004; Bernstein, 1977; Bourdieu & Passeron, 1977; Young, 1971) crafted a more multifaceted conception of what schools do, one that incorporates the component of cultural power as well. Schools were now conceived of as a site for the production of knowledge that boosts and bolsters cultural domination, alongside economic domination, resulting in new focus on the forms of curriculum, pedagogy, and evaluation, which facilitate that domination. And since the cultural forms prevalent in the school are not "neutrally" selected as such, but specifically chosen to advance those with the power to select them and thus define their knowledge as legitimate for production, schools should be understood as a terrain of ideological conflicts. There, cultural hegemony's domination is continuously contested and negotiated, with the dominant groups—such as segments of the new middle class (Bernstein, 1977) or dominant fractions of the dominant class (Bourdieu, 1984)—in a constant wrangle amongst themselves, as well as with the subordinated groups, over the contents and shape of that hegemony and to secure and entrench their particular interests. These cultural and ideological battles can exist in the framework of the school since, as we explain below, it has relative autonomy from the needs of production as an apparatus of the state (Bernstein, 1977). Schools thus are a site of conflicts and contradictions in which the dominant culture can be and is acted against, consciously or unconsciously, whether by students, as demonstrated in Willis's ethnographic work (1977), or by teachers (Apple, 1995). And as such, they are not simply subject to domination through mere imposition, coercion, from above. Here we see at play the reciprocal dynamics of the relations between the rulers and ruled. As Apple (2000) explained, the dominant groups must always be attentive to the subordinated culture; through a process of "cultural incorporation," they consolidate their domination by "reaching out" to the dominated culture and reshaping it to support the culture of the dominant.

Schools are not merely reproductive, then; they engage in cultural *production* as well. They *produce* the knowledge of dominant groups and subject-matters that reinforce the cultural form of those groups. However, schools, as sites of struggle, can also participate in the production of alternative or oppositional culture. To some extent, counter-hegemonic culture and struggle derive from individual agency and resistance, but they are also the result of the relative autonomy schools enjoy as a state apparatus. This autonomy is manifested and exercised in the education system's attempts to cope with and balance among multiple needs and demands, a task faced by all state apparatuses, related not only to the economic and cultural spheres but also to the political sphere and its legitimacy needs. In considering the role of the state in the education system and the conflicts around and over education, it is important to grasp the importance also of the political sphere and the ruling regime's need for political legitimation in the hegemonization process.

Furthermore, class is not the only dynamic at play in the process of domination and subordination and the constitution of subjects. Each of the social spheres—economy, culture, politics—are comprised of many additional dynamics, such as race and gender, that are relevant for comprehending domination and differential power (Apple & Weis, 1983). These dynamics cut across the various spheres, each bringing its own tensions and struggles and further nuancing the broader tensions in society. An important development in critical education thought was the reconception of the state as a crucial player in the formation of public education systems (Apple, 1995, 2000, 2003; Curtis, 1992; Dale, 1989; Green, 1990), not a merely neutral "vessel" of the hegemony in this process. While state education policies were seen as serving to legitimize and advance dominant groups' interests, the state and its apparatuses were also understood as having to contend with and deliberate certain conflicting interests when executing or, accordingly, modifying policies. Building on theories of the state and its crisis (Habermas, 1973; Offe, 1976, 1984), Dale (1989) described the state as under siege from many conflicting pressures, which are very present in the education policy-making process. Thus, the dominant powers and tensions in schools are the result of the power structure and conflicts in the state in the framework of its attempt and need to deal with its political and legitimation crisis.

This understanding rests on Dale's notion of the state not as a monolith but as a "set of publicly financed institutions, neither separately nor collectively necessarily in harmony, confronted by certain problems deriving from its relationship with capitalism, with one branch, the government, having responsibility for ensuring the continuing prominence of those problems on its agenda" (p. 57). The capitalist state, then, has to both contend with internal contradictions that are an inevitable part of its nature as a complex of loosely connected institutions, each with competing needs and demands (fighting each other over budget or resource allocation, for example), as well as respond to the needs of capital accumulation, while also securing legitimacy for its actions from the people, who, at times (quite often), have to pay the price and are loath to bear it. The education system, as one of the state's "publicly financed institutions," is "expected to contribute to the meeting of the economic, political, and legitimatory needs of the State," while "at any and every level of education, just as in the State as a whole, the simultaneous solution of these problems is impossible" (p. 48). Since educational apparatuses are crucial for meeting production needs, their policies are a major "tool" for the state in responding to and maneuvering between the sometimes incompatible demands and are thus fertile ground for struggle over their control.

This understanding of the relationship between the state and public education was elaborated by Green (1990) and Curtis (1992) in their works on education and state formation. While Curtis took a Foucaultean, centralization of power approach to state formation,[3] Green (1990) asserted that the process of state formation, in which various social groups struggle for control over social power, has a profound influence on the shape and nature of the state education system. He defines state formation as "the historical process by which the modern state has been constructed . . . includ[ing] not only the political and administrative apparatuses of government . . . but also the formation of ideologies and collective beliefs which legitimate state power and underpin concepts of nationhood and national 'character'" (p. 77). Thus, the education system, as one such apparatus, is construed as part of this process and as promoting (or supposed to promote) these legitimating ideologies and beliefs and underlying concepts. The link between public education and state formation is so strong that the analysis of the development of state education systems "can only be understood in relation to the process of state formation," but in a "non-reductive way which gives due weight to both political forms and their economic and social conditions of existence" (p. 77).

In other words, to fully grasp the development of public education and how its policies were and are negotiated and formed, we must look at the political, economic, and cultural struggles, the players, tensions, and compromises, during the process of state formation, that gave shape to the state itself—and continue to do so. This is not to say, however, that education is molded and guided solely by the state formation process in a "top-down" direction. As explained, public schools are a perpetual and partly independent site of struggle and mediation in themselves and, hence, do not always follow or "comply" with the demands and needs emanating from "above," the state level, during state formation. Indeed, Bernstein (1977, 1996) pointed out the reciprocity of the state–school relations, in showing how the internal feature of the pedagogic device can in fact profoundly moderate the process of state formation. For the process of state formation is not a chronological stage in the state's "life," a single, complete moment in time in which the state is "born," its construction completed. Rather the state is forever evolving through formative struggles, shaped by the conflicting pressures, tensions, and needs it faces and must respond to, including in the context of educational policy-making (Apple, 1979/2004, 1996, 2000; Dale, 1989). And just as public schools are in many respects the embodiment of these tensions and conflicts and the results of the concessions reached over the course of the process of state formation (and nation-building), so can the public education system influence, moderate, the process of state formation.

As noted, the addition of the cultural dimension and the role of the state and its formation process to the understanding of the dynamics and operation of public education was significantly influenced by Gramsci's (1971) concept of hegemony. Wong (2002), in turn, infused a further subtlety into the concept of cultural hegemony and its strategies, particularly in the context of education, in his comparative analysis of the complex power relations between the ruling regime and dominated groups in multicultural societies. Wong's insight is that the hegemonic strategies for contending with subordinate groups can vary from place to place; they are not uniform, as assumed in the predominant approaches, universal, or automatic and can lead to different, sometimes surprising, results. Contributing a deeper understanding of the racial dynamic in cultural hegemonization and nation-building, Wong's work reveals the possibility and ramifications of the hegemonic forces failing to remake or transform counter-hegemonic oppositional or alternative culture through incorporation: what happens when the ruling regime fails or opts not to incorporate, rearticulate, or accommodate the culture of a subordinate group and is "forced to exclude" its cultural traditions (p. 251).Wong offered preliminary insight into the potential impediments and outcomes of implementing cultural exclusion and replacement: strong, perhaps insurmountable, resistance from the subordinated group or, alternatively, the risk of creating a cultural vacuum if exclusion (eventually) succeeds.

Opposition is too complex to be understood by its immediate rami-fications and results. Cultural hegemonization is a multilayered, subtle process, with many, at times unexpected, outcomes. Wong demonstrated that incorporation and rearticulation are not bound in Catholic marriage. Dale suggested that it is not necessarily the active consent of the people that is required; at times passive acceptance of state policies and actions suffices for legitimation and political control. Gramsci (1971) was aware of this option, asserting that since consciousness consists of two parts, one actively explicit and the other superficially explicit, it can produce a situation in which "the contradictory state of consciousness does not permit of any action, any decision or any choice, and produces a condition of moral and political passivity" (p. 333). This can explain the success of the state, cultural hegemony, and the education system in securing legitimation while pro-moting certain cultural forms and the interests of certain groups and subordinating others; it also explains the need for strategies to maneuver and mediate between demands and tensions.

These insights and understandings are crucial to the analysis of public education systems in multicultural societies. The Israeli public education system is a particularly illuminating case in point. Beyond being a society divided along a multiplicity of lines—culture, ideology, ethnicity, race, religiosity, nationhood—Israel is a unique instance of two-pronged cultural hegemonic domination. As will be discussed, some of the current blocks in the way of democratizing the Israeli education system are, like Israeli society, the fruits of the state's attempts to contend with the cultures of two subordinated groups: the non-European Mizrahi Jews and the non-European, non-Jewish Palestinian citizens of the state. The dual hegemonic practices and policies directed at these two groups, manifested most prominently in the education system, have added another scenario to Wong's anatomization of hegemonic strategies: the possibility of the *same* ruling regime using different strategies with regard to different dominated groups, marginalized in the Israeli case on the basis of ethnicity and nationhood.

In Israel, the different strategies have resulted in different outcomes to the cultural hegemonization process. With regard to the Israeli education system, "it was the different forms of hegemony operating between the dominant and subordinated classes which were ultimately responsible for what schools did, for who they allowed to go to what type of school and for what they taught them when they were there" (Green, 1990, p. 311). Specifically, the Israeli hegemonic attempt to establish and gain legitimacy for its control and ideology led to strategies of incorporation and rearticulation of Mizrahi culture and marginalization and coercion yet remaking of Palestinian culture. This agenda, as well as the struggles that revolved around it and the conflicts it embodied, essentially determined the shape of Israeli public education.

The Birth of the Israeli Public Education System

The Israeli space is the site of "a violent, creative, inter-cultural" meeting, with a multiplicity of contradictions (Gur-Ze'ev, 1999, p. 19). Indeed, Israeli society is commonly described as suffering from five main types of rifts: national (between Arabs and Jews); ethnic (between Mizrahi Jews and Ashkenazi (European) Jews); religiosity (between secular and religious (Jews)); political ideological; and social economic (Lissak & Horowitz, 1989).[4] The Israeli public education system is afflicted with and manifests all of these social rifts. The complexities of the frequently intertwined and interrelated tensions and clashes can be understood from two different perspectives of their origins and impact. The one perspective looks at the historical formation of the hegemonic alliances, the state, and its education system in Israel as distinctly manifested in the 1953 State Educational Law. This exposes certain aspects of the national, political, ethnical, and religious rifts and their relevance to the shape of the national education system and its policies, as well as the consolidation of cultural hegemony and its struggle for control over social power in the process of state formation.

The second perspective looks to the ideology that guided the European, Zionist, Jewish ruling regime in forming the Israeli state and its education system. Building on Said's (1978) concept of orientalism, two simultaneous binaries that still exist in Israel can be identified: East/West and Jewish/Arab.

This pair of binaries underlies the national/ethnic ideology that shaped the public education system and drove the cultural incorporation and subordination that transpired there. We must qualify our appeal to binarism, with its limited and, at times, reductive nature. While we are well aware of and, indeed, generally favor the more nuanced hybrid analysis of power relations, such as that developed by Bhabha (1990), binarism has crucial explanatory power here, in grasping much of the conflicting legitimation needs and pressures the Israeli state faced and still faces. As a new regime that, in its fight for independence, had both expelled and subordinated another nation, the Israeli state urgently required legitimation and consent for this subordination from its (Jewish) subordinating citizens and for its existence from its (Palestinian) subordinated citizens.

The state's attempts to win legitimacy for its rule and the new hegemonic culture from one non-hegemonic and (culturally and economically) dominated group (Mizrahis) through incorporation was ironically executed largely by way of the subordination and exclusion of another non-hegemonic (culturally, economically, and politically) dominated group (Palestinians). This was clearly manifested in the education system from its outset.

Indeed, embedded in the very formulation of the 1953 state Educational Law, the legislation that laid the foundations for public education in Israel, were these cultural, political, and economic conflicts and tensions, as well as the compromises reached amongst the different fighting factions. The Law embodied the state's incorporation of the hegemonic alliance's agenda—the European Zionist Jewish aspiration to create a Western, Jewish democracy—into its official agenda and reflected the negotiated arrangement amongst the different hegemonic groups on the shape public education would take in Israel. This represented the state's official monopolization of educational authority and consolidation of a national education system. After the establishment of the state in 1948, as part of the process of transition to statehood, Prime Minister David Ben-Gurion sought to create such a unified system and to abolish the system of different so-called educational "trends" that had prevailed in the pre-state Jewish community in Palestine (Avidor, 1957, p. 54).

The ensuing "struggle over education," as it was called, resulted in intense clashes between the coalition parties in the new government, each of which represented a different educational trend. The 1953 Law constituted a compromise amongst these hegemonic groups. While the elimination of the trend system "relieved educators from the distractions of Trend rivalries and bickerings" (p. 59), it also facilitated the continued domination and control of official education and the exclusion of any other, counter-hegemonic "trend."

The three main Jewish educational trends that had existed in pre-state Palestine had been affiliated with the different political parties and movements that had comprised the hegemonic alliance in the Jewish community there, known as the "*Yishuv.*" All had been founded by Zionist Jews who had immigrated to Palestine from Europe in the late nineteenth and early twentieth centuries. The General Trend ("*Hazerem Haklali*") espoused a secular Zionist ideology and liberal-traditional values, while the orthodox-religious *Mizrahi*[5] Trend had been established by European Jews affiliated with the religious Zionist socialist movements and incorporated Zionism and modernism (science, humanities, and languages). The third trend, the secular Labor Trend ("*Zerem Haovdim*"), with its adjunct Religious Labor Education Branch, identified ideologically with the General Federation of Jewish Labor and was politically affiliated with the dominant (and, later, ruling) *Mapai* Party ("The Workers of the Land of Israel" Party), whose Zionist-socialist ideology prevailed in the *kibbutz* and *moshav* collective settlements.[6] Each of these trends had the authority to set their curriculums, pedagogies, and training for teachers based on their ideologies and doctrines (Avidor, 1957, p. 28; Nardi, 1945, p. 46; Zameret & Yablonka, 1997).

While during the pre-state period, a certain balance had been maintained amongst the different trends, the struggle over education intensified with statehood in 1948 and an ensuing surge of Jewish immigration (mainly from Arab and Muslim countries but also displaced Holocaust survivors). Most of the new immigrants were not affiliated with any of the Zionist parties or movements upon their arrival. Consequently, it was not automatically clear to which educational trend their children should or would be affiliated. During this period, under the 1949 Compulsory Education Law, parents were allowed to choose the educational trend in which their children would learn. This right, however, was not extended to the new immigrants living in immigrant transit camps, who were required to send their children to state-run, so-called "uniform schools."[7]

These schools were originally intended to provide immigrant children with a "basic" education as set by the state and to teach them the core concepts of Zionism and history of the Jewish People and State. A product of the state's "melting pot" policy, this system was established and over-seen by the Ministry of Education's "Department for the Imparting of the Language and Cultural Absorption," which was early on accused of representing and advancing the interests and ideologies of the ruling secular and socialist *Mapai* Party. A struggle followed between the different political parties representing the different ideological and educational trends, grasping the electoral potential of educating the immigrant children. The *Mizrahi* movement, for example, asserted that since the new immigrants had largely come from traditional communities and practiced a religious way of life, they should be channeled to the religious trend and not secular education.

This claim became the "common sense," the rule of thumb, regarding the appropriate placement of immigrant children from North African and Middle Eastern countries (and was later applied also to Ethiopian immigrants in the 1980s and 1990s). This struggle was, of course, more a battle within the hegemonic alliance over dominating education, through which the character of the state, its agenda, and the people could be shaped, than a genuine attempt to accommodate the incoming communities and provide them with culturally appropriate education. And while purportedly equalizing access to all streams of education, the 1953 State Educational Law in fact was no more than a compromise between the dominant Jewish, Zionist, European hegemonic groups. Although allowing for the incorporation and integration of non-hegemonic populations into the public system, it ensured the reshaping and exclusion of their cultures and ideologies in line with culturally and politically hegemonic needs and interests. In this way, the Law consolidated hegemonic control over the state and education, both mirroring and reinforcing the course of state formation and its outcomes.

Already during the early years of Jewish "nation-building" in pre-state Palestine and the transition into statehood, an attempt was made by the *Yishuv* leaders to integrate and incorporate all the Jewish political streams into the ruling regime. This process was reflected in the establishment of two official state educational trends, state education and state religious education, under the 1953 Law, embodying the agreement reached amongst the secular General Trend, the Labor Trend, and the religious *Mizrahi* Trend. Furthermore, the Jewish ultra-orthodox religious trend, a private (non-public) educational stream, was granted the status of a "recognized but not official" trend, under government coalition agreements,[8] while the *kibbutzim* and *moshavim* were allowed to operate a separate, segregated education system, due to and based on their "unique educational ideology."[9]

In contrast, the Palestinians, whose school system had constituted the public education system since the time of Ottoman rule (serving mostly the Muslim Arab population) and who had fought hard battles for Arab and local content in their schools,[10] were denied any recognition in the 1953 Law as an autonomous ethnic group or as a unique educational trend. Instead, they had the option of either attending Jewish, Zionist state education schools that were segregated from the state schools attended by Jewish children or attending private, usually Church-run schools. In this way, the national education system, from its birth, deepened the rift between Arab and Jew, pursuing an agenda of segregation, exclusion, and delegitimization of the former's culture and educational institutions.

Thus we see that from the foundation of the Israeli education system, there was official recognition only of educational streams and ideologies that were tied to fractions of dominant hegemonic relations. The story of the formation of the Israeli system is illustrative of Green's (1990) assertion of the strong link between state formation and the formation of the public education system and how education is a major and accelerated priority for countries undergoing the particular process of national reconstruction after war or a successful struggle for independence. As in the case of Israel, external military threats, territorial conflicts, and national independence are factors in a "compacted process of . . . 'nation-building,'" where the relevant countries have "emerged from major conflagrations with an urgent task of national reconstruction . . . to establish a new social order which will reflect the principles for which the struggle was originally undertaken" (p. 310). From the very outset, the Israeli state education system was part of the hegemonic compromise towards forming such a new social order and building a "unified" country.

The education system, like the state, was constructed on the premises of this compromise: Western (non-Eastern) oriented and predominantly secular, with room for only *European* Jewish religious, ethnic, and national elements. This hegemonic vision of a modern democratic state as the homeland for all the Jewish People necessarily excluded and was threatened by both the "primitive" "Oriental" "Diaspora" Mizrahi culture and the distrusted, "dangerous" "enemy" Arab-Palestinian culture and nationhood. The next part of this chapter looks at the dual binaries that underpinned the ideology guiding this vision and the resulting strategies and policies taken to secure its legitimation and domination.

Culture, Nationalism, and Ideology

As we saw, since its very establishment, the Israeli public education system has both produced the state's citizens and reproduced inequalities amongst them to serve hegemonic interests, as well as controlling and subordinating select groups of citizens, to prevent the emergence of any competing culture or nationhood within the state's midst that could imperil the regime. The hegemonic ideology that has driven and enabled the education mission in executing these strategies on the economic, cultural, and ideological fronts rests on two overlapping binaries: East/West and Arab/Jew. This ideology has provided the "justification" for tracking certain dominated groups into vocational, "non-intellectual" education, leading to their a-priori economic subordination, for unequally distributing public resources in general and specifically in education, and for producing "official knowledge" that is embedded with and supports this ideology and the interests of hegemonic relations.

Under the first dichotomy, running along Said's (1978) West/East binary, the West represents, or is represented by, European (Ashkenazi) Jews, who monopolized power already in pre-state Palestine; the East represents, or is represented by, the native Arab population in Palestine as well as the Mizrahi Jews who immigrated from Arab and Muslim countries following long centuries of cultural influence in those countries. This binary was brought with the European Zionist settlers, espousing European social, political, and cultural ideals, values, and ideology inherent to their Zionism; accordingly, they situated themselves as the West and cast the Palestinians they encountered and, subsequently, Mizrahi immigrants as the East. Ironically, in the original form of this imported binary, the same Ashkenazi Jews had been the (despised and oppressed) foreign "Oriental," "East," in the European midst—the West they later claimed to represent and sought to reproduce in a national and cultural colonization project.

This binary, with its accompanying assumptions of Western superiority, modernity, enlightenment, and rationality versus the inferiority, irrationality, and primitivity of the East, was thus borrowed by the very victims of its violence and redirected at what they now constructed and construed as the East. Aziza Khazzoom (2003) has asserted an interesting perspective on the construction of this ethnic/cultural dichotomy between Ashkenazi/West and Mizrahi/East. She argues that the past two centuries of Diaspora Jewish history "can be conceptualized as a series of Orientalisation" in which Jews came to view all Jewish tradition as Oriental. It was only in Palestine/Israel, she claims, that Ashkenazis constituted the "Mizrahis" as a part of the former's "intense commitments to Westernization as a form of self improvement" (p. 482). It was from this Eastern-ness, this Oriental identity, that the European Zionists sought liberation in a new homeland. Thus the "New Man," the "Sabra," that the Zionist hegemony and, later, its state education system sought to create was one who would erase the Diasporic Jew, a "New Israeli" constituted against the cultural construct of the Arab/Oriental as the "Other," whose backwardness and cultural inferiority justified the "civilizing" (i.e., culturization) mission.

This East–West binarism, which has dominated Israeli state ideology and the state's education arena, at times overlaps and at times runs parallel to the second dichotomy—that separating Arabs and Jews into two different national groups. The latter binary both complicates the distinction between East and West and augments the perception of the Arab/Oriental as the feared and inferior "Other." Dividing the two "Eastern" communities down the national line of Jew and Arab, the second binary situates the Mizrahis on the Jewish side of this dichotomy along with Jews from the "West," as the ruling cultural colonizers, and the Palestinians on the Arab side, as the colonized, dominated. This second dichotomy, and the fears and rifts it represented and entrenched, underlay the divergences in the Israeli state's policies and agendas regarding the two non-hegemonic "Oriental" groups.

While the hegemonic cultural apparatus, especially at the time of state formation, sought to transform and reshape Mizrahi culture, like *all* Jewish Diaspora cultures (Ashkenazi included), into the mold of the "New Israeli" and thus pursued and encouraged assimilation, the Palestinians were perceived to be part of the existential threat to that New Israeli and the new state.

Ironically, many of the early Ashkenazi Zionist settlers embraced the local Palestinian culture, customs, practices, and even garb; they admired their rootedness to the land, how they worked and lived off the land, and their earthiness (Eyal, 2005). Shohat (2006) notes that "the return to the homeland of Zion, led at times to the exotic affirmation of Arab 'primitiveness' as a desirable image to be appropriated by the native-born sabra. The Arab was projected as the incarnation of the ancient, the pre-exiled Jews . . . the authentic Jew" (p. 220). Thus, despite tensions between the Jewish and Arab populations in Palestine, there was also a semblance of symbiosis in the interaction between the two, a coexistence, for a time, which was long-gone by the time the Jewish state formation process was underway and the Arab was construed as the enemy. As will be shown, this complexity of binary distinctions and the ideology they shaped fed and served the different strategies employed to contend with and neutralize the (cultural and political) threats posed to the cultural hegemony by the Mizrahis on the one hand and the Palestinians on the other.

The Public Education of Mizrahis and Palestinians in Israel

What, then, did and do Israeli public schools do and who benefited and benefits from this? The structure, curriculum, and pedagogy of the Israeli public education system and its relationship with the state, as well as the struggles of social movements and ensuing reforms in the system, all reveal how hegemonic authority maintained economic and cultural domination in a fluid, if not necessarily uniform, process.

Despite any cultural affinities between the two "Eastern" communities, the Mizrahis and Palestinians were treated differently by the state and educational system. They experienced different forms of domination, with the Jews thrown into a "melting pot" in an attempt at incorporation and the Palestinians segregated and excluded, conceived of and constructed as "enemies of the state" and a "fifth column." And though both communities underwent a *racial formation process* (Omi & Winant, 1994), they were racialized in different ways too, with the Israeli hegemonic power bloc seeking to assimilate one "racial" group (the Mizrahis) while rejecting the other (the Palestinians).

Accordingly, a combination of different hegemonic strategies was applied to culturally marginalize and repress these two groups in society. Comparing the education of the two, we unravel below how this was manifested in and was executed through and by the public education system and the conflicts, rifts, and concessions that emerged in the process. The system's treatment of and relations with each of the two groups, guided by the hegemonic ideology described above and shaped by the ongoing state-formation process, illuminate the operation of cultural hegemony in Israel in particular as well as the force of Wong's observation regarding these dynamics in general. We will see that the Israeli case exemplifies his assertion that not all ruling regimes possess "equal capability to incorporate the culture of the dominant," nor do they necessarily use "the same strategies to constitute hegemony" or are "haunted by similar types of contradictions," with clearly diverging political and cultural results (Wong, 2002, p. 3).

Education and the Cultural Threat: The Mizrahis

Karl Frankenstein, a driving force in the Israeli public education system well into the 1980s, articulated in 1947 the Eurocentric notion that was to underlie and shape the new state's education system. Based on his deeply entrenched conceptions of the inferiority of "Eastern," Mizrahi culture, Frankenstein's approach quickly became official state policy:

> The Jews of the East lag behind, they do not yet have the capacity to understand the contents and values of Western culture except by way of imitation and passive reception . . . they are not capable yet of joining productively the path sought by the majority of the Jewish population in building their lives.
>
> (in Chetrit, 2004, p. 77)

Similarly, Zalman Shazar, one of Israel's early political leaders and its third president, ominously warned in 1951 of the dangers inherent in Mizrahi immigration:

> We will pay dearly. . . . This immigration has not tasted the taste of the gymnasium, they are not used to so much education, so much studying. . . . Assuming the best, we will be able to influence them to finish elementary school, but what then will be the level, how will the community be, will we be able to be a light unto nations? . . . Will the community in Israel be able to exist without a European and Anglo-Saxon addition, Jews of our own kind?
>
> (in Chetrit, 2004, pp. 64–65)

The Ashkenazi Eurocentric/Western hegemony represented by these two public figures made sure that Mizrahi children would not go very much beyond elementary education. From the outset, the education system rested on, produced, and reproduced differential treatment of Mizrahis and a discriminatory ideology that promoted cultural and economic disparity as well as hegemonic domination of the state and its apparatuses. This led to an ethnically based tracking system in public education, in official and unofficial forms, under which the overwhelming majority of Mizrahi students were streamed to vocational schools (with no possibility of matriculation and higher education) and Ashkenazi students to theoretical schools. This was justified as responding to the production needs of the new state and the Mizrahis' particular educational and economic needs, with educational experts claiming vocational education to be a "special blessing" for them (Yonah, 2005, p. 67). The hegemonic ideology and agenda were openly expressed by Zalman Aran, then Minister of Education, in a speech to Parliament in 1956: "A country cannot exist when [only] one-third of its breadwinners are productive and they must support the unproductive remaining two-thirds [of the population]" (p. 67). This ratio must be changed, he claimed, by channeling two-thirds of the students to skilled labor training and agricultural studies and one-third to intensive theoretical preparation for continued education.

In fact, however, this educational tracking policy secured the interests of the dominant hegemonic groups, serving the needs of capital, producing cheap labor for exploitation, and allowing the professional and managerial sectors to maintain control over the state and economy. It enabled the hegemonic groups to reproduce and produce economic disparities and thereby entrench an economic and cultural advantage. This domination was reinforced by the deliberate attempt to reshape the cultures and identities of all immigrants at the time, through education amongst other things. A tactic of cultural incorporation was employed to "remake" or "reorganize" the cultures of immigrant groups so as to advance the interests of the Israeli cultural hegemony. But although Mizrahis, like Ashkenazi immigrants, were incorporated into the hegemonic public education system, it was a Western-oriented education (values, principles, basic subject-matter, ideology) that was imposed on them (already in the transit camps) to reconstruct their identities.

In the late 1950s, the first real counter-hegemonic opposition emerged, directed at the state's discriminatory approach to and treatment of Mizrahis in both public life and education. This was initiated with the organization of the Union of North African Emigrants, a social movement comprised mostly of new immigrants from Morocco, which called for economic, cultural, and educational equality. A violent revolt in 1959, known as "the

Wadi Salib events" and instigated by Union activists, was a major trigger of the government's open concession, for the first time, of the existence of a "disparity problem." Although denying any actual policy of discrimination, the state and the hegemonic bloc had to respond to the disparity and the struggle against it. The reforms to the educational system implemented in the period following Wadi Salib and continuing through the next outbreak of Mizrahi activism and protest between 1971 and 1973 (led by another social movement, the Black Panthers) exemplify and embody how hegemonic control over the state and its apparatuses is preserved.

It is in this context that the mediating capacity of the state and its relative autonomy become apparent, even while it continues to preserve hegemonic interests. The Israeli state had to contend with the competing demands commonly faced by such states. On the one hand, it had to meet the needs of capital and the dominant class; it had to ensure both highly educated professionals and bureaucrats to run and administer the modern economy as well as control of that economy—and privileged access to the education system—for the dominant class. On the other hand, the Israeli state had to secure and retain its political legitimacy, which was being challenged by the Mizrahi struggle against their cultural, political, and economic subordination.

Such an amalgamation of pressures on the state, which seeks to maintain its autonomy and not be a mere tool in the hands of the dominant groups, forces it to "incorporate some of the other diverse perspectives both within other elements of elite groups and from those groups with less economic, cultural and political power" (Apple, 2000, p. 64) into its decisions and policies, including in the educational context. This understanding of the state as an independent player in the social struggles mediating between the different interests and agendas recalls Dale's (1989) conception of the state under siege. It is further augmented by Apple's (2000) description of the state's strategy in contending with the pressures it is caught between: "the key is to form an accord that acts as an umbrella under which many groups can stand but which basically still is under the guiding principles of dominant groups" (p. 64).

Accordingly, the Israeli state's gradually implemented education reforms incorporated some of the Mizrahi protesters' demands and language, using their "good sense" in rearticulating the hegemonic position, but leaving the dominant culturally hegemonic ideology in place. In the early 1960s, following official recognition of the educational achievement gap between Mizrahis and Ashkenazis, differential education programs were developed, as it was articulated, to respond to the different needs of the two groups. In 1962, an official government decision led to the introduction of two educational tracks in public high schools: a theoretical track leading to a matriculation diploma and access to post-secondary education and a vocational track with no or only partial diploma and, thus, the end of the educational path.

This measure impacted mainly the Mizrahi community. The addition of a vocational stream in the high schools was purportedly intended to open the door to secondary education for Mizrahis, in supposed response to their demand for equal access to this education but while accommodating the community's special need for what was termed "rehabilitation and development." Until that point, access to secondary education had been a highly limited possibility for Mizrahis due to their almost automatic tracking to vocational education and training. This was in stark contrast to the Ashkenazi community, which was generally tracked to theoretical schools and therefore had always been able to continue to (the solely theoretical-based) high schools. Furthermore, in 1965, the extension of compulsory education from eighth grade to ninth grade was presented as expanding the state's commitment and duty to educating Mizrahi children and to equalizing access to education and education opportunities. In practice, however, this became a legal tool for ejecting Mizrahi (and Palestinian) students from the public education system once they had reached the end of compulsory education. This mechanism, although applying formally to Ashkenazi students as well, in practice had little impact on them as the majority still learned in theoretical streams in strong high schools with minimal drop-out rates (Chetrit, 2004).

A second measure, adopted in 1965, was allegedly aimed at closing the education gap and responding to counter-hegemonic demands for equal education: the institution of educational "groupings"[11] of students in the elementary schools according to proficiency in the basic subjects. This new practice in fact only further entrenched the differential power relations and the culturally and politically hegemonic bloc's advantageous position in education and society. Svirsky has noted the unquestionably political nature of this move—a segregation arrangement that essentially catered to the ruling elite's social-political needs and "whose practical ramification is the advancement of only certain students" (Svirsky, 1995, as cited in Chetrit, 2004, p. 122).

Then, in 1968, in further response to the Mizrahi demand for greater access to secondary education, a radical structural change to the education system was decided on to enable integration of Ashkenazi and Mizrahi students. Elementary schools would be decreased from eight grades to six and middle-schools, with three grades, would be created as the space in which social and educational integration would occur, with the declared aim of improving both Mizrahi scholastic achievements and inter-ethnic relations. "To ensure a meeting of hearts between the population groups, to nurture a collective consciousness of belonging, and to reinforce the sense of Israeli unity and the individual's responsibility for upholding that unity," pronounced the Minister of Education at the time (Yonah, 2005, p. 68). This program, not immediately implemented, was hailed for its great potential to equalize Mizrahi access to education and narrow the cultural and ethnic gap. It received "active consent" and legitimation from Mizrahi activists, constituting a central demand in their social struggles for education in equality through the 1970s.

But this program of physical integration of students in fact simultaneously advanced a completely different agenda as well. On the one hand, it served the goal of incorporating Mizrahis into the dominant culture with its values and agenda of "collective belonging" and social "unity" and of transforming their worldview so as to consolidate existing power relations; on the other hand, it offered the possibility of entrenching those power relations through "segregation within integration." For no special curricular programs were developed to level the educational playing field in these schools or to introduce Mizrahi contents and culture, which would have challenged the differential cultural and power relations. And inevitably, ways of bypassing the ethnic integration were found, most prominently in the effective creation of different learning tracks within the schools and, in some schools, the formation of ethnically homogeneous classes. This reform is, thus, a distinct example of the strategy of responding to the needs of the people by offering them certain advancements, while rearticulating their demands for change so that they can be incorporated into practices of production and repro- duction of social inequalities.

Finally, public schools in Israel played an important role in producing and reproducing these disparities by "maintain[ing] privilege in cultural ways by taking the form and content of the culture and knowledge of powerful groups and defining it as legitimate knowledge to be preserved and passed on" (Apple, 1995, p. 38). This was accomplished by way of the hegemonic strategy of cultural replacement or exclusion described by Wong (2002). For example, there was no representation of the Mizrahi in the Zionist historical- cultural super-narrative and its official knowledge (Apple, 2000). The history textbooks taught[12] in the state schools largely ignored the culture and narrative of Mizrahi Jewry in the history of the Jewish People (Shenhav, 1999), as well as their role in the State of Israel. The state, its educational apparatus, practices, and official knowledge drew clear ethnic boundaries, which composed what Yonah (2005) calls the "ethno-republic" State of Israel: Jewish, thereby excluding all non-Jewish citizens of the state, and Eurocentric, creating and maintaining an internal hierarchy amongst the two Jewish ethnic groups based on their (real or perceived) contribution to the building of the state.

The hegemonic alliance amongst the Ashkenazi secular and religious Zionist streams framed a narrative that purported to describe and represent the entire history of the People of Israel (Jewish culture), the State of Israel (Jewish polity), and the Bible of Israel (Jewish tradition and religion), all consolidated into one super-narrative of Zionism (Ram, 1995; Yonah, 2005). This soon became the "common sense" regarding the legitimacy of the formation of the State of Israel. The collective memory of the Jewish community in Israel was forged under this Zionist-Ashkenazi hegemonic super-narrative, devoid of Mizrahi and Palestinian contents and used as a tool by the state to suppress, marginalize, and control both populations culturally and economically (Pappe, 1999).

Education and the Security Risk: The Arab-Palestinian Citizens of Israel

Let us return to the binarism between Mizrahis and Palestinians. The discriminatory and differential treatment and construction of the Mizrahis in the context of the West/East binary was only one aspect of the cultural oppression and domination of the Arab-Palestinians in Israel.[13] This was augmented by the Israeli state's perception of its coerced Palestinian citizens as a fifth column, otherwise known as the "security issue." Thus they have been situated on the dominated, counter-hegemonic sides of both binaries: the East in the West/East binary and the nationally and culturally subordinated Arab versus the Jewish-Zionist subordinator in the second binary. As noted, in line with the hegemonic super-narrative, the Arab-Palestinians were denied any recognition in the State Educational Law as an autonomous ethnic group. Only after a long struggle did they gain some, albeit very limited, recognition.

Most recently, a 2003 amendment to the Law recognized the "Arab" citizens of Israel as having a "unique language, culture, history, heritage, and tradition," but as a "population group," not an ethnic minority. This exclusionary education policy reflected and produced the divergence in the state's "colonizing" and legitimation mission and strategies with regard to the two "Eastern" groups. The so-called cultural threat posed by the Mizrahis who had "not tasted the taste of gymnasium" to the character and shape of the new Israeli community was nothing compared to the security risk the Arab-Palestinians supposedly posed to the very existence of the Israeli state and its nationhood. Whereas the state sought to incorporate and assimilate the Mizrahis, its agenda was not always as clear-cut with regard to the Arab-Palestinians. Alongside the open attempt to "neutralize" the risks allegedly posed by the latter, by controlling and subordinating them through exclusion, there was an unexpected or perhaps ambivalent attempt to re-shape and accommodate their culture as well. Indeed, the tension-fraught Arab-Palestinian case entailed more than a mere choice between integration and reshaping or subordinating and rejection. Rather, *a combination* of hegemonic strategies was employed by the *same* regime to contend with the *same* population, with different strategies applied in different contexts (a possibility Wong raises).

This was clearly manifested in the education arena in the ways the state "decided" to educate its Palestinian citizens in the face of conflicting strategies, ideologies, and interests regarding how the Other is treated and conceived in Israeli society. How can "we" incorporate, accommodate, the Other for the purpose of removing the peril he/she poses to "our" society, but at the same time keep him/her at a distance and under control because he/she will never be completely like "Us" or aligned with "Us"? This is a still-predominant tension in Israeli society, which is partly expressed in its aspiration to be simultaneously Jewish and democratic.

The treatment of the Arab-Palestinian citizens of Israel in general and particularly in the public education context was strongly debated amongst officials and educators from the outset. It was not their intellectual or academic abilities that occupied political leaders and the education system, but the Arab-Palestinian national (and perhaps religious) identity. Their perceived threat to Jewish nationhood and statehood was the foremost concern in the decision on what shape the curriculum for Palestinians would take, with policymakers weighing which education approach would best defuse this risk, assimilation or segregation and control, or, in other words, "how to achieve the goal of educating the Arab young generation for loyalty to the state of Israel" (Benor, 1951, p. 8, as cited in Al-Haj, 1995, p. 123).

An assertion made by a (Jewish) superintendent in the Arab public schools in 1949 is illuminating, claiming assimilation to be the best strategy:

> in giving the Arab schools the same structure which exists in the Hebrew schools as far as possible, the same methods, the same class hours, the same atmosphere, and if possible also a similar curriculum . . . we can hope not only to bring our Arabs closer to us but also to take them away from the Arab world surrounding us.
> (State Archives 145/1733/G, as cited in Al-Haj, 1995, p. 122)

This reflects not only a semi-assimilationist strategy (only "closer to us," not "one of us") but also the prevailing attitude at the time: the need to distance the Palestinians from the "Arab world," from Arab identity, as well as to distance from and reject in *Israeli* society, culture, and identity everything that is "Arab."

However, the more dominant stance with regard to how to "educate" the Palestinian population was that it would be virtually impossible to educate them into being Israelis (in Bhabha's (2004) terms, to transform, or "purify," them, their identity, into Israeli identity). They would never be "like us," "close to us," or "one of us"; any attempt at incorporating them into the dominant culture would imperil the latter. The "colonial authority requires modes of discrimination (cultural, racial, administrative . . .) that disallow a stable unitary assumption of collectivity" (Bhabha, 2004, p. 158) in order to establish and maintain its control over the colonized: domination through disavowal. Proponents of this stance thus supported an exclusion/ segregation/control strategy, seeking to "diminish the sense of deprivation (among the Arabs) on the one hand and to intensify the control over Arab education on the other" (State Archives 145/1292/GL, as cited in Al-Haj, 1995, p. 123).

Under this strategy, the segregated Arab public schools underwent a transformation, with the culture and knowledge of the cultural (and territorial) dominator (Jewish, Zionist, Western-oriented hegemony) replacing the local contents and form. The Arabic textbooks that had been used in the Arab public schools since the early 1900s[14] were seen by the state as a potential catalyst of national awareness and forging of a national identity amongst the Arab-Palestinians; they were thus replaced with Israeli textbooks in Arabic. Oral literature with any Arab/Palestinian national context or Arab history and geography contents defined as nationally oriented were forbidden and removed from the curriculum (Al-Haj, 1995). Notably, Arabic remained the language of instruction in the Arab state public schools, but was used for teaching the core curriculum of (European) Jewish history, literature, and culture. This contributed to the Palestinians' continued economic and cultural subordination, as Hebrew was the language of economic and academic progress. However, the combination of a curriculum based on and promoting the Jewish-Western hegemonic narrative and culture, on the one hand, but taught in Arabic by Arab-Palestinian teachers in segregated schools located in politically and economically oppressed communities, on the other, can be seen as a central factor in the emergence of ambivalence and ambiguity in the individual and collective cultural and national identities of Arab-Palestinians in Israel.

Active and effective Palestinian resistance to this process of cultural domination and colonization was not quick to surface and, when it did, faced many obstacles. While policies of cultural exclusion run a substantial risk of strong opposition arising at some point (Wong, 2002), the concurrent (limited) accommodation and incorporation of Palestinian culture in the public education system (incorporation of Arab schools, Arabic language instruction) as well as the cultural reshaping (teaching the hegemonic official knowledge, values, and aspirations) led to their seemingly becoming integral participants in Israeli society, despite their subordinate economic and cultural status. Moreover, during the first years of Israeli statehood, up until 1966, the Palestinian community was subject to military rule, which wielded enormous power over every aspect of their lives and acted forcefully and swiftly to prevent the emergence of opposition.

In the educational system, for example, teachers and school principals had to undergo a thorough security screening, and any teacher suspected of "disloyalty" (usually socially activist teachers) was removed (Al-Haj, 1995, pp. 163–171). The first prominent outbreak of opposition only occurred following the Arab-Palestinian "cultural renaissance" in Israel, which began with the 1976 Land Day Protests. These protests marked the first broad Arab-Palestinian resistance and took the form of a general strike and large demonstrations against Israeli expropriation of Arab lands and discrimination. But what had begun as peaceful demonstrations escalated into violent clashes between protesters, the police, and Army, resulting in the death of six Arab-Palestinians.

In recent years, a new leadership has emerged in the Arab-Palestinian community, originating in civil and political movements and establishing new bodies such as the High Follow-Up Committee for the Arabs in Israel and the National Committee for the Heads of the Arab Local Authorities in Israel. This development is the product of a conscious decision on the part of the Palestinian citizens of Israel to take an active role in transforming their subaltern position in Israeli society. A very recent expression of this activism is the 2006 initiative "The Future Vision of the Palestinian Arabs in Israel,"[15] which presents and formulates the Palestinian narrative of Israel as a colonial state and the outcome of a settlement process "initiated by the Zionist-Jewish elite in Europe and the west and realized by Colonial countries contributing to it" and as implementing "policies derived from its vision as an extension of the west in the Middle East" (p. 9).

Alongside an outline of the social and political missions of the Arab-Palestinians in Israel, the Vision describes the changes that have transpired in their collective identity. It describes how Palestinian culture in Israel has begun to lose its uniqueness and identity. This culture is not surviving the processes of modernization, globalization, and Israelization and is undergoing individuation and disengagement from the Palestinian community outside Israel's borders. This stage in the collective identity and culture of the Arab-Palestinian in Israel is one of "setback, it starts from 1991 when the gulf war broke out and continues with the Oslo agreements up until the second Intifada, in 2000 . . . [and] is characterized by Arab Palestinian lack of sense of unity" (pp. 31–32).

The Palestinian community in Israel is, indeed, facing a huge challenge. Its leaders and, primarily, social movement activists and intellectuals feel the need to unite the community. However, attempts to essentialize this community are complicated by the historical circumstances that led to its creation. The community sees itself as part of the Arab nation, part of the Palestinian nation, yet also (unwilling) citizens of the State of Israel. Even the declaration of the Vision's aim to establish the community as a national minority clearly speaks of being a community *in* the State of Israel, separated from their sisters and brothers in the future state of Palestine and the refugees in the Diaspora. Thus, Arab-Palestinians in Israel are emerging as a community with a distinct collective identity and national awareness not only vis-à-vis the Israeli majority, but also vis-à-vis the rest of the Palestinian nation.

Nowhere are the ambivalence and complexity of Arab-Palestinian identity in Israel and the community's struggle to contend with this more apparent than in the concrete educational initiatives that have emerged from within this community over the last few decades. This has been part of, or in conjunction with, a broader phenomenon in Israel of educational frameworks being initiated or evolving in counter-hegemonic communities. The unprecedented growth of new and unique education projects since the late 1980s is the product of both counter-hegemonic awareness and a drive to confront the dynamics of the Western hegemonization process in education and society as well as the need to contend with the complexities brought on by intensifying global processes and flows. The question, however, is whether these initiatives have succeeded where their predecessors—counter-hegemonic social movements—failed. Have they made a lasting and sustainable impact on the hegemonic domination of the public education system?

Counter-Hegemonic Schools

Like other public spheres and apparatuses of the state, the public education system in Israel has undergone great transformations over the last two and a half decades. As was described, some progress was made in areas related to inequality and disparity on the basis of ethnic origin, religion, and gender. These gains were often the result of specific counter-hegemonic struggles that succeeded in putting some pressure on the state, forcing it to incorporate some of the demands of historically oppressed groups. Unfortunately, the results were meager and, overall, never amounted to a tangible and concrete challenge to hegemonic control of the official curriculum or pedagogy in the public system. The emergence in recent years of concrete counter-hegemonic educational initiatives and frameworks—and the evolution of identities and identity politics—have not been merely the product of local factors and circumstances. Looking at the Israeli case in the global context, the double nature of the Western influence is apparent.

Just as occurred in many other countries swept by neoliberal ideology, since the 1980s the Israeli education system has experienced a process of decentralization and privatization (often followed by a backlash of recentralization). At the same time, it has been subject to a process of global cultural politics that "continue to perpetuate an unequal flow of cultural commodities, ideas, and discourses from Western centers to the rest of the world, affecting the cultural and racial identities of the marginalized populations both within and outside the West" (Takayama, this volume). However, these global influences and forces have opened up a space for new discourses of identity, difference, and multiculturalism, as well as generated the structural change that has enabled individuals and social movements to challenge the hegemonic official curriculum and pedagogy. Indeed, complexities and contradictions abound all around us.

The continuing economic and cultural oppression of the East and South by the West was intensified by the process of globalization. Yet the complexity of global powers carries with it a (limited) liberating potential alongside the oppression. From the Israeli perspective, although it was long-standing structural and bureaucratic forms[16] that provided the "crack" through which non-hegemonic education could emerge in the form of "recognized but not official" schools (an option originally made available by the state mainly in order to keep the ultra-orthodox community(ies) under the gaze of the Ministry of Education and as a part of the political coalition), it was only in the 1980s that the wave of globalization facilitated the establishment of new "alternative" secular schools. From the late 1980s, with the erosion of the power and status of the welfare state, many new schools were established by organized groups of activists and parents who wanted to provide their children with an alternative education that they viewed as better, in quality and approach, than the official public education.

Certainly, the labels "alternative," "progressive," "open,"[17] and even "democratic" that were used to describe these new schools have contested meaning and application. There is a decided tension between two perspectives of these schools, the one regarding them as the vanguard of progress in a long process of change, clearing the way for other counter-hegemonic or alternative schools, the other seeing them as merely a new elite. Most of these schools started out as private organizations and struggled to achieve the Ministry of Education's recognition and financial support. Hence, it was mostly privileged communities with the necessary kinds of capital to secure the success of their children that were able to embark on such endeavors. This notwithstanding, some of these initiatives have succeeded in challenging the Jewish and/or Eurocentric orientation of the hegemonic curriculum and educational structure, offering a more democratic framework that does not privilege (or at least tries to level the playing field for students and communities) based on class, ethnic, national, or other categories of divergence.

Three such counter-hegemonic educational projects are particularly prominent in these contexts and illustrate the different forces at play—local, regional, global—in the successes and failures of such initiatives. Each project emanated from different political commitments and ideologies and from different structural locations; each is the result of different forces from below and above. Two of the schools, the Kedma School and the Bridge over the Wadi (BOW) School, started out as private initiatives; they then fought for "recognized but not official" status from the state and subsequently gained full recognition as official schools. As semi-private schools when under the category of "recognized but not official," they retained a significant extent of autonomy. While they were required to teach the official core curriculum, they could supplement it with counter-hegemonic contents and develop and use pedagogical practices suited to the school's population and/or ideology. The transformation into a fully official school could compromise this autonomy. Indeed the state's response to such initiatives is in itself part of the hegemonization process. It at first denies recognition and support to these schools, marginalizing them. Once they have succeeded in standing on their own two feet for a few years and have persisted, the state begins to pull them in from outside, to bring them into its hegemonic purview, by granting partial recognition tied to partial supervision. At this stage, the schools still maintain a degree of (perhaps illusory) educational autonomy and freedom.

The final step in this process, which the majority of such schools paradoxically strive for,[18] is the dangling sword of full recognition—and full state supervision. In fact it could be argued, convincingly, that the establishment of such schools, followed by the state's support of them, is actually part of a sophisticated hegemonic strategy. On the one hand, the state keeps intact cultural hegemony in "regular" public schools, which most children attend, while on the other hand, it enables the hegemonic elite at one end of the spectrum to go to private schools, with partial state funding, and counter-hegemonic initiatives, situated at the other end, to survive in the margins, without ever really endangering hegemonic relations.

Both the Kedma School and the BOW School were initiated by social activists. They were also both actively supported by a social movement that has sought to set up a network of schools across the country as alternatives to the hegemonic educational system. The Kedma School was established by Mizrahi intellectuals and educational activists as a secondary school that challenges the Eurocentric official curriculum, but at the same time strives to provide working-class students access to higher education. The BOW School was created by activist middle- and upper-middle-class Israeli Palestinian and Jewish parents, in an effort to provide elementary bilingual and multicultural education to their children while challenging the Jewish-centered official curriculum.

In contrast, the third school, the Bialik School in South Tel Aviv, was a public elementary school that, due to demographic changes in the neighborhood where it was located, started to serve mostly children of migrant laborers. At this unique school, a charismatic principal and her school staff independently developed a multicultural curriculum within the public system and adapted their pedagogical practices and approaches to the unique needs of the diversified student body. All three schools have distinguished themselves as concrete frameworks that have succeeded where counter-hegemonic social movements failed in their fight for general social and educational change in Israeli society. Yet all three have ultimately had a narrow scope of impact, posing only a limited—in time and space—challenge to the hegemonic educational system. Despite grassroots pressure from below and global pressure from above, the existing hegemonic alliance continues, through various ways, to withstand significant erosion of or threat to its domination and monopolization of public education in Israel.

The Kedma School

The Kedma[19] School in Jerusalem is a unique example of an organized educational project that mobilized a community, parents, and activists to challenge the inequality of the Israeli public education system. The initiative of Mizrahi social activists and educators, themselves from underprivileged backgrounds, the School opened in 1994 in the predominantly working-class Mizrahi neighborhood of Katamonim, one of the poorest and most underserved Jewish areas of Jerusalem. These activists had formed the "Kedma Foundation for the Advancement of Egalitarian Academic Education in Israel," an association whose creation was authorized by the Israeli parliament in 1993[20] to establish autonomous schools that would advance the education level of Mizrahi children. The Foundation sought to create schools that would serve as an educational model[21] addressing the disparities and discrimination from which Mizrahi populations and culture suffer in the public education system.

These schools would raise the educational level of young Mizrahis in peripheral and disadvantaged communities and, in turn, empower these communities by improving educational achievement. The central concrete goal would be to prepare students for academic matriculation while providing an education that is meaningful and connected to the students' cultural and personal frames of reference (http://kedma-edu.org.il/main/site New/index.php?langId=1). The segregative national public system would be challenged in three central spheres: curriculum, pedagogy, and access. Not seeking to essentialize "Mizrahism," the Kedma schools would rather "reconstruct" Mizrahi identity by integrating elements of Mizrahi culture, history, and traditions into the curriculum and building a pedagogy that would be suited to and supportive of the school's populations and their needs, that would develop the children's "ability to belong concurrently to their close culture and community, to the surrounding culture, and to the wide world" (Yona et al., 2004, p. 117, as cited in Resnik, 2006).

This reconstructed Mizrahi identity would be aimed at empowering the children, at transforming the negative self-image that accompanies "Mizrahi" in the Israeli reality into a positive one. This would be achieved by exposing— and remedying—the Eurocentrism of the official curricula and adapting teaching methods, school structures, and institutions to a multicultural conception of education (Resnik, 2006). Finally, no child would be turned away: there would be open enrolment on a first-come-first-served basis, with preference based only on residence in the community.

The first such school to be established was the Jerusalem Kedma School, with the Foundation choosing to begin its activities in the Katamonim neighborhood "where the JEA [Jerusalem Education Administration] has thrown in the towel." The existing public schools there were (and are) amongst the most prominent examples of the disparities between socio-economic and ethnic groups in education. Overcrowded, underserved, and of poor quality, their students either dropped out of school before matriculation or else pursued (or were streamed to) purely vocational studies that did not lead to matriculation and, therefore, higher education. In the same year that the Jerusalem School was founded, another was opened in a similar socio-economic neighborhood in Tel Aviv and one was planned (but never opened) in Kiryat Malachi, a poor Southern development town. The Tel Aviv school closed after only five years of operation, and the Kiryat Malachi school was never launched, in both cases, due to strong opposition from local authorities and local interests. Thus, the only school to survive and flourish is the flagship Jerusalem Kedma School, whose student body continues to expand to this day.

From the outset, the Kedma School in Jerusalem attached great importance to its bond with the local community and parents[22] and strove to be an organic part of that community (Bar Shalom, 2005, p. 96; Yona, 2002, p. 102). The Kedma activists (none of whom were from inside the education system) began by going from door to door in the neighborhood to tell parents about the school they wanted to open with the cooperation and involvement of the parents and community. They spoke to them about education, tracking, discrimination, and the importance of academic matriculation. They told them the school would provide quality secondary education (grades 7 to 12) without tracking; there would be only one track— an academic track to full matriculation. They made contact with the local community center, where they held group meetings with parents, and recruited parents who were PTA members at the local elementary school to be active in the endeavor. They appeared on local television, distributed flyers in the neighborhood mailboxes, and put posters up. They also met with potential students, trying to gain their enthusiasm and agreement to going to a school that did not yet exist. Making strong parental and neighborhood involvement a fundamental part of its operation, the school has aimed at reinforcing the students' identification with their families, neighborhood, and community (Bar Shalom, 2005).

The journey to opening the Jerusalem Kedma School was not an easy one. It was no simple task convincing parents and students to support a school that had yet to even find facilities and that the Jerusalem Municipality was refusing to approve. They faced significant local and official obstacles, as well as opposition and criticism from academic circles, which depicted the school as a segregative Mizrahi school serving "juvenile delinquents, wild, criminals, and the retarded" (Yona, 2002, p. 104).[23] The Municipality's refusal to grant the new school approval meant that not only was there no agreement in principle to the school's establishment, but also no facilities or funds would be provided to run the school. In its first year, the Kedma School was thus forced to operate as a completely private school under the authority of the Ministry of Education's Jerusalem District, which did not provide any funds or a building either. Kedma's founders had to raise the funds for the school's general budget by themselves and find facilities. During its first two years, the school moved around, renting different rundown facilities in different parts of town, searching for a permanent home, preferably in the neighborhood itself.[24]

At the end of the second year of operation, the Jerusalem Municipality agreed to support the school and provide facilities in the Katamonim neighborhood, but on the condition that it would become a municipal school and would cease to be run privately by the School association. At this point, the Kedma group's funds had run out. The staff had been working without pay for over half a year and had even been paying school expenses, supplies, and maintenance out of their own pockets. The school was on the verge of closure. But the students wanted to continue learning at Kedma; "they felt they were building the school." Thus, the school administration and PTA agreed to the Municipality's terms, but still maintained pedagogical and curricular autonomy.

At Kedma, the official state curriculum is taught in order to provide an academic education and prepare students for succeeding in the matriculation exams. This, however, is supplemented by a curriculum that reflects the history and culture of the majority of the students, both on the individual level of family background and origins and from a broader Mizrahi perspective. The Kedma curriculum seeks to foster in the students a sense of identification with their families, the surrounding community, and their cultural backgrounds, as well as a sense of belonging to Israeli society and the world (Bar Shalom, 2005). Social, cultural, and literary materials are taught that both reflect and broaden the students' cultural perspectives; they are encouraged to supplement the lack of official materials on their family and ethnic histories and culture by conducting interviews with family members and investigating their personal family histories and backgrounds, as well as topics that relate to their community and personal experiences (Dahan & Levy, 2000, p. 431).

Three special programs developed by the school have been central in transforming the basic curriculum at Kedma: its Language and Literature Program and its unique Social Education and Social Studies Programs. The Language and Literature Program, aimed at developing reading and comprehension abilities, combines materials from the core curriculum with texts by Mizrahi authors, on the assumption that the latter are more related to the students' worlds and therefore easier for them to understand and more relevant to them (Yona et al., 2004, as cited in Resnik, 2006). The Social Education Program integrates subjects related to such issues as human rights, democracy, and coexistence. As explained by the school principal, this Program seeks to expose the students to the social structural difficulties that prevent them from succeeding. The curriculum is geared to instilling awareness of their rights as well as their state of submission and oppression. "[T]hey will be able to understand that when many people fail in a society, it is not a personal failure but the result of unequal social conditions that do not permit people to develop and flourish, as in the case of unequal educational conditions" (Yona et al., 2004, p. 191, as cited in Resnik, 2006). The Program aims at developing social awareness in the students, a sense and experience of activism, and to provide them with tools to combat oppression; it seeks to teach them that social change is possible in a broad set of circumstances and situations. In the framework of the Program, the students, teachers, and parents participate in community day projects.

One such event was "Katamonim Day," for which the students researched and documented the history of the neighborhood, including its social activism, and then presented what they had compiled to the community, which was invited to the school to view displays and participate in symposia and activities. Another social-education project was "Human Rights Day," when the students conducted a human rights fair on education rights.

Thirdly, the Social Studies Program is an interdisciplinary framework that includes elements of sociology, history, and cultural studies, with emphasis on the connection between family, neighborhood, and community. The Program curriculum melds Western cultural studies and traditional subjects with subjects neglected in the core curriculum such as Mizrahi Judaism, Christianity and colonialism, Arab national movements, and Asian and African cultures and histories. This is intended to instill in the students a sense of pride, identity, and belonging with their families and past, their community and culture, their country and the world (Yona, 2002). In the framework of this Program, the seventh-grade students do independent research projects on the history and culture of their families' countries of origin; in eighth grade, in the context of nationalism and national movements, the students do independent studies on a country in the Middle East and study Arab national movements. In ninth grade, the topic of Jewish-Arab relations is studied, with stereotypes and prejudices clarified and the commonalities between Arab culture and the culture of their parents, homes, and community raised and considered, aiming at the eventual understanding that much of Jewish culture, particularly Mizrahi culture, originates in Arab culture. This attempt to deconstruct the dichotomy between Jewish and Arab culture has the powerful potential to create a "third space" in which both cultures are reconstructed.[25]

The school's curriculum is reinforced by a pedagogical approach of dialogical learning that is heavily influenced by Freire's pedagogy of liberation, with the school regarding itself as liberating both the students and the community. The teachers develop and maintain close personal relationships with their students that stretch beyond the school walls, to their realities at home and in their neighborhood. Life in school is understood as based on meaningful relationships, and dialogue between students, parents, and teachers (Yona, 2002) is a foremost priority. This is achieved by keeping classes relatively small in size, allowing teachers to give individual attention to the students. There is no screening or streaming based on academic ability or chances of success. Classroom study is further broken down into small heterogeneous groups of eight to ten students, who sit around a large circular table and read texts together, talk, and write.

A pillar of its pedagogical approach is the school's special mentoring program. At Kedma, in addition to classroom instruction, some of the regular teachers serve as mentor-teachers. The mentors are responsible for monitoring and guiding the progress and well-being of twelve to fifteen of their students. They monitor the students' attendance records, home situations, social adjustment at the school, and academic development and attend to any special needs or challenges that might arise—academic, social, or personal. The mentoring relationship transcends the physical boundaries of the school, extending into the home. Mentors must be aware of what is occurring in the child's home and personal life and offer a sympathetic ear or external intervention if necessary. Many of the teachers—who are from a diversity of ethnic, and religiosity, backgrounds—are university graduates who themselves grew up in disadvantaged neighborhoods and development towns and, as such, also serve as role models with whom the students can identify and strive to emulate.

Ultimately, the Jerusalem Kedma School has flourished and grown. From two classes in 1994, it now has 150 students in grades 7 to 12 and is widely regarded as a landmark academic success story. Before Kedma was founded, on average, only 10% of high-school-age children in the Katamonim neighborhood matriculated. Ten years after its opening, the percentage of twelfth-grade students from Kedma who completed a full matriculation exceeded the national average (Yona, 2002). The Jerusalem Kedma School serves as an outstanding example of a successful counter-hegemonic project, described as transforming the identity of its students from marginalized to emancipatory (Resnik, 2006) while enabling them to succeed in hegemonic terms. Its overall impact, however, as a national counter-hegemonic educational movement has been limited. This was clear from the circumstances surrounding the closure of the Tel Aviv Kedma School and the failure in opening a school in Kiryat Malachi. The Tel Aviv school, which ironically did not encounter the same initial resistance from local authorities that the Jerusalem school experienced, was closed after five years due to strong ideological opposition from within the local municipality, which came to regard the school as excessively radical.[26] The Kiryat Malachi project was grounded due to the fierce opposition of the only existing high school in the town, a state vocational school that belongs to one of the largest and most powerful national public vocational school networks in the country (Yona, 2002).

As the project gained impetus in Kiryat Malachi, the vocational school realized that the planned Kedma School, with its academic matriculation orientation, would be a significant threat in that it would draw away students. Not only would this eat away at the vocational school's dominant presence and influence in the town, but its diminished size would result in less public funding and lost teaching positions (even though Kedma had promised to employ teachers who would lose their jobs). The vocational network thus (successfully) brought great pressure to bear on the Kiryat Malachi Municipality to stop the opening of Kedma (Yona, 2002). Here, too, were clearly manifested the powerful economic and ideological institutions and forces to which the state has to respond, which, in the long-run, thwarted the operation of these schools.

The Bridge over the Wadi School

The Bridge over the Wadi School (BOW), similar to the Kedma School, arose as the endeavor of a group of activists—parents in this case—seeking to challenge the discriminatory bias and segregative nature of the public education system, here on the basis of national group. On the one hand, the school represents an attempt to remedy the lack of representation of Palestinian culture, history, and narratives in public education, and on the other, it seeks to expose Israeli Jewish children and Israeli Palestinian children to the national "Other." An integrated, bilingual, and dual culture school, the BOW School is one of four similar schools in the Hand-in-Hand Educational network. Founded in 1997, the Hand-in-Hand Center for Jewish-Arab Education in Israel was created to build peaceful coexistence between Jews and Arabs in Israel through the development of bilingual and multicultural schools that would serve as a model for egalitarian Palestinian-Jewish cooperation in education (Bekerman & Horenczyk, 2004). Hand-in-Hand currently educates over 800 children in its four schools across the country, under a unique model integrating five principles: academic excellence, bilingualism, civics, diversity, and educating the entire community (http://www.handinhandk12.org).

The BOW School is unique in that it was founded on the immediate background of unprecedented violent political and social clashes between Israeli Palestinians and Jews. Located in Kfar Kara, a Muslim town in the center of Israel, the school lies in the heart of a region torn by conflict between the two groups—the Wadi Ara region. The Wadi (meaning "valley" in Arabic) crosses through small and large Arab towns, agricultural land, and small Jewish towns and agricultural communities. In October 2000, violence erupted in this region, beginning with a general strike in the Arab sector, intensifying with stone-throwing and riots, and culminating in the killing of thirteen Israeli Palestinians by the police during demonstrations. In the wake of this violence and the resulting deterioration in Jewish-Arab relations, a small group of ten Jewish parents and ten Palestinian parents from the region came together to formulate a solution that would enable coexistence and overcome the violence and hatred: a framework where their children could live and learn together.

The declared common denominators of the founding parents were a desire to develop democratic life in the region, the belief in universal human rights, and the willingness to establish a system of communal life between the Jewish and Palestinian members of Israeli society. The common ground between the two communities is set on democratic principles of action: respect for divergence and the desire for daily and practical coexistence between the communities. This group of parents joined with the Hand-in-Hand organization to create and open the BOW School based on the Hand-in-Hand model (http://www.handinhandk12.org/index.cfm?fuse action=content.display&pageID=73).[27] However, what makes the school particularly unique is that, unlike its three counterparts,[28] which are all located in Jewish areas (in Jerusalem, the Galilee, and Beersheba), the Bridge over the Wadi is the only Hand-in-Hand school to be established in an Arab town. Thus for the first time, children from the hegemonic culture exit the (geographical and cultural) safety of their environment and are "visitors" in the home of the counter-hegemonic culture.

The Bridge over the Wadi School opened its doors in September 2004 with 105 pupils from kindergarten to grade 3 and has since almost doubled in size. Like the other Hand-in-Hand schools, in both its curriculum and pedagogical approaches, it challenges the Jewish national aspect of the Israeli hegemonic education. It breaks down the walls excluding the narratives, practices, culture, and history of the Palestinians in the region, seeking to create a balanced representation of the two nations. This is manifested in the composition of the student body, school staff, teaching methods and practices, and curricular contents and form, ensuring that students learn a curriculum and experience a learning environment that they identify with as well as being exposed to and made familiar with the world and culture of what is perceived of as the national Other. The school has an equal number of Jewish and Palestinian students and teachers, with the latter coming from Jewish and Arab towns in the area, and two co-principals, one Palestinian and one Jewish, female and male respectively. The classes are conducted in Arabic and Hebrew simultaneously, with both a Palestinian teacher and Jewish teacher present in the classroom. The students learn the narratives, folklore, and histories of the two cultures, as well as how to read and write in Hebrew and Arabic. As part of the curriculum, the students learn from one another how to pray according to their respective traditions—Muslim and Jewish. They learn to sing each other's folk songs in music class and celebrate and observe the traditions and holidays of the two cultures and religions.

The curriculum does not only look to shared or neutral grounds. Indeed, the divergences lie at the heart of the curriculum. The school does not shirk from the challenges of the political-social-historical tensions existing between the two groups. The highly charged subjects and issues at the foundation of these tensions are taught, with the perspectives of both groups, often strongly and sensitively at odds, presented and discussed. One of the most illustrative examples is how the school deals with Israel Independence Day, which celebrates the establishment of the State of Israel, clearly a very loaded occasion in the Arab-Jewish context. The Israeli Jewish narrative of this day speaks of the 1948 War with the Arab states, victory, and the establishment of the Jewish State of Israel on lands settled and owned by Jews or abandoned during the War by Palestinians as well as lands on which Palestinians remained. The Palestinians, however, mark this day as the *Nakba*—"the Catastrophe"—a day of national disaster and mourning for the conquering of the lands and exodus of Arab refugees from Palestine during the War. The Jewish perspective is the hegemonic perspective, given exclusive representation in the public curriculum, while the Palestinian perspective is completely absent, in many respects delegitimized as falsehood. At the Bridge over the Wadi School, both narratives are taught and the clash between them—often unresolved in the emotional class discussions between the students—is not masked.

This is a unique phenomenon in the Israeli social and cultural experience, shared only by the few bilingual schools, for this day constitutes one of the biggest rifts between the two populations. In Israeli society, for both groups, merely listening to the other narrative can be interpreted as giving legitimacy to its construction of the events and outcome. The BOW School, in many contexts like this, not only seeks to expand and supplement the hegemonic perspective taught and represented in the official curriculum with Palestinian counter-hegemonic perspectives and contents; it also tries to directly challenge the hegemonic version, question its legitimacy or at least its monopoly on legitimacy.

This project has not been without limitations, of course. Some of the criticism, which emanates mainly from the academia, indeed refers to the issue of identity formation, as well as the impediments that counter-hegemonic struggles face. The BOW School, while it seeks to enhance each group's culture and history alongside exposure and acceptance of the Other, does not create a space to dispel the concept of Otherness. The Other that is encountered and the boundaries of Otherness that are lowered are quite narrow, perhaps misleading, in many respects. The school, in addition to bilingualism, places emphasis on teaching and celebrating each group's culture and traditions with all the accompanying religious aspects, giving religion a much stronger presence than in secular schools.

However, the majority of the parents are secular, so this does not necessarily represent the particular culture or identity of the individual students. Moreover, there is a lack of full symmetry between the languages, with Hebrew emerging as the dominant one—something that has surfaced in all four Hand-in-Hand schools. Since Hebrew is spoken by all the students and teachers, while most of the Jewish students and some of the teachers do not speak Arabic, students and teachers alike see Hebrew as the convenient middle-ground and switch to it frequently.[29] In addition, the majority of students, from both groups, come primarily from middle- and upper-middle-class families (Bekerman & Nir, 2006). Even if this is not a case of "more powerful and privileged communities breaking off from the public system" via this school (like charter schools in low-income neighborhoods), the BOW School tends to serve students who are "better off" in that their parents "are actively engaged in their education" (Wells et al., 1999, p. 174). This has meant that only a limited segment of the two populations experience what the school offers. Thus, there is nonetheless a certain element of (cultural and economic) privilege attached to attending the school, making this, from the outset, a limited and private case of challenge to hegemonic cultural and political relations.

This said, the school does represent a genuine and original desire on the part of members of both groups to break free of the confines of the identity community, to have contact with other identity groups and learn about them, while rearticulating their own national identities and cultures. There is an attempt to enrich and/or replace parts of the hegemonic curriculum and pedagogy to include Arab and Palestinian contents and forms, to give the counter-hegemony a place. As part of the successful and growing Hand-in-Hand network, the BOW School is part of a broader, more far-reaching challenge to the hegemony than Kedma. More people are reached; the dialogue is brought to more places, to more homes. But like Kedma, Bridge over the Wadi is still "outside" the sphere of general public education, resulting in narrow and individualized impact.

The Bialik School[30]

In some respects, the Bialik School in South Tel Aviv is the most unique of the three projects described here. For rather than the product of political and ideological forces and activism, it was a purely organic and natural phenomenon that emerged out of global and local changes and the individual initiative of certain educators within the public school system. The school was (until September 2005) an existing official public elementary school serving a traditionally underserved neighborhood in Tel Aviv, which transformed and adapted itself to the changing demographics of its students. The new circumstances and environment in which the school found itself in the 1990s were reflective of the multilevel forces at play in the general economic and demographic shifts that Israel, like many other countries, underwent over the previous two decades.

Set in the poor and highly polluted vicinity of the central bus station in South Tel Aviv, the story of the Bialik School was shaped by local, national, regional, and global political agendas and economic forces. Until the first Intifada, in the late 1980s, the majority of cheap labor in Israel had been performed by Palestinians from the Occupied Territories. With the outbreak of the Intifada, the Israeli government began to pursue a deliberate and direct policy of encouraging the replacement of Palestinian workers with migrant laborers from elsewhere. Bolstered by the general global flow of labor migration, this set in motion an influx of tens of thousands of migrant laborers, many of whom came to reside in the city of Tel Aviv, concentrated in the neighborhood in which the Bialik School was located. Thus from the mid-1990s, the working-class veteran population that had resided there for decades began to leave, and mini-communities of laborers from all across the world (mostly Africa, Asia, South America, and Eastern Europe), the majority undocumented, turned the neighborhood into a global village.

By the early 2000s, children of migrant laborers accounted for over 50 percent of the Bialik School student population (Knesset Research & Information Center, 2004; Lavi, 2003). The rest of the student body was no less a product of global flows and forces. This included children of new immigrants from the former Soviet Union, mainly the Asian republics, whose emigration to Israel from the early 1990s was the product of the collapse of the regime in which they had lived and who now sought either a new home with which they identified nationally (as Jews) or else (sometimes also) political and economic stability and prosperity. The school also served the children of Palestinian and Lebanese "collaborators" with the Israeli state, themselves victims and participants in the regional tensions and changes. These were Palestinians from the West Bank and Gaza who had collaborated with the Israeli forces during the Occupation and Christian Lebanese who had been members of the pro-Israel South Lebanese Army, which was disbanded when Israel withdrew from South Lebanon in 2000 (Bar Shalom & Hayman, 2003; Bar Shalom, 2005). Both groups were forced to flee their homes, in the wake of the geopolitical shifts in the region, for they would have been killed as traitors and enemies, and now live in the periphery of Israeli society as complete outsiders. Finally, the school also served a declining number of veteran Israeli-Jewish families, whose children comprised only 15 percent of the school population (Lavi, 2003). These were families who could not afford to move out of the neighborhood and were "left behind" to become the minority there, to live in one of Israel's most economically and socially peripheral areas, on the one hand, yet most multicultural, multi-national, and global, on the other.

Thus, the Bialik School was both the essence and the outcome of the processes that had led to the "natural" demographic changes in the neighborhood. Moreover, as an alternative educational framework, it also was the direct result and manifestation of global pressure brought to bear on the state by supranational institutions to comply with certain inter-national norms and practices. The fact that Israel is signatory to international treaties and conventions, such as the Convention on the Rights of the Child, that protect children's fundamental rights and liberties means that the basic needs of even the children of undocumented migrant laborers should be provided by the state, including education[31] (Bar Shalom, 2005). Thus, laborers, along with the other diverse residents of the South Tel Aviv neighborhood, could register their children at the local public school—the Bialik School. By the 2002/03 school year, the Bialik student body consisted of 350 children aged 3–13, speaking nineteen different languages and originating from thirty-three different countries (Knesset Research & Information Center, 2004; Lavi, 2003).

When a new school principal, Ofira Yahalom, was appointed in 1992, Bialik was a typical underserved, "low-achieving" school serving a disadvantaged neighborhood. As she described it, she arrived to find "a dump with a tin shack as the restroom" (Lavi, 2003). The Ministry of Education, she claimed, like the Tel Aviv Municipality, was supportive of her efforts to rehabilitate the school. The Municipality invested millions in refurbishing the building; the Ministry backed her up in implementing the international conventions that enabled the registration of migrant laborers' children (Lavi, 2003). Acknowledging the dramatic change in the school's demographics and concerned over poor academic achievements, the Ministry also offered Yahalom the opportunity to replace some or all of the teaching staff. However, she declined, stating that "educators should be given a chance to prove themselves, with the assistance of a professional and supportive process" (Bar Shalom, 2005, p. 41).

Together with the original staff, Yahalom transformed the school, its curriculum, and pedagogy into a model of successful multicultural, multinational education within the public system and of high academic achievement. To begin with, the curriculum contents and pedagogical approach had to be adapted to the variety of languages and dialects spoken and the variety of national and cultural identities in the school (Ben-Yosef, 2003). The school also had to adjust itself, without official guidance, to the diverse and changing community and surroundings. Yahalom realized that the school's approach must be altered to be more respectful of, and in a dialogue with, the students, their families, and the environment. The school perceived itself as a part of the surrounding community, defining itself as a "multicultural community public school" and emphasizing "pluralistic multicultural concerns of equal rights and tolerance, respect for difference, and acceptance of the other without preconditions" (Resnik, 2006, p. 595). The "transnational identity" that was fostered at the Bialik School addressed the particular needs of its diverse population, many of whose parents had illegal status in the country, making their lives in Israel uncertain and migratory (Resnik, 2006).

Since the official curriculum in no way accommodates such a diverse and international body of students, the school had to find ways to modify some of the hegemonic Israeli contents to reflect or at least respect other cultures. In many subjects, such as history, literature, and geography, the curriculum was expanded to incorporate the various backgrounds and traditions of the non-Israeli, non-Jewish cultures represented in the school. The teachers altered the official curriculum to internationalize and transnationalize it. For example, in teaching the Old Testament unit of study, part of the core curriculum, different cultural and religious versions of the Biblical stories were presented and discussed to give them relevance to the different students, as well as to show and teach respect for diverging traditions and narratives.

Thus, from "agents of socialization," the teachers became "cultural mediators" (Bar-Shalom, 2005, p. 49). The school allowed and stressed the need for teacher "flexibility" in their pedagogical practices and with regard to the curriculum, especially in relation to Education Ministry "norms." The teachers learned to follow the Ministry's curriculum and norms in an interpretive way, not to "blindly" follow official guidelines and requirements, as one teacher stated (p. 47). Yahalom gave them the leeway and encouraged them to develop the curriculum in conjunction with the students over the year and to use innovative, non-traditional teaching methods, such as mixed-ages study groups of children speaking the same language. As one teacher explained, "The subject is built through the learning. We don't know where we will get to by the end of the year—we only know where we start. We create mixed-age study groups and we also pay attention to the children's interests" (p. 50).

Language and cultural maintenance was a central element of the school's approach. Newsletters to parents, reports and certificates, and school ceremonies were translated into English, Spanish, Russian, Turkish, and Arabic (Bar-Shalom, 2005; Resnik, 2006). Along with the Jewish holidays, the children learned about Ramadan and Christmas. A unique Religious Program dealing with Judaism, Christianity, and Islam was developed at the school to supplement the Jewish context of the official curriculum. This preservation of the cultures of origin was intended to build the children's self-confidence and prepare them for reintegration when and if they returned to their parents' countries of origin. It also cultivated a transnational identity and awareness that would allow them to integrate anew were they to move to another foreign country, mitigating the fragile and unpredictable reality of many of them.[32]

Alongside this multicultural, multinational education, it was seen as paramount to provide the children with "Israeli skills" as well—Hebrew language proficiency and knowledge of Israeli culture—so that they would be able to integrate and function in Israeli society. Lastly, the children were taught "universal adaptive" tools applicable anywhere in the world: practical tools such as home economics and health-care and learning skills such as self-teaching (text analysis, library research, internet use) and critical and creative thought (Ben-Yosef, 2003). The school had to address and respond to the harsh world in which migrant laborers and their children live: the "Non-Place of Exploitation" (Hardt & Negri, 2000, p. 208).[33] As Yahalom explained, "We will prepare them for life, with no relation to where they might be in the future" (Bar-Shalom, 2005, p. 233).

The Bialik School is the story of how a public elementary "low-achieving" school can be transformed by an administrator and staff into a "success story" on a number of levels. The school was lauded as a "flourishing multicultural establishment"; its graduates were pursued by secondary schools in the area due to their high academic performance. In directly challenging the Jewish-Israeli-centered curriculum, Bialik facilitated the construction of a transnational identity for its diverse and multinational body of students (Resnik, 2006). Similar to the Kedma and Bridge over the Wadi Schools, Bialik strived to foster in its students the ability to "succeed" in hegemonic terms (i.e., to gain the necessary certificate for acceptance to any secondary school in Tel Aviv) and thereby enhance their ability to reach matriculation. But at the same time, the official curriculum was adjusted to reflect the cultures, origins, and narratives of the students and their families, and the school transformed into a community school. The Bialik teachers and school administration knew that they had to work hard to gain the parents' trust, especially as the school represented one of the branches of the very entity that was seeking to deport many of them.[34]

Moreover, quite often, parents were not very accessible, working multiple jobs or shifts, absent from the home from early morning until late at night. In most cases, their trust and confidence was won due to the long and committed efforts of the school staff, which included many outreach activities and the creation of a supportive community together with other social organizations in the neighborhood. Unfortunately, the 2005 relocation and merging of Bialik with the nearby local secondary school, Rogozin, might be a lethal blow to the warmth, intimacy, community, and success that was achieved at Bialik. The official reason for the school's closure and relocation was the poor condition of the building and its infrastructures. Rogozin, an "underachieving" school, had itself recently returned to traditional public school format after a brief detour as a democratic school.

The fact that Bialik could have been renovated by the Municipality or Ministry or moved to new facilities rather than being annexed to an existing school (itself under threat of closure due to low registration) raises the question of whether this would have happened had the school served a different population, had it been less viable as an alternative to the hegemonic forms of education. In fact, the relocation of the Bialik population can perhaps be understood as an expression of the hegemonic tactic of segregation-integration, which was used in contending with the "threat" posed by the Mizrahi counter-hegemony. In shattering the community of Bialik and preventing the dispersal of its graduates to more "successful" (affluent) secondary schools than Rogozin, the school merger maintained socio-economic segregation but "integrated" (submerged) the counter-hegemonic framework into the hegemonic framework and culture.

The Bialik case also perhaps reveals an inherent flaw to alternative educational frameworks that emanate entirely from below: the dependence on specific individuals to sustain them. It raises the question of the long-term viability of completely organic and grassroots initiatives without parallel or complementary pressure and change from above to support it. The Bialik School on the one hand highlights the inherent potential of the public system as a space where diversity can be negotiated, accommodated, and embraced, of the public system as a true neutral mediator. Yet on the other hand, we see the Education Ministry's persisting domination in these struggles, its ability to neutralize the "threat"—in the Bialik case, by merging it with Rogozin—and submerge the counter-hegemonic supposedly in an act of embracing.

Conclusion

This chapter began with the question of what schools do and the relationship between education and differential power in society. Building on a long tradition of neo-Gramscian work, we used the formation of the Israeli state and formal education system as a case study to show that one regime can use different hegemonizing strategies toward different groups, leading to different outcomes. This discussion of the forces and processes at work in the nation-state, its formation, and the many conflicting pressures brought to bear on the state focused mostly on the state level. The current global reality makes it vital to expand our understanding of how public schooling (and the state) is being challenged from both above and below. While attention must be devoted to counter-hegemonic educational projects coming from below, analysis of public schooling must look beyond the nation-state to the intensification of global powers as a source and sphere of pressure from above.

The rise of informational technology and global economy and the global spread of Western neoliberalism have shaken the state's hold over (national) identity formation as well as the (local) cultural hegemony's influence in this process. Israel has been no exception. Pressure from above impacting education now also emanates from the supra-state level, while at the same time, global forces and flows have changed the shape and identities of the grassroots and local levels, of the counter-hegemonic.

With these understandings and perspectives, we looked at progressive schools that have presented concrete challenges to the official curriculum and pedagogy in Israel, each driven by a different political and moral commitment and from a different structural location. Yet, as we saw, in the current neoliberal reality, endeavors to challenge the official curriculum face greater obstacles when attempted from inside the walls of the public system. Indeed, many such schools start out as "non-governmental-not-for-profit organizations" (NGNPOs), usually initiated by activists and parents with the necessary cultural and economic capital to participate in the project. Of the three specific schools we described, the public official Bialik School was the exception in this respect. The two other schools, Kedma and Bridge over the Wadi, began as NGNPOs, later finding their way into the gaze of the Ministry of Education.

These three schools are part of a growing phenomenon of attempts to create counter-hegemonic schools. In Israel, like elsewhere, counter-hegemonic schools tend to be problematically connected to the categories of "experimental" and "unique," alternatives to the general public education system. The proliferation of such non-public, at times semi-private schools undermines the public system, which is, we believe, the right place to fight for equality and social justice, for a real and comprehensive project of politics of redistribution and recognition (Fraser, 1997). The decentralization and privatization processes in the Israeli education system over the last decades have been roundly criticized from many quarters (Ichilov, 2006; Yonah & Dahan, 1999). What have emerged are schools that, like Kedma and the Bridge over the Wadi, are public in principle but with a growing part of their budgets funded by the parents, some even operating as private schools. Supported by a neoliberal, managerial ideology, this phenomenon, like charter schools and home-schooling, is at odds with the principle of equal opportunities and erodes the social fabric (Apple, 2006).

This raises, of course, questions about the complex relations amongst and within (as well as the shifting meanings of) the "public," "private," and civil society in education: What are the consequences of liberation projects and do these projects contribute to social justice or do they, in fact, exploit or marginalize other people and communities? And do they dichotomize and reinforce artificial barriers of Otherness or do they tear them down, creating a true third space?

But the three schools discussed here are not merely examples of counter-hegemonic educational projects. They are also clear evidence of global influences on educational policy and practices, as well as on identity formation. The flow of ideas and its impact on the politics of borrowing and lending of educational practices and policies have added to the already complex dynamics at play. While the transformation of time and space, or at least their social meaning (Castells, 1996), has led to the illusion, for some, that we live in a global village, in fact, the walls dividing people by class, race, gender, nationality, ethnicity, sexuality, ability, religious and cultural belonging have only been raised higher. Yet at the same time, global flows have brought with them the fertile soil on which new multilayered, liberating identities can be sown. This was not only clearly the case with the Bialik School, but also true of the Kedma and Bridge over the Wadi Schools.

Alongside the apparent commonalities between the three schools, which are seemingly different forms of the same phenomenon, there are compelling divergences—most significantly, as different counter-hegemonic responses or strategies. For all three schools offer a different prism through which to understand the various ways in which alternative schools come into being. We saw that this can take the form of a social movement: the endeavor of committed activists, educators, and intellectuals who seek and succeed to motivate and organize working-class parents and the community to take on the challenges of establishing a school, as in the case of Kedma. A second model is the self-organization of active middle-class parents who join an existing organization. This was the framework of the Bridge over the Wadi School initiative and what the Hand-in-Hand organization seeks to facilitate and foster. The third type of endeavor is based on the concerted efforts of individuals already operating within the education system—like the Bialik principal and the teachers she succeeded in motivating, engaging, and supporting in their task. Each of these strategies, as we saw, results in different outcomes as well as being plagued by different flaws.

Similarly, each of the schools reminds us of the limits of counter-hegemonic projects. They do not act in a vacuum. They are exposed to constant political, economic, and ideological challenges. In the case of the Bialik School, merging it with Rogozin effectively prevented the continuation and reproduction of the former's success at creating a unique, nurturing multicultural environment for its students. The expansion of Kedma as a network of schools, of which the Jerusalem Kedma School was the pilot project, was similarly resisted. The two other endeavors at establishing alternative Kedma schools (Tel Aviv Kedma and the failed Kiryat Malachi project) could not withstand local official and political opposition, and further attempts to open new schools elsewhere suffered similar fates.

It is still too early to predict what the future holds for the Bridge over the Wadi, for the school is a young, growing school, annually expanding by a grade level to accommodate its continuing students. At this early stage of development, it is still unclear what long-term counter-hegemonic impact it will have, if any, and what obstacles the neoliberal state will place in its way. One challenge that could arise is a problem faced by the more veteran schools in the Hand-in-Hand network: growing beyond the ninth grade while maintaining an equal ratio of Jewish and Arab students. This has proven to be very problematic, as the majority of the Jewish students opt to go to other, "high quality" secondary schools upon completing eighth grade at the Hand-in-Hand schools, so as to ensure acceptance to higher education. This has been one of the manifestations of what can be understood as the narrow, or short-term, undertaking of the Jewish families to the inter-mingling of the counter-hegemonic with the hegemonic.

On the one hand, there is an ideological and political commitment to what the schools represent and to exposing their (hegemonic) children to counter-hegemonic form and content. Yet on the other hand, they see this as a limited venture in terms of their personal involvement. They have not relinquished their middle-class aspirations for their children to "succeed" in hegemonic frameworks that ensure their advancement in hegemonic terms. The result is that at the secondary-school stage, the Arab students are left behind by their Jewish friends and counterparts in this project, thereby hindering systemic long-term impact.

Indeed, perhaps any real educational challenge to the hegemonic process is doomed to remain on the fringes of the public system. Perhaps educational autonomy and uniqueness can be realized in the periphery of society only when it falls under the gaze of the state apparatus, as with all three schools. Moreover, it appears that any attempt to create a revolutionary (or at least alternative) world of concepts and constructs even fully within the state framework, as in the case of Bialik, must be prepared to contend with harsh resistance and obstacles (Markovich, 2007). As Markovich (2007) has noted in the context of the Jerusalem Kedma School, there are strong ideological and structural obstacles that must be overcome by any counter-hegemonic challenge to class and ethnic marginalization in education in order to be more than a "footnote" or anecdotal anomaly.

But we would like to end on a positive note. The significance of the fact that the educational projects described here exemplify the "politics of curriculum and teaching" in constructive motion cannot be denied. In all three cases, there has been an invaluable "conscious building of coalitions" between the school and communities it serves. All were "bottom-up movements" for change, much more than a "technical vision." Rather, each can be seen as what one of us has described as a "political project: enhancing democracy at the grassroots, empowering individuals who had heretofore been largely silenced" (Apple, 2000, p. 39). Having said this, however, we still need to ask whether such still relatively small and scattered attempts at building solidarities across differences, in a time when the tensions within Israel and between Israel and Palestine are so charged, can contribute in powerful ways to a just and democratic solution to what seems to be almost intractable conflicts. What we can be certain of is this, however. Without trying to change education in counter-hegemonic ways, and without connecting these counter-hegemonic educational practices and institutions to the larger struggles against dominance, we will never be able to answer that question.

Notes

•Assaf Meshulam would like to thank ISEF for its generous support.

1   This usage of "Mizrahi" refers to Jews who immigrated to Israel from a variety of different countries, mostly from the Middle East and North Africa, that do not necessarily share a common culture. On the way that this group "became" a distinctive social group, see Levy (2002).

2   This will be discussed further on in this chapter.

3   Curtis defines state formation as the process of "centralization and concentration of relations of economic and political power and authorities in society" (as cited in Wong, 2002, p. 19), whereby the state monopolizes control over violence, taxation, administration, and symbolic power.

4   Genderial rifts exist as well (Hertzog, 1994, 1999; Rapaport, 1993).

5   Ironically, this trend was in no way connected to Mizrahi ethnicity in the sense referred to in this paper. The label "*Mizrahi*," meaning "eastward" in Hebrew, was chosen by the Ashkenazi founders of the *Mizrahi* movement to symbolize the geographical direction of the state of Israel from the European perspective and the longing for the eastern "Holy Land."

6   In 1951, a huge ideological conflict divided this stream over the shape of the educational system, revolving around whether to maintain the socialist traditions and ideological affiliation and ties with the Soviet Union or to shift to "Western-modern" values and orientation. This conflict was part of the above-mentioned "struggle over education" and was also economically rooted—it marked the beginning of the departure from an agricultural-based economy to industry ("non-productive work"), a shift that was, in fact, initiated by Ben-Gurion.

7   At first, the Compulsory Education Law's requirement that parents declare their choice of education trend applied also to the new immigrant residents of the transition camps. But this was amended by the Israeli Parliament to halt the persistent battling amongst representatives of the different trends for students.

8   The 1949 Compulsory Education Law already offered parents who did not wish to send their children to any of the official schools the option of establishing non-official schools, providing that "the Minister may, by regulation, prescribe a procedure and conditions for the declaration of non-official institutions" (as cited in Avidor, 1957, p. 56). The practical ramifications have been that non-official schools are not required to teach the full official curriculum and are not under full Ministry supervision; hence they are only partially funded by the state. Under this category, quasi-private schools were established in the late 1980s and 1990s, a trend that is discussed further on.

9   This education system, which was part of the Labor Trend, had many progressive elements to it. For a deeper discussion of the education in the Labor Trend, see Reshef (1980), Dror (1997). For a recent study of national education in Israel focusing on secular Zionist education from the 1880s to the end of the 1990s, see Dror (2007).

10 Christian and Jewish private schools were allowed to operate alongside this system, with this arrangement prevailing both under British Mandate rule and into Israeli statehood, up until the 1953 Law. Non-Jewish private schools continued to be operated even after the Law's enactment.

11 A system by which children of similar proficiency levels were grouped together to learn together at the same pace.

12 Limited progress in this respect has been made over the years to reverse this.

13 Different terms are used to describe the Arab-Palestinian community in Israel. In the Arab media, terms such as "the Arabs of 48" or "the Palestinians of 48" are in use; the Israeli media uses terms such as "Israeli Arabs." A term often used by Palestinian scholars as well as Palestinian citizens of Israel, however, is "Arab-Palestinian residents of Israel," to indicate that any "Israeliness" or Israeli citizenship had been imposed on this community. We use "Arab-Palestinians in Israel" here to distinguish the community from Arab-Palestinians outside the borders of Israel as well as to give expression to all aspects of their identity.

14 From the Ottoman period, through the British Mandate period, and into the first two years of the Jewish state, until the establishment of an official state education system.

15 See http://www.adalah.org/newsletter/eng/dec06/tasawor-mostaqbali.pdf.

16 The 1953 State Educational Law allowed parents to send their children to "non-official" schools. These schools, at the time mostly ultra-orthodox religious seminaries, were semi-financed and semi-supervised by the Education Ministry (Avidor, 1957).

17   A few "open schools" were founded in the 1970s, but did not endure long (Caspi, 1979).

18   The only exception thus far has been another Arab/Jewish school, Neve-Shalom/Wahat al-Salam. The first bilingual school to be granted full official recognition, it subsequently declined this recognition, not wishing to bear the burden of full supervision and its ramifications (http://nswas.org/rubrique32.html).

19   "Kedma" is a Hebrew literary term for "eastward."

20   This official legitimation was granted mainly in order to enable the incorporation of parental choice into the education system (Ayalon, 2004). Ironically, it was neoliberal agendas that supported the establishment of this school.

21   One of the more immediate goals has been to develop and document the Kedma model so that it can be applied as an educational alternative in other disadvantaged communities in Israel. It is widely regarded as a model for providing top-quality education in the heart of a community, accepting all students without discrimination or classification, and working in collaboration with the entire community (students, parents, teachers, neighborhood residents) (http://kedma-edu-org.il/main/siteNew).

22   Like the Bialik School to be discussed further on.

23   The long and continuous challenges that the Kedma School in Jerusalem (and the other two Kedma schools) faced as well as the persistent and deep commitment of its founders is well documented in *Voices from the Katamonim* (Yona, 2002).

24   It was thrown out of its first "home," a former bank that the group renovated at great cost, after only a few months, when both the Municipality and the other residents of the building got court orders preventing the school from operating. For a period of time, the school held classes outside, in the town square across from the Jerusalem Municipality, but eventually returned to the neighborhood, to a rundown "shack" provided by the Municipality after significant pressure was placed on the Mayor.

25   Here perhaps we see Bhabha's (1990) concept of hybrid "Otherness" in action: "the 'other' is never outside or beyond us; it emerges forcefully, within cultural discourse, when we think we speak most intimately and indigenously 'between ourselves'" (p. 4).

26   The founders and administrative staff of the Tel Aviv school were, indeed, more radical than at the Jerusalem school. A good and well-documented example of this is the commemoration of Holocaust Memorial Day at Tel Aviv Kedma. At the ceremony, in addition to the traditional six candles lit to symbolize the six million Jewish victims, the students lit a seventh one in memory of all other (non-Jewish) victims of the Nazis. The ceremony, which received great public attention, was highly criticized for tampering with one of Israeli society's most sensitive days (Levy & Barkay, 1998). On the Tel Aviv Kedma School, see Chetrit (2004, pp. 281–289).

27   The first bilingual school, in Neve-Shalom/Wahat al-Salam, was established two decades earlier, and although it is not part of the Hand-in-Hand organization, there is collaboration between the two. For a fascinating study of the Neve-Shalom/Wahat al-Salam school, see Feuerverger (2001).

28   This is true regarding other Arab-Jewish schools that are not part of the Hand-in-Hand network.

29   This imbalance in bilingual schools between the hegemonic language and the non-hegemonic one is not unique to the BOW School. On the power relations between the two languages in bilingual schools, see, e.g., Valdes (1997).

30   In September 2005, the Bialik School was relocated to its new home, merging with the nearby secondary school Rogozin, which was renamed "Rogozin-Bialik."

31   Recently, the government began to set the criteria for granting special "family status" to parents of children either born in Israel or who have lived in the country for a long period of time. Israeli citizenship is not granted automatically to children of migrant laborers upon birth in Israel. (Knesset Research and Information Center, 2004).

32   A report prepared for the Israeli Parliament on migrant laborers in Israel noted a similar approach to this as having guided Germany's education system in dealing with a comparable situation. This could be an interesting instance of "borrowing" if the Israeli government does adopt the German solution to contend with this social "problem" in setting its own policy.

33   In their book, *Empire*, Hardt and Negri (2000) use the term Empire not as a metaphor but as a concept "characterized fundamentally by a lack of boundaries: Empire rule has no limits" (p. xiv).

34   In 2002, in response to national panic over what has been coined the "foreign workers problem," the government decided to take action by establishing the Immigration Administration and to deport tens of thousands of laborers.

References

Al Haj, M. (1995). *Education empowerment and control: The case of the Arabs in Israel.* New York: State University of New York.

Apple, M. W. (1995). *Education and power* (2nd ed.). New York: Routledge.

Apple, M. W. (1996). *Cultural politics and education.* New York: Teachers College Press.

Apple, M. W. (2000). *Official knowledge* (2nd ed.). New York: Routledge.

Apple, M. W. (2003). *The state and the politics of knowledge.* New York: RoutledgeFalmer.

Apple, M. W. (1979/2004). *Ideology and curriculum* (3rd ed.). New York: RoutledgeFalmer.

Apple, M. W. (2006). *Educating the "right" way* (2nd ed.). New York: Routledge.

Apple, M. W. & Weis, L. (Eds.). (1983). *Ideology and practice in schooling.* Philadelphia, PA: Temple University Press.

Avidor, M. (1957). *Education in Israel.* Jerusalem: Youth and Hechalutz Department of the Zionist Organization.

Ayalon, A. (2004). Successful urban school reform for marginalized groups—a case comparison. *Curriculum and Teaching,* 9(1), 83–103.

Bar-Shalom, Y. (2005). Educating Israel: Educational entrepreneurship in Israel's multicultural society. Basingstoke: Palgrave Macmillan.

Bar Shalom, Y. & Hayman, R. (2003). Bialik school—a warm heart in the middle of the town. *Social-Education Work Encounter,* 18, 53–71.

Bekerman, Z. & Horenczyk, G. (2004). Arab-Jewish bilingual education in Israel: A long-term approach to intergroup conflict resolution. *Social Issues,* 60(2), 389–404.

Bekerman, Z. & Nir, A. (2006). Opportunities and challenges of integrated education in conflict-ridden societies. *Childhood Education,* 82(6), 327–333.

Ben-Yosef, E. (2003). *What does it take to learn to read? A story of a school with love* (unpublished dissertation, Hofstra University, New York).

Bernstein, B. (1977). *Class, codes and control* (Vol. 3). London and Boston: Routledge & Kegan Paul.

Bernstein, B. (1996). *Pedagogy, symbolic control and identity: Theory research and critique.* London: Taylor & Francis.

Bhabha, H. (1990). Narrating the nation. In H. Bhabha (Ed.), *Nation and narration* (pp. 1–8). London and New York: Routledge.

Bhabha, H. (2004). *The location of culture.* New York: Routledge.

Bourdieu, P. (1984). *Distinction: A social critique of the judgment of taste.* Cambridge, MA: Harvard University Press.

Bourdieu, P. & Passeron, J. C. (1977). *Reproduction in education, society and culture.* London: Sage.

Bowles S. & Gintis, H. (1976). *Schooling in capitalist America.* London: Routledge.

Caspi, M. (1979). *Education tomorrow.* Tel Aviv: Am Oved Publishers.

Castells, M. (1996). *The rise of network society.* New York: Oxford University Press.

Chetrit, S. S. (2004). *The Mizrahi struggle in Israel, between oppression and liberation, identification and alternative.* Tel Aviv: Am Oved Publishers.

Curtis, B. (1992). *True governance by choice man? Inspection, education, and state formation in Canada West.* Toronto: University of Toronto Press.

Dahan, Y. & Levy, G. (2000). Multicultural education in the Zionist state—the Mizrahi challenge. *Studies in Philosophy & Education,* 19(5), 423–444.

Dale, R. (1989). *The state and education policy.* Philadelphia, PA: Open University Press.

Dror, Y. (1997). Labor trend. In Y. Kasti, M. Arieli, & S. Shlasky (Eds.), *The lexicon of education* (pp. 163-164). Tel-Aviv, Israel: Ramot.

Dror, Y. (2007). *"National education" through mutually supportive devices: A case study of Zionist education.* Bern: Peter Lang.

Eyal, G. (2005). *The disenchantment of the Orient.* Jerusalem: Van-Leer Institute (Hebrew).

Fraser, N. (1997). *Justice interruptus.* New York: Routledge.

Feuerverger, G. (2001). *Oasis of dreams. Teaching and learning peace in a Jewish-Palestinian village in Israel.* London and New York: RoutledgeFalmer.

Gramsci, A. (1971). *Selections from the prison notebooks* (1st ed.). New York: International Publishers.

Green, A. (1990). *Education and state formation: The rise of education systems in England, France and the USA.* New York: St. Martin's Press.

Gur-Ze'ev, I. (Ed.). (1999). *Modernity, postmodernity and education.* Tel Aviv: Ramot.

Habermas, J. (1973). *Legitimation crisis.* London: Heinemann.

Hardt, M. & Negri, N. (2000). *Empire.* Cambridge, MA: Harvard University Press.

Hall, S. & du Gay, P. (Eds.). (1996). *Questions of cultural identity.* London: Sage.

Hertzog, H. (1994). *Realistic women: Women in local politics.* Jerusalem: Institute for Israel Studies.

Hertzog, H. (1999). *Gendering politics—women in Israel.* Ann Arbor: University of Michigan Press.

Ichilov, O. (2006). The Trojan horse of globalization. In D. Inbar (Ed.), *Toward educational revolution?* (pp. 88–104). Jerusalem: Van Leer Jerusalem & Hakibbutz Hameuchad.

Khazzoom, A. (2003). The great chain of Orientalism: Jewish identity, stigma management, and ethnic exclusion in Israel. *American Sociological Review,* 68(4), 481–510.

Knesset Research & Information Center. (2004). *Children of foreign workers—state of affairs and ways to contend with the future.* Jerusalem. Retrieved March 3, 2009, from http://www.knesset.gov.il/mmm/data/pdf/m01317.pdf.

Lavi, A. (August 29, 2003). What I learned at school. *Ha'aretz Daily Newspaper.* Retrieved March 13, 2008, from http:http://www.haaretz.co.il.

Levy, G. (2002). *Ethnicity and education.* London School of Economics and Political Science. Unpublished dissertation.

Levy, G. & Barkay, T. (1998). How to commemorate the Holocaust: Ethnicity, class and education in Israel. *Politika: The Israeli Journal of Political Science,* 1, 1.

Lissak, M. & Horowitz, M. (1989). *Trouble in Utopia: The overburdened polity of Israel.* Albany: State University of New York Press.

Markovich, D. (2007). *Ethnicity, education and identity: The case of the Kedma academic community high school.* Jerusalem: Hebrew University. Unpublished dissertation.

Nardi, N. (1945). *Education in Palestine, 1920–1945.* Washington, DC: Zionist Organization of America.

Offe, C. (1976). Crisis of crisis management: Elements of a political crisis theory. *International Journal of Politics,* 6(3), 29–67.

Offe, C. (1984). *Contradictions of the welfare state.* London: Heinemann.

Omi, M. & Winant, H. (1994). *Racial formation in the United States: From the 1960s to the 1990s.* New York: Routledge.

Pappe, I. (1999). Educational implications of multiculturalism in Israel: The case of Israeli historiography. In I. Gur Zeev (Ed.), *Modernity, postmodernity and education.* (pp. 233–259). Tel-Aviv: Tel-Aviv University Press.

Ram, U. (1995). Zionist historiography and the invention of modern Jewish nationhood: The case of Ben-Zion Dinur. *History and Memory,* 7(1), 91–124.

Rapaport, G. (1993). *On feminism and its opponents.* Tel Aviv: Dvir Publishing House.

Reshef, S. (1980). *The workers trend in education.* Tel Aviv: Hakibbutz Hameuchad.

Resnik, J. (2006). Alternative identities in multicultural schools in Israel: Emancipatory identity, mixed identity and transnational identity. *British Journal of Sociology of Education,* 27(5), 585–601.

Resnik, J. (2007). Discourse structuration in Israel, democratization of education and the impact of the global education network. *Journal of Education Policy,* 22(3), 215–240.

Said, E. (1978). *Orientalism.* New York: Pantheon.

Shenhav, Y. (1999). Analyzing Jewish history text books. *News from Within,* 15(8), 32–35.

Shenhav, Y. (2002). Jews from Arab countries and the Palestinian right for return: An ethnic community in realms of national memory. *British Journal of Middle Eastern Studies,* 29(1), 27–56.

Shenhav, Y. (2006). *The Arab Jews.* Stanford, CA: Stanford University Press.

Shohat, E. (2006). *Taboo memories, diasporic voices.* Durham, NC: Duke University Press.

Valdes, G. (1997). Dual-language immersion programs: A cautionary note concerning the education of language minority students. *Harvard Educational Review,* 67(3), 391–429.

Wells, A. S. et al. (1999). Charter schools as postmodern paradox: Rethinking social stratification in an age of deregulated school choice. *Harvard Educational Review,* 69(2), 172–204.

Willis, P. (1977). *Learning to labour.* Farnborough, UK: Saxon House.

Wong, T. H. (2002). *Hegemonies compared.* New York and London: RoutledgeFalmer.

Yona, I. (2002). Kedma—an academic high school in the community. In I. Yona (Ed.), *Voices from the Katamonim neighborhood* (pp. 76–133). Ramat Gan, Israel: Association of Friends of Kedma School.

Yonah, Y. (2005). *In virtue of difference: The multicultural project in Israel.* Jerusalem: Van Leer Jerusalem Institute.

Yonah, Y. & Dahan, Y. (1999). The educational system in a transition period from governmental collectivism to civilian individualism. In E. Peled (Ed.), *Fifty years of Israeli education* (pp. 163–179). Ministry of Education, Culture and Sport and Ministry of Defense, Israel (Hebrew).

Young, M. F. D. (Ed.). (1971). *Knowledge and control.* London: Macmillan.

Zameret, Z. & Yablonka, C. (Eds.). (1997). *The first decade—1948–1958.* Jerusalem: Yad Ben-Zvi.

CHAPTER 5

Popular Education Confronts Neoliberalism in the Public Sphere

The Struggle for Critical Civil Society in Latin America

JEN SANDLER AND ERIKA MEIN[1]

Introduction

Neoliberalism, one of the major topics of this volume, is a particular set of economic and social relations that privileges the market as the chief structural and ideological governance mechanism. Structurally, it is a radical reconfiguration of class relations, a form of capitalism through which state and international governance are brought into the service of producing and maintaining markets that maximize the power of corporations dedicated to capital to exploit labor, move freely, and consolidate power. Neoliberal policies have brought these structural mechanisms to the so-called "developing world" with disastrous effects. But, in addition to structural aspects, there is an ideological component of neoliberalism the significance of which must not be underestimated. The ideological aspect of neoliberalism is best understood, as David Harvey notes, with reference to Antonio Gramsci's concept of "common sense" and the need for "consent" for state rule in non-totalitarian societies. In the powerful liberal democracies of the United States and the United Kingdom, as Harvey shows, the "neoliberal turn" was accomplished largely through the construction of an ideological "common sense" that centered around notions of individual freedom, the incompetence of government, and the inherent value of private competition and its outcomes (Harvey, 2005). Harvey further notes that neoliberal "development" has been extremely uneven, particularly in the "developing" world.

The uneven and unstable imposition of neoliberal structures in the developing world begs the question: How does the *ideological* dimension of neoliberalism work—and how is it contested—in nations where poor people have borne the greatest costs of neoliberal structural reforms? While much has been written about the brutal structural effects of neoliberalism on poor communities within "developing" countries, these analyses usually focus on the decisions and conundrums of states. Because of the central role that ideology plays in neoliberal reforms, there is a need to understand how the ideological battle between neoliberalism and critical social justice work has been waged not simply upon but *within* the spaces of poor communities in the developing world, *within* the non-state, non-market sphere known as "civil society." In Latin America, the struggle for consent within civil society is in fact a struggle to define the nature and role of civil society itself.

At the forefront of this struggle to define the role of the popular sphere in Latin America lie two dynamic movements. The dominant movement— by dint of sheer power—is a re-configured neoliberal development industry, which has developed increasingly ideological mechanisms designed to go beyond the state to address and incorporate as much of Latin American *society* as possible. Popular power, however, has also shifted and evolved to address these new characteristics of neoliberal power. In fact, the *social space* of civil society—communities and networks of communities—has become an important front in the struggle against neoliberalism in Latin America. Critical educators, working in the tradition of popular education that evolved within the region to address both the structural and ideological aspects of injustice, have long worked within these spaces now targeted by neo-liberalism. Community-based popular education, a critical movement located outside of schools and in the "popular" sphere of civil society that in Latin America has always been a vital front for regimes seeking "consent," thus finds itself working in resistance to neoliberalism in a social space that is increasingly important to the development industry.

This chapter examines the struggle on the part of community-based popular educators in Latin America to define the nature and role of civil society in the face of neoliberal power. In order to do this, we will first explore some of the particular ways that neoliberal policies have affected Latin America. We will outline the well-documented economic instability and undermining of nascent democratic welfare states and public services in Latin America before turning our attention to *civil society* and the way that neoliberal policies have developed an articulation of a popular social space that is functional for the economic and structural aims of neoliberal models of development. We thus explore both the material-structural and ideological aspects of the neoliberal development agenda, and we begin to situate this agenda within Latin America and within Mexico, in particular.

Our discussion of the development industry's turn toward civil society in the 1990s is presented as a backdrop for the particular "alternative civil society" development agenda that is the focus of this chapter: community-based popular education in Latin America. We introduce a conceptual framework from Howell and Pearce that distinguishes two "genealogies" of civil society. The "alternative genealogy," where the work that we will discuss in the main sections of the chapter lies, is thus not simply situated as resistance but as an alternative conceptualization of non-state social space. We will further delineate this social space by describing and defining *community-based popular education.*

We will then turn to the main three sections of the chapter, in which we describe and explore community-based popular education efforts. The first of these sections calls attention to a systematic and comprehensive effort to create a Latin American network that addresses neoliberalism explicitly in its efforts to delineate an alternative model of critical popular participation. Finally, we will turn to an in-depth examination of the projects of two community-based popular education organizations in Mexico, both of which see their work as enacting critical responses to the neoliberal development agenda. In our analysis of the first organization we focus on how community-based popular education constructs the *social space* for an alternative civil society that is critical of the neoliberal reforms. In our analysis of the second example of community-based popular education, we examine the development of local educator-organizers and the important aspect of critical identity work involved in this alternative civil society agenda.

Neoliberal Globalization in Latin America

Latin America has been the site of deep and lasting social, political, and economic transformations during the last three decades. One aspect of these transformations has been the turbulent transition from the authoritarianism that dominated in the 1960s to the uneven process of democratization that is present today. These political shifts have been accompanied by equally powerful economic, social, and technological shifts attributable to globalization. In social and economic terms, Latin American countries have been deeply affected by globalization in at least two fundamental ways: (1) through the trade liberalization and accompanying movement of labor and capital resulting from regional free trade agreements such as the North American Free Trade Agreement (NAFTA), implemented in 1994; the Central America–Dominican Republic–United States Free Trade Agreement (CAFTA), passed in 2005; and the *Mercado Común del Sur* (Common Market of the South or Mercosur) between Argentina, Brazil, Paraguay, and Uruguay, originally passed in 1991; and (2) through the changes in public sector spending resulting from the structural adjustment programs recommended by the Bretton Woods institutions (the

International Monetary Fund and the World Bank) following the Latin American debt crisis of the early 1980s.

One of the key symbols of trade liberalization in Latin America has been NAFTA, which was passed in 1992 and implemented in 1994. Opening up trade relations between the United States, Mexico, and Canada, NAFTA has had a politically charged history, with much discussion and debate about its impact. Mexico, in particular, has experienced mixed results, and the policy has tended to hurt the poor more than any other group. Immediately following the implementation of NAFTA in 1994, for example, the country experienced a massive devaluation of the peso, sending the country into a downward spiral. In spite of the promises of growth, Mexico has only experienced 1% growth on average, as compared to 3.2% between 1948 and 1973 (Stiglitz, 2004) and job creation has also fallen below expectations (Audley, 2004). On the whole, it is fairly widely agreed upon that inequality has increased in Mexico since NAFTA, with economic elites experiencing more gains and the vast majority of citizens becoming more impoverished, particularly in rural areas (Esquivel & Rodriguez-Lopez, 2003; Stiglitz, 2004; Audley, 2004).

Another manifestation of globalization has been the structural adjustment programs that came into effect in the 1980s, when international lending agencies such as the World Bank and the International Monetary Fund— which came to be known as the Washington Consensus because of their geographical/political location in Washington, DC—provided policy recommendations for former military regimes in Latin America to reduce massive external debts and to revitalize their economies (Williamson, 1997). Structural adjustment programs ushered in the neoliberal framework under which trade policies like NAFTA became sensible to states by changing the relationship between the state and its citizens. According to several scholars of Latin American education, the social and educational policies associated with structural adjustment programs fundamentally altered the relationship between the state and society (Puiggrós & Torres, 1995; Puiggrós, 1999; Apple, 2001; Fischman et al., 2003). Neoliberal policies throughout Latin America have emphasized privatization, decentralization, and the drastic reduction of state spending on education and other social services.

Such policies have both *structural-material* and *ideological* dimensions; they involve not only changing the role of the state, but also altering public understanding of the role of the state. In its ideological dimension, neoliberalism involves the belief in the free market as not only the mediator of social and economic life but also the means to solving social and economic problems (Apple, 2001, 2006). In Mexico, specifically, the neoliberal shift has marked the decline of the Corporatist state, which according to Morales-Gómez and Torres (1990) "refers to a form of State that, being the result of a popular revolution, has a broad mass-base of popular support despite its capitalist character" (p. 41). Thus, while neoliberal policies have undermined nominal and inchoate social democratic processes everywhere and have thus encountered some resistance, because of the popular support enjoyed by the Corporatist state in Mexico neoliberal policies have encountered particular ideological challenges in the popular sphere.

Neoliberalism and Civil Society: The World Bank

As a result of some of the challenges to the brutal effects of initial neoliberal policies centered around structural adjustment, during the past two decades large-scale development organizations have mounted aggressive campaigns to accommodate diverse contexts and attend to diverse social institutions. The World Bank is a prime example of the development industry's protracted soul-searching toward what might be called a kinder, gentler, and more totalizing neoliberalism—a neoliberalism that is more hegemonic than imperialist.

To be clear, the World Bank's approach to education as well as community development contains implicit—and often explicit—conceptions about knowledge, identities, and social change. Many of these conceptions fit rather neatly the Bank's broad economic development agenda that favors corporate growth over human development and the freedom of capital over the political and social liberties of people. However, it is a mistake to characterize the Bank as unified in this agenda, or as wholly (or even mostly) uninterested in what occurs outside of financial and other state institutions. In fact, World Bank leadership has been quite aware of the critiques of structural adjustment policies and of the costs more generally of failing to attend to how its development agenda relates to non-state, non-market actors. Indeed, the Bank's internal dialogue, as recorded in its own extensive web and document archives, paints a picture of a neoliberal institution that is very much attempting to assimilate "participation" (beginning in the early 1990s) and "civil society" (from the mid to late 1990s to the present) into its discursive as well as structural model of economic progress.[2] For example, the following is a characteristic World Bank explanation of the importance of civil society for development:

> The World Bank's partnership with civil society is built upon the recognition that civil society organizations often have closer contact with the poor and can offer valuable insights and perspectives that differ from other stakeholders. CSOs may be better able than government or official actors to help the poor through the provision of direct services and through assisting the poor to identify their

most pressing concerns and needs. CSOs' local knowledge, expertise and ability to foster and promote people's participation often give them strong comparative advantages in addition to making them valuable and experienced allies in development. CSOs can also help strengthen the effectiveness of development policy through the promotion of transparency and through efforts to monitor policy impact.

(World Bank, 2000, p. 8)

Over the past two decades, the leadership—not simply the fringes—of the World Bank has in many ways exhibited a keen awareness of Antonio Gramsci's conviction that civil society is key to governmental (and in this case international) power (Gramsci, 1971). The Bank has opened entire programs to gain greater popular participation in policy-making, to "partner" with civil society organizations more rigorously, and to use these partnerships to more successfully integrate neoliberal reforms into developing countries. The Bank studies all aspects of these projects, working ever more diligently to integrate a focus on "participation" and civil society into its assessment, lending, and social development projects. In this way, civil society has become a principal space for neoliberal economic policy implementation, and the "participation" of those affected by policy has become a prized component of contemporary versions of neoliberal policy-making.

Alternative Conceptions of Civil Society

In this section we situate concepts of civil society rather differently than has the World Bank. Of course, the development industry has come to its recognition of the importance of civil society rather late in the concept's post-cold war resurrection by social theorists (see Cohen & Arato, 1992). Civil society is a concept of a sphere—a space, a set of non-state institutions and socio-institutional relations—that is relatively autonomous from (and often considered functional for) the state or international agencies and agendas. But if theories of civil society have experienced a resurgence since the 1989 end of the Cold War and the beginning of the neoliberal economic policies, such theories have been distinct from nineteenth and early twentieth-century theories of civil society in an important sense. Contemporary civil society theories are about the normative dimensions of civil society—they are not about *what civil society is*, but instead about *how to build it and for what purposes*. But as "civil society" has become an important front in neoliberal policy development, so too have popular movements developed their own vision and structure for the popular sphere.

The project of "civil society building" in Latin America, in particular, has taken two very distinct forms. The first, as we have glimpsed in the previous section, is expounded by the World Bank and other development agencies, and has been taken up by states in collaboration with these agencies. This is a concept of civil society as functional for a particular development agenda. Civil society here is a space to be "won over," a "front" in the struggle for hegemony, and a necessary partner in a non-totalitarian state. This is the dominant paradigm of civil society. However, it is not the only conception of the role of the popular sphere.

For its champions in social movements in developing countries and on the margins of (over)developed nations, civil society is the space where ordinary people enter into dialogue about power, privilege, and rights; come together to develop and express local cultural, economic, and gender identities and needs in ways that go beyond voting or consuming; act collectively to make demands on the state (particularly in the form of protest movements) and the market (particularly in the form of labor unions); and proactively seek to fulfill their own interests and needs with others who share these interests and needs. Howell and Pearce suggest that an "alternative genealogy" of civil society theory paves the way for these contemporary civil society activists (Howell and Pearce, 2002). The theorists in this genealogy are not liberal democrats seeking social cohesion. Rather, they comprise an eclectic group that have as their common threads radical criticisms of power inequalities deriving from capitalist exploitation, an emphasis on civil society as a space of agency (Escobar, 1992), and an ambiguous relationship with the state and political mechanisms.

We understand Howell and Pearce's "alternative genealogy" of civil society as a theory that incorporates a range of critical theorists and researchers who address issues of power, governance, and the role of popular movements in the processes of "development." Alternative genealogy scholars are openly critical of the concept of civil society as a romantic space of possibility, as a call for universalizing particular (Western) social and cultural forms, and as an apolitical and ahistorical concept. Nevertheless, these theorists often *use* the concept of civil society, or the space of non-market, non-state agenda-setting and action, as a way to make visible the variety of individual and potentially counter-hegemonic collective social and cultural forms that "development" discourses often obscure. For example, Laclau and Mouffe use a Gramscian framework to analyze contemporary social movements, focusing on civil society as a means of contesting both hegemonic and political structures (Laclau & Mouffe, 1985). Their work, like that of many cultural Marxists following Gramsci, foreshadows Howell and Pearce's elaboration of a way of understanding a civil society that functions to *contest* rather than legitimize state and capitalist hegemonic power. Gilbert Rist traces the growth of the religion-like structural myth of development and its disastrous effects on the global South. He concludes his insightful book with some thoughts on what can be done, including the strengthening of social movements and the promotion of creative citizen-action groups that are based on local experiences of oppression (Rist, 1997). His suggestions, aside from those aimed at transforming academia, all revolve around the type of alternative-civil-society collective movements that Howell and Pearce describe.

Gareth Williams's work on Latin America brings specificity and focus to how this "alternative genealogy" of civil society is particularly relevant to contestations of neoliberalism in the region. For Williams, what is needed in response to neoliberalism is a re-claiming of the notion of difference rather than an attempt to patch up the original myth of common interest that served as a nation-building tool in Latin America. The notion of difference that would provide a viable mechanism for the popular (non-elite) classes to negotiate neoliberalism is, according to Williams, to be found in the post-colonial concept of "subalternity" (Williams, 2002). It is this concept of subalternity that guides the foundation of civic, popular knowledge-production in contemporary Latin America. And it is within this critical space of "alternative" civil society in Latin America that falls the range of knowledge-production, educational, cultural and local/critical economic activities that characterize contemporary community-based popular educational practices.

We have found Howell and Pearce's notion of an alternative genealogy of civil society quite helpful. It allows us to retain a focus on institutions outside of the state and the market, but at the same time to begin our examination with a keen attention to *power*, with the notion that civil society is an intensely political space. It allows us to articulate the distinction between functional civil society that presume that deliberation, critique, popular participation, and the cultural context can only be understood as instrumental for some broader ideological end, and civil society agendas within which the propagation of such qualities are goods (if not ends) in themselves. In Latin America, deliberation, critique, popular participation, and an integral notion of context are at the core of what we consider to be the most interesting effort to respond to the neoliberal development agenda. This effort is community-based popular education.

Community-Based Popular Education

Rooted in the theoretical commitments and elaborations of renowned popular educator Paulo Freire, contemporary community-based popular education has a rich history with a coherent theoretical thread. In La Belle's

(2000) account of the history of non-formal education in this region, he discusses popular education and similar "political consciousness"-oriented educational projects that primarily target marginalized populations. Although he organizes his article in terms of large historical shifts in political movements and economic policies and the non-formal educational policies that correspond to each era, he acknowledges popular educational movements' presence in each of the past four political-economic eras. While clearly popular education takes somewhat different forms and has different agendas in the authoritarian nationalist 1960s, the reform and revolution 1970s, the "structural adjustment policy"-initiated economic stagnation and downturn of the 1980s, and the neoliberal politics from the 1990s into the present that form the backdrop for this chapter, the abstract objectives of *individual liberation* and *community empowerment* have been present in each era's popular education movements (La Belle, 2000). That these movements are in some political climates taken up by state apparatuses while in others are marginalized and occur only in local civil society contexts speaks as much to the resiliency of the movements and their appeal to the disenfranchised masses *across* political contexts as it does to the importance of the state and economic climates in shaping the form and strength of such education agendas.

For the purpose of this chapter, it is important simply to note that community-based popular education is based on Freire's notions of a pedagogy based on the experiences and critical insights of the oppressed (Freire, 1970). Popular education takes the experiences of the oppressed as its basis, elaborating a dialogic process through which learners develop a critical understanding of the politics of their oppression and develop an analysis along with the skills to *act* to transform their circumstances and to promote justice and liberation. These elements—oppression, critical dialogue and consciousness, collective action, and social transformation—are all essential components in contemporary community-based popular education. In addition, as the term implies, community-based popular education goes beyond—and generally is based outside of—formal educational institutions like public schools. It is thus inherently multi-generational, involving adults as well as youth in working to understand, learn, and act to transform the oppressive circumstances they face.

CEAAL: Community-Based Popular Education Network in Latin America

One regional collectivity that organizes community-based popular educators in Latin America is the Consejo de Educación de Adultos de América Latina (Latin American Council of Adult Education) or CEAAL—a network of nearly 200 Latin American adult education NGOs established in 1982. With Paulo Freire as its founding president, CEAAL—as an organization rooted in Latin American popular education representing the interests of the majority "popular" or "base" segments of Latin American societies—was intended to be a "foil" to UNESCO (Austin, 1999).

Within CEAAL's wide base of membership there have emerged diverse, and sometimes contradictory, articulations both about the nature of popular education and about the relationship between NGOs and the state. These articulations are conceptually interrelated: NGOs that see themselves as playing a functionalist role in relationship to the state have tended to de-emphasize the political aspects of their educational work, whereas those that take a more oppositional stance in relation to the state have tended to highlight the politicized elements of their work and to view their work as part of a larger grassroots or popular struggle against the neoliberal state. The organizations that comprise CEAAL, then, represent a spectrum of positions—some very clearly enunciated, others not—about civil society–state relations and about popular education.

CEAAL represents a site of contestation, particularly about questions regarding the role of popular education in relation to civil society and the state. That CEAAL represents a site of contestation is visible in its positioning as intellectual arbiter of popular education in the region: the organization serves as a platform for knowledge generation and dissemination via not only regional meetings and general assemblies but also through the publication of its journal, *La Piragua*. The journal has been widely distributed in print form throughout the CEAAL network since its inaugural issue in 1990, and CEAAL's website (www.ceaal.org) contains an archive of all of the issues published until the present day.

One recurring theme found in the volumes of *La Piragua* is the importance of popular educators assuming a critically deliberative stance in the face of neoliberal dominance and reflecting on the nature of the popular education movement itself. This effort at deliberation over the identity of popular education plays out in the opening article of the 2000 edition of *La Piragua*, where then Secretary General Carlos Zarco Mera synthesizes key themes that emerged during discussions among CEAAL affiliates that occurred at regional workshops between April and July 2000. The conclusions of these discussions, as described in his article, can be interpreted as revisionist: where popular educators once viewed their movement as a struggle to create "a new society," by 2000 there came to be more of a focus on creating "a new paradigm"—one rooted not so much in an abstract notion of liberation, but rather grounded in gender-based, ecologically minded, citizenship-oriented perspectives. Yet in response to neoliberal approaches that are ever more hegemonic, a new paradigm that is rooted in profoundly situated perspectives is in some sense a precisely appropriate shift for popular education.

The emphasis on creating a new paradigm—rather than a new society—spurs questions about the relationship among popular education, civil society, and the state, and these very questions are addressed head-on in this document. While the popular education movement had traditionally viewed itself as working in opposition to the state, Zarco Mera presents a more complex, ambivalent stance appropriate to the de-centering of the state in a neoliberal era. On the one hand, he argues that in this particular historical moment of democratic transition, civil society now more than ever "should be preoccupied with the construction of democratic institutions" (2000, p. 10). He suggests the need for popular education organizations to be strategic—if not opportunistic—in their relationship with the state, particularly at the local level, where he sees the greatest possibilities for intervention. He goes on to outline specific roles for popular education organizations, especially in the areas of civic education, training of local authorities, fostering of civic participation through cultural projects, advising local authorities, and helping to design public policy (2000, p. 10). At the same time, he draws attention to the ways in which popular education organizations are deeply preoccupied with concerns about becoming functionalist for the neoliberal state, and he suggests the need to embrace the ambiguities of their positioning, working both within and outside the system but always maintaining a reflexive stance, one that is continuously guided by questions about "how far to go, when to stop, with whom to advance, and what to strengthen" (p. 14).

CEAAL has, if nothing else, identified through its deliberative critique the heart of the effects of neoliberal *ideologies* as well as the material effects of its policies within Latin America, and brought to bear this critique on local community-based popular education's diverse local responses. We now turn to an examination of two such local projects.

Community-Based Popular Educational Responses to Neoliberalism in Mexico

In this section we will explore some manifestations of this alternative conception of civil society by looking at case studies of two community-based popular education organizations in Mexico. Both of these organizations are active members of CEAAL, and both have been engaged in popular education practice for more than two decades. The two organizations work in rural areas of Mexico that have suffered the brunt of neoliberal policies, and both focus particularly on working with women to develop a critical, collective response to the neoliberal hegemony that has not only contributed to economic decline in their respective regions but has also contributed to the breakdown of social ties.

The first organization, the Center for Education in Support of Economic Production and the Environment (Centro de Educacion en Apoyo a la Producción y al Medio Ambiente) or CEP, was located in the border state of Coahuila in northern Mexico and worked primarily with rural women in desert *ejidos* (communal lands/communities) who have suffered economically in part because of the onslaught of agribusiness in the region. The second, Ayuda Mutua, was located in the central mountainous state of Michoacán and worked primarily with rural indigenous women whose communities have experienced breakdown because of the massive outward migration of men and women seeking opportunities in the United States. Our understandings of these organizations comes from our own ethnographic fieldwork: one of us (Mein) spent nine months as a participant-observer with CEP (2005–2006) and the other (Sandler) spent the summer of 2003 as a participant-observer with Ayuda Mutua.[3]

Centro de Educación en Apoyo a la Producción y al Medio Ambiente (CEP)

CEP was a community-based popular education organization located in a small town in northern Mexico's Chihuahuan desert. The organization, which was founded in 1993, was made up of four full-time popular educators as well as an extensive network of volunteer collaborators who assisted in a wide range of activities. Those activities included, but were not limited to, running women's education classes in marginalized urban *colonias* and rural *ejidos*; overseeing training programs to prepare community leaders; facilitating the formation of community-based women's savings groups; organizing local, regional, and national popular education workshops; and sponsoring Ferias Pedagógicas (Pedagogical Fairs), an activity that will be explained in greater detail later in this section. The founders of CEP, who came from a mix of socioeconomic and educational backgrounds and whose completion of formal schooling ranged from primary school to university, had been involved in education work in Mexico's rather isolated northern region since the 1980s, first as leaders of ecclesiastical base communities associated with the liberation theology movement and later as literacy teachers with the national literacy program, before forming their own popular education organization.

The desert context in which CEP popular educators worked is a region marked by stark internal and external contrasts. On the one hand, the region contains several key industrial cities whose large *maquiladora* industry forms an important part of Mexico's domestic economy. The North of Mexico, in fact, is considered the most prosperous region of the country and is distinct from the central and southern regions not only in terms of its economic makeup but also its ethnic makeup, as the Indigenous groups of the North were historically nomadic and the number of remaining Indigenous groups is minimal compared to the South. In spite of these regional economic contrasts, the North's urban areas face acute economic disparities—disparities that have been exacerbated by the presence of low-wage, low-skill *maquiladora* jobs, where workers earn on average $4.50/day in the service of both domestic and transnational corporations.

Another stark contrast can be found between the North's urban and rural areas. The industrial centers are surrounded by vast rural areas, whose harsh desert landscapes and climatic conditions make agricultural production difficult. Compounding these geographical limitations are deeply entrenched problems related to the lack of access to credit, unequal water rights allocations, and conflicts surrounding land distribution and ownership. These difficulties have intensified in recent years with the influx of agribusiness in the region and the accompanying entry of cheap agricultural goods produced by foreign (usually US) corporations into local markets—both as a result of NAFTA. On top of these changes, upon the initiation of fieldwork in 2005, the region was suffering the fourth year of a massive drought that had all but strangled production in the rural *ejidos* of Coahuila. With the combination of a shifting political-economic landscape and the ongoing drought, then, economic conditions in the rural areas were abysmal, and hardship was in abundance in the communities involved in CEP programming.

The work of CEP was deeply rooted in this northern desert context, and the CEP popular educators were keenly aware of the economic shifts that impacted the daily lives of families in the communities with which they worked. In keeping with the Freirean principle of starting with the lived experiences of those who are oppressed, the CEP educators designed educational activities that not only drew on the knowledge and experiences of participants but also addressed the realities of their economic situations. One such activity was the Feria Pedagógica (Pedagogical Fair), which will be explored in detail in the next section.

Pedagogical Fairs

The Pedagogical Fairs were festive, loosely structured events that were designed to bring together different groups, organizations, and individuals involved in various types of education and social change work into one physical space—usually a community square or city plaza. The CEP educators invented the concept and practice of the Pedagogical Fair in 2003 with the intention of creating a "synergy among civil society organizations"

(Alvarez Serna, 2005, p. 1) in order to facilitate collective critical reflection and action (Freire, 1970) to address the economic and social breakdown faced by northern Mexican communities. Feria activities included the dissemination of information about participating groups and organizations, the buying and selling of locally produced goods, the presence of educational games for young people, and artistic performances ranging from poetry readings to song and dance competitions.

The ferias were open to the public, with the goal of attracting as many people as possible. The smaller, community-based ferias attracted, on average, 60–100 attendees, while larger ferias that took place in city plazas tended to attract between 100–200 attendees. Throughout a one-year cycle, CEP popular educators would sponsor, on average, 20–25 ferias in a variety of locales. Fieldwork for this project involved attending eighteen CEP-sponsored ferias, ranging from community-based ferias in Coahuila to regional and national ferias held in Saltillo, the state capital, and in Mexico City's Zócalo (central plaza).

In a 2005 publication called *La Feria Pedagógica: Una mirada ciudadana* (*The Pedagogical Fair: A citizen viewpoint*), the director of CEP makes explicit the purposes of the Pedagogical Fairs, the articulation of which emerged from a process of research and documentation of feria activities throughout 2004. Based on this account, the purpose of the feria was threefold: (1) to promote a broad vision of "education" oriented towards the "humanization of current society"; (2) "to promote dialogue and the full participation of different social subjects and sectors" oriented towards the construction of a "citizen agenda"; and (3) "to promote cooperation, collaboration, trust, and community-building as an elemental factor to imagine and cultivate alternative, popular, solidarity-based economic forms, which are essential to the humanization of economic processes" (Alvarez Serna, 2005, p. 1). This same publication also describes the necessary components of a Feria Pedagógica as the following: "the presentation and exchange of information; the dimension of popular solidarity-based economy; full participation and collective work; that which is subjective and playful; the aesthetic (culture and identity); and reflection, analysis, and critique—[resulting in action] proposals" (p. 79).

This description of the Feria Pedagógica was borne out on the ground. In practice, the ferias did the work of carving out a particular kind of social space that not only expanded notions of teaching and learning but that also enacted a particular notion of participation that was inclusive and grounded in community. The CEP educators' emphasis on democratic forms of inclusiveness suggests a notion of participation that counters the dominant neoliberal conception of self-maximizing individuals who produce and consume in their own interest and who act in a competitive relationship with similar individuals. All of the ferias, for example, included an array of organizations, community groups, and individuals who exchanged information about their own work and about relevant social issues. The ideal of full participation was also visible in physical layout of the booths that made up the feria, which provided all participants with equal standing, regardless of whether one was a representative of a large organization or a tiny grassroots association. The booths were set up in a square formation, where attendees could browse along, reading information provided by organizations or groups and asking questions of the representatives at the booths. The physical layout of the event underscored the CEP educators' emphasis on inclusiveness, which was accompanied by collective sense of cooperation, where all participants worked together to ensure the success of the event; everyone—regardless of affiliation—actively participated in the set-up, execution, and dismantling of the feria.

Pedagogical Fairs and the Local Economy

This inclusive notion of participation was even more evident in the ferias' promotion of a particular form of commercial relations that emphasized strengthening the local economy, which had experienced intense hardship in part as a result of NAFTA and other neoliberal policies. For the CEP educators, the concept of building a "popular, solidarity-based" economy— one that ran parallel to the formal market and that involved the exchange of locally produced goods and services—was vital to their educational work. One of the most compelling examples of CEP's effort to help construct a popular economy in northern Mexico was a project known as "Chains of Commercialization and Production" ("Cadenas de Comercialización y Producción"), which involved the buying and selling of poultry among networks of neighboring communities that rotated in the production and consumption of chicken. The overriding objective of this project was to create alternatives to corporate brands of livestock products (such as Tyson chicken), which could instead be raised locally. For the CEP educators, the importance of popular economy was captured in a comment made by one of the CEP's co-founders, who explained that their role as practitioners was not only about helping rural women to read and write and finish school but also about "providing support for the family economy" (RS, 5/2/06).

The emphasis on building a solidarity-based economy played out in a large way in CEP's women's education classes, which in turn were closely connected to the ferias pedagogies. The classes incorporated a variety of dialogue-based activities around key themes related to health, economics, citizenship, and leadership. In addition to these activities, each class session contained a segment devoted to the hands-on creation of domestic products such as generic versions of Vicks VapoRub, Vaseline, and popular household cleaning solutions. The CEP educators leading the session would provide the instruction and materials, and the women participants would learn to produce these domestic goods. More importantly, participants had the opportunity to sell these types of goods at the Ferias Pedagógicas, which devoted physical space as well as moral support for the buying and selling of local products, particularly those produced by participants in their community education programs. In distinct contrast to the prevalence of corporate goods and the emphasis on efficiency and profitability above all else within the neoliberal context, the commercial relations that formed part of the Feria Pedagógica instead emphasized local production and consumption in an effort to promote "the humanization of economic processes" (Alvarez Serna, 2005, p. 1) first and foremost. This focus mirrors Freire's humanist legacy, where education is understood as a mutual process of "humanization" for both teachers and learners (Freire, 1970, 1992).

The presence of an explicitly humanist theoretical framework in CEP's work is one that can be found across Latin American popular education. As we shall see as well in the discussion of Ayuda Mutua in the next section, humanism as a liberatory framework has persisted within Latin American popular education movements, ultimately to find new relevance in popular educators' community-based responses to neoliberal discourses and policies. Just as we saw in the previous section that CEAAL's focus on liberatory paradigms can be seen as at once revisionist and remarkably appropriate to a contemporary neoliberal political context, so humanist discourses have been reappropriated by many of CEAAL's members and deployed to address precisely the de-humanizing instrumentalization of local knowledge that contemporary neoliberal policies of "participation" promote.

Pedagogical Fairs and Democratic Knowledge Production

The "pedagogical" aspect of the ferias signals a broad notion of what counts not only as "education" but also as legitimate knowledge—notions that go beyond the confines of school-based learning. In CEP's large body of educational practice—of which the ferias were only a part—there seemed to be an acute awareness on the part of the popular educators about the politics of knowledge and knowledge production, which was likely tied not only their involvement in the popular education movement but also the related participatory action research movement in Latin America (see Fals-Borda and Rahman, 1991). In their practice, CEP educators explicitly sought to democratize both knowledge production and dissemination; the feria happened to be one of the most visible instances of such efforts. Within the feria, crowds could find a large selection of books, pamphlets, and other kinds of printed materials on display; most were accounts of practice and organizational information published by the participating organizations.

CEP itself was prolific in its publication; during fieldwork for this project, the CEP educators produced three major publications, all of which resulted from their research on and with the communities with whom they worked. One was an account of the conditions in ninety urban *colonias* around the northern city of Torreón based on a diagnostic study that CEP educators conducted in 2004/05; the second was a compilation of prose, poetry, and photography written by CEP educators and program participants; and the third was an educational manual called *Demand Your Rights*, which emerged out of CEP's community education work and which emphasized the formation of active, engaged citizens. The publications were disseminated not only through public events like the ferias but also through regional- and national-level networks, workshops, and forums in which CEP educators participated.

In addition to these publications, there were a handful of activities in the feria that involved the spontaneous production of knowledge on the part of participants. At one community-based feria, for example, a participant walked around with markers and a sandwich board containing the open-ended question, "What can we do to fight apathy, indifference, and mistrust?" Feria attendees had written a variety of answers, including: "spend time [*convivir*] with other people," "trust in people," and "pay attention to the most important things in life" (Documents, 10/23/05). At another Feria Pedagógica that occurred on the basketball court of a middle school, one key activity involved participants—most of whom were of middle school age—writing answers to open-ended questions about the things that they would like to see transformed in their school and the things that they would like to see remain the same. The responses varied: some wrote about the need to clean up the school setting and to have more resources and supplies, while others wrote about the need to conserve water and the environment (Fieldnotes, 11/17/05).

Both of these instances—the community-based feria and the middle school feria—represented an effort on the part of the CEP educators to solicit the perspectives of feria attendees on a range of issues. It seemed to represent an attempt to collect informal data related to the most basic questions of what was happening in a particular place and how people were responding on an everyday basis. The CEP educators used the responses as a way of gauging both the relevance of their events and possible courses of action, taking as a starting point the problems as they were defined and understood by participants themselves.

This informal data collection was complemented by the more formal process of data collection, reflection, and analysis about CEP projects and programs that the CEP educators understood as *sistematización*. For the CEP educators, *sistematización* was a democratic process that brought together all participants in a project or program—such as the feria—to systematically reflect on and find patterns among their experiences with the program. While dialogue among participants was a vital dimension of the process, so too were documentation, writing, and dissemination. One important outcome of this process, then, was a written report, which sometimes was converted into a publication, as in the case of the CEP book *Feria Pedagógica: Una mirada ciudadana* referenced above. This emphasis on grassroots research in conjunction with project participants is an illustration of the "experiential methodology" described by Fals-Borda and Rahman (1991) in their explanation of participatory action research (PAR). In this sense, the CEP educators' process of *sistematización* was oriented towards the "acquisition of serious and reliable knowledge upon which to construct power, or countervailing power, for the poor, oppressed, and exploited groups and social classes" (p. 3).

What is significant about both the formal and informal acts of knowledge production associated with the ferias is that they were facilitated not only by the CEP educators but also by the particular kind of social space that the Feria Pedagógica served to create—a space that could be understood in terms of Howell and Pearce's (2002) notion of an "alternative genealogy" of civil society, which provides room for the work of locally based movements. In this case, the CEP educators' emphasis on democratic knowledge production and the construction of a solidarity-based economy—both of which were embodied in the feria—can be seen to mirror Escobar's (1992) description of "new social movements of grassroots orientation," which are characterized not only by their situatedness in the everyday lives of participants and their questioning of "expert" knowledge but also by their emphasis on both the material and aesthetic aspects of social life. The CEP educators' approach to participation and movement-building, then, served to interrupt the traditional hierarchies associated with knowledge production and consumption, as well as the neoliberal discourses that appropriate local participation for the purpose of mainstream "development" ends.

Ayuda Mutua

If CEP's Pedagogical Fairs are an example of how community-based popular educators produce an alternative social space where local perspectives, critique, and economic activity can arise, Ayuda Mutua's School for Promotores is an example of how the identities of community-based popular educators who organize such alternative civil society spaces are themselves produced. Ayuda Mutua ("mutual help") is an organization with headquarters in Morelia, Michoacán, in the mountainous zone approximately five hours west of Mexico City. The director of Ayuda Mutua, Elena,[4] has integrated Freire's theories as well as her own community-based work to create a process through which local educator-organizers—"promotores" and "promotoras"—plan and implement extremely diverse projects to address the specific needs of diverse urban neighborhoods and rural communities. Ayuda Mutua, founded in the late 1980s, has developed within the historical and theoretical context of popular education programs and debates in Latin America. The development of promotores through a systematic two-year curriculum, initiated in the mid-1990s, remains at the core of an organization that involves myriad local development projects in dozens of urban neighborhoods and rural towns. The director's self-published book details the theory and practice of the "School for the Comprehensive [*Integral*] Development of Promotores and Promotoras" (Galván 2000). Elena emphasizes that this book is the culmination of a great deal of work, thought, research, and collaboration with other Latin American popular educators.

The book explores the history of Ayuda Mutua, its objectives and what type of work it has done in different places. It also places Ayuda Mutua within the context of a popular sphere that has grown, become more diverse, and taken on a more precise meaning and a sense of a unified purpose (in the— at that time— 14 years since the organization's founding (p. 48)). In addition, the book discusses the political and economic shifts over this period, including the emergence of neoliberal policies and their effects on the Mexican economy and in particular on the communities of Michoacán. The state's encouragement of the development of NGOs to take on much of the public welfare and local development work coincided with policies that increased the wealth disparity between different regions of the country and policies that decreased the capacity for sustainable local development by encouraging emigration north to the *maquilas* and to the United States (pp. 50–54).

At the same time, increased state support for grassroots community-based education and organizing in the late 1990s created a public space that has made Ayuda Mutua's work more visible and has increased the possibilities for the organization to work with a wide variety of government agencies and NGOs. In the case of Ayuda Mutua, civil society entities have gained strength as their ties to the state have increased. Nevertheless, from the perspective of Ayuda Mutua's founder, the functionality of Ayuda Mutua for the state is limited and incidental; indeed, Elena frames the story of the organization as one in which they happen to use various state forms and policies where necessary to advance a critical and independent civil society agenda defined by its popular education practices. At the center of these practices are promotores and promotoras who organize within their communities to develop a space for participation and community-driven development.

The objective of the Ayuda Mutua School for Promotores and Promotoras is primarily to bring students together to share, reflect on, and learn from one another's experiences in Ayuda Mutua and other projects in their local communities. Yet Elena emphasizes the importance of "comprehensive (*integral*) formation" in the school's name, saying that the curriculum is set up so that "the people involved acquire the knowledge, capacities, abilities, skills, attitudes, and values necessary to allow them to respond to the specific requirements of their activities inside the communities" (section 3.1.2). According to her description of the curriculum, students develop these qualities and abilities through activities designed to draw upon and analyze their own experiences as community members and as organizers. She describes a quite Freirean dialectical "praxis," where learning occurs as an ongoing critical relationship between theory and practice.

The curriculum has an explicitly "humanist" orientation, placing the "social subject" at the center of the analysis. The lessons begin with the individual (including lessons on personal development, human rights, and the role of the promotora in interacting with individuals), shift to an analysis of groups (including conflict resolution, leadership, meeting facilitation, and participation), and then move toward spending the better part of a year and a half on community issues: analyzing regional/national/international contexts in relation to local communities, studying sustainable development issues, reflecting on gender issues in communities, exploring local community cultures and histories, and developing specific community organizing skills.

School for Promotoras: Pedagogy and Exams

Since fieldwork for this project did not allow for the observation the School for Promotoras in action (they were on a 6-month break between 2-year cycles during fieldwork for this project), this analysis relies upon archival materials from the organization, including lesson plans, activity sheets, exams and other promotore writing, evaluation reports, Elena's descriptions, and promotoras' oral recountings of their experiences in the school. The school's pedagogy is basically Freirean, with many creative twists. Most lessons begin by eliciting experiences or concepts from the student-promotores themselves, drawing on their personal life experiences and on their experiences working in their communities. Often lessons include creative activities, and they usually involve working in small groups to come up with some sort of final product or plan. The school curriculum places a heavy emphasis on written and oral articulation skills, with promotores-in-training expected to become more and more able to use words to describe their work, their identities in multiple ways (as women/men, as indigenous people, as educators, etc.), their communities, their beliefs, and their hopes. The development of skills revolves around increasing the ability of promotores to talk to one another about their own experiences and ideas, to become skilled at engaging in discussions in their communities, and to orally relay analysis and strategies related to issues in their individual communities.

What follows is a brief analysis of the exams given to a twelve-student cohort after they completed the first of their two years at the school. These are presented as examples of promotores' self-reflection on their role and the meaning of their work as community-based popular educators. Analyzing these exams several months after returning from fieldwork provided a way of triangulating the clarity and directness with which the promotores talked about their work and about themselves as promotores. Indeed, the explicit and open style of self-reflection of promotores in both rural and urban areas, from all class backgrounds, who talked about their work—analyzing what it means, how it works in their community, how it relates to their own sense of self, etc.—is demonstrated in these promotora exams.

The promotores who took the first-year exam (and hence who comprise this "sample") are from eight different communities, five of them rural and three urban or semi-urban. Ten of the twelve are women. Two of the promotores in this group have such limited writing skills that it is difficult to analyze or even decipher the content of many of their responses. Based on cross-checking the names of these students with the director's memory as well as (incomplete) records of adult literacy classes, approximately five of the twelve learned to read and write as adults.

The exam questions are all open-ended and are meant to encourage promotores-in-training to reflect on their communities, their work, and their own identities as promotores. The exam is five pages long. The presence in the exams of reading and writing activities that ask students to use language to move between concrete description and abstract analysis reveals a particular orientation to the development and improvement of literacy skills for promotores. The exams require many of the students to reach beyond their current writing skills, to attempt to put into words on paper original work plans, definitions, connections between concepts, and justifications. All ten students who have basic writing skills wrote at least a few lines—and in most cases closer to a paragraph—in response to each question.

There is a great emphasis on the importance of *talk* in the responses to hypothetical scenario as well as in the responses to questions that ask students to reflect on their experiences at the school or in their communities. All of the exam responses refer to talking with the people in their communities, learning from discussions with one another in the school, and using discussions as a way to involve more people in solving community problems. Dialogue, in some form, is recognized by ten of the twelve promotoras as an important aspect of being a promotora. The following excerpts from responses represent five instances of promotora reflection on dialogue or collective reflection:

> The cultural center—we meet there to have our meetings with everyone who wants to accompany us to the discussions. That is how we come to agreement on what we are going to do, how we are going to do it . . . we don't distinguish between people, everyone who wants to have discussions [can attend].

> For me [the School for Promotoras has] been a small grain of sand to improve my community, in that I have better communication with my family, that they have more communication with their family, and discussion is something that has helped us because discussing and listening is how we are going to understand and, in this way, learn and improve each day.

> We would have to have a meeting, and for this I would invite everyone in the community and we would talk about the problems in our community.

> In the [projects] in which I participated as promotora I'm trying so that when there are people who don't want to participate in the work that they reflect about what we now need to accomplish.

Like the answers that emphasize talk and the importance of listening to the ideas and experiences of community members, the students' emphasis on human rights and literacy frameworks manifests itself both as something they feel has been an important aspect of their own learning and as an educational agenda they think ought to be imposed on their communities. In none of the following examples does the context of the response indicate that these ideas or frameworks would be elicited from the people in the communities themselves.

> For me the task is that the children learn to read and write so that they know how to defend themselves in other communities, that the community moves forward, that it doesn't stay like it was before, that the community changes itself or knows how to defend itself.

> [The School for Promotoras] offered more education to learn my rights as a person and this helped me to live in peace. Because what we have learned about our teaching to the people is that this way the community will have more education and knowledge.

[A promotora is] a person who is charged with advocating or introducing to the community certain themes by different media, at the same time helping to resolve problems, doubts, and to offer a little more education to the people.

Human dignity is the most important of all for the people. Because it makes us such that there would not be distinctions, whether they are poor or rich, and that we would live with equality and with the same rights—the children, elders, and everyone in general already would be in our house, in our community, and in our country.

These exam responses allude to the human rights focus that runs throughout Ayuda Mutua's curricula and projects. There is an explicit "human rights" unit in the School for Promotoras curriculum, and the theme of ensuring human rights and human dignity runs throughout the two-year curriculum. Furthermore, several Ayuda Mutua projects that focus specifically on domestic violence and sexual assault utilize a human rights framework in each education and action activity.

Ayuda Mutua's promotores are diverse, and they live in communities that are affected by neoliberalism in diverse ways. In some of these communities neoliberalism is experienced as extreme economic stress and familial instability, leading to increased violence. In other communities neoliberal policies affect the resources of schools, while in others these policies result in de-regulated manufacturing and severe ecological and public health consequences. The task of the School for Promotores and Promotoras is to institute a comprehensive focus on the individual, group, community, and larger regional and global issues, and to give local community educator-organizers the tools to engage others to address their concerns at various levels.

What emerges out of this type of community educator training are promotores who work with their communities to build health clinics and promotores who focus on indigenous language preservation, promotores who develop local produce and artisan marketplaces in isolated rural areas and promotores who work with women to respond to domestic violence with legal action and awareness campaigns. At the "micro" level there are puppet shows and self-help groups, savings groups and literacy classes. Ayuda Mutua's projects can be so wildly diverse, developing in direct relation to the *specific* needs in diverse social spaces, because, unlike the civil society initiatives of the World Bank, *there is no overriding development agenda that must unify or "guide" them.* The agenda for community-based popular educators is to facilitate alternative spaces of critical participation in economic and educational activity that has meaning and relevance not for some abstract "development agenda," but for the communities themselves.

Community-Based Popular Education: An Adequate Response?

CEAAL's network of popular educators is vast and comprehensive in its aims. The individual projects we have highlighted in CEP and Ayuda Mutua are only a small piece of each organization's work, and these are only two organizations among hundreds of member organizations that comprise CEAAL. There are many efforts throughout Latin America to develop forms of civil society that are consciously critical, offering alternative spaces for thick participation in defining and carrying out alternative structures and alternative ideologies to those being offered by the neoliberal development industry as well as many Latin American governments.

It is difficult for us as critical educators to conclude this chapter—indeed, any writing on neoliberal globalization—without an impassioned call for unified resistance. Indeed, we are compelled by the need to resist what we have here described as an increasingly astute and comprehensive neoliberal development agenda that is able to reach with its instruments of co-optation, knowledge appropriation, and management into the very social spaces that, in Latin America, have traditionally served as the greatest resources for popular social movements. But we are also compelled by the notion that the struggle against neoliberalism is not the same as the struggle against imperialism. There is no final moment, no single front. Moreover, as we have shown, there is this particular social space of the Pedagogical Fair, open now for critical deliberation that is not trained on developing producers and consumers for the global economy. There is this educator from the school for promotores and promotoras, armed now to go into her community and ask questions that lead to discussions and action without the imposition of development principles or funding criteria. These are actions that answer the World Bank's instrumental deliberation over how to reach into communities to institute its agenda more deeply and effectively. These are actions that counter the nominal efforts of the World Bank to situate its agenda within civil society.

Community-based education responds to the neoliberal development agenda in precisely the "local" sites this agenda claims to reach. Moreover, community-based popular education in Latin America responds with critical deliberation and alternative paradigms of progress to precisely the new terms (both political and rhetorical) that neoliberal development institutions like the World Bank impose upon the region. But—is it enough? Is it sufficient to topple the agenda? No, of course not. Community-based popular education in Latin America—and particularly in Mexico—is literally starving for resources. Indeed, what we have articulated here is a quintessentially contemporary agenda that is based on a long and rich history within Latin America, but this agenda is barely recognized (indeed, because of the near-exclusive vocational focus of adult education in the US and in the UK, it is barely *recognizable*) in the seats of neoliberal power outside the region.

But progressive educators and activists outside of Latin America would do well to understand the particular strengths and relevance of focusing on social space and social subjects articulated by community-based popular educators in Latin America in their regional discourses and in their local projects. These are characteristics well tailored—even uniquely tailored—to respond to the remarkable flexibility and ideological strength of neoliberal policies and discourses. Progressive educators would do well to listen, to learn, and to join in the struggle for the role of civil society as a critical social space necessary (if not sufficient) to address the challenges of neoliberalism.

Notes

1 Both Sandler and Mein contributed equally to the research and writing of this chapter.
2 While a full exploration of the civil society and participation initiatives is beyond the scope of this chapter, the following additional documents have been particularly instrumental to our understanding of these initiatives that led to the framing of this chapter and the brief characterization in this section: "Nurturing civil society at the World Bank: An assessment of staff attitudes toward civil society," Social Development Papers, Paper 24, Sept 1998; "World Bank—civil society engagement: Review of fiscal years 2002–2004"; "Participation in practice: The experience of the World Bank and other stakeholders," World Bank Discussion Paper 333, December 1996; "Participation and the World Bank: Successes, constraints, and responses," Social Development Papers, Paper 29, 1998. All are accessible through the World Bank website's "Publications" section.
3 Data collection in each of these two organizations was conducted in conjunction with each author's distinct ethnographic project. However, for the sake of stylistic consistency, we have retained the plural first-person ("we") throughout the text of this chapter.
4 All names of individuals are pseudonyms.

References

Alvarez Serna, J. L. (2005). La Feria Pedagógica: Una Mirada Ciudadana. Saltillo, Mexico: PATTimpresiones.

Apple, M. W. (2001). Comparing Neo-liberal projects and inequality in education. *Comparative Education*, 37(4), 409–423.

Apple, M. W. (2006). *Educating the "right" way: Markets, standards, God, and inequality* (2nd ed.). New York: Routledge.

Audley, J. J. (2004). Introduction. NAFTA's promise and reality: Lessons from Mexico for the hemisphere. Carnegie Endowment for International Peace. Retrieved May 23, 2006, from www.ceip.org/pubs.

Austin, R. (1999). Popular history and popular education: El consejo de educación de adultos de America Latina. *Latin American Perspectives*, 26(4), 39–68.

Cohen, J. & Arato. A. (1992). *Civil society and political theory*. Cambridge, MA: MIT Press.

Escobar, A. (1992). Reflections on "development": Grassroots approaches and alternative politics in the Third World. *Futures*, 24(5), 411–436.

Esquivel, G. & Rodriguez-Lopez, J. A. (2003). Technology, trade, and wage inequality in Mexico before and after NAFTA. *Journal of Development Economics*, 72, 543–565.

Fals Borda, O. & Anisur Rahman, M. (1991) *Action and knowledge: Breaking the monopoly with participatory action-research.* Bogotá, Colombia: Cinep.

Fischman, G., Ball, S., & Gvirtz, S. (2003). Toward a neoliberal education? Tension and change in Latin America. In S. Ball, G. Fischman, & S. Gvirtz (Eds.), *Crisis and hope: The educational hopscotch of Latin America* (pp. 1–19). New York: RoutledgeFalmer.

Freire, P. (1970). *Pedagogy of the oppressed.* New York: Continuum.

Freire, P. (1992). *Pedagogy of hope.* New York: Continuum.

Galván, A. S. (2000). Jarhuajperakua (Ayuda Mutua) A.C.: Re-Pensando Nuestro Trabajo. Morelia.

Gramsci, A. (1971). *Selections from the prison notebooks of Antonio Gramsci* (Q. Hoare & G. N. Smith, Trans.). New York: International Publishers.

Harvey, D. (2005). *A brief history of neoliberalism.* Oxford: Oxford University Press.

Howell, J. & Pearce, J. (2002) *Civil society and development: A critical exploration.* Boulder: Lynne Reiner Publishers.

Kamat, S. (2002). *Development hegemony: NGOs and the state in India.* Oxford: Oxford University Press.

La Belle, T. J. (2000). The changing nature of non-formal education in Latin America. *Comparative Education,* 36(1), 21–47.

Laclau, E. & Mouffe, C. (1985). *Hegemony and socialist strategy: Towards a radical democratic politics.* London: Verso.

Morales-Gómez, D. & Torres, C. (1990). *The state, corporatist politics, and educational policy making in Mexico.* New York: Praeger.

Puiggrós, A. (1999). *Neoliberalism and education in the Americas.* Boulder, CO: Westview.

Puiggrós, A. & Torres, C. (1995). The state and public education in Latin America. *Comparative Education Review,* 39(1), 1–27.

Rist, G. (1997) *The history of development: From Western origins to global faith.* London and New York: Zed Books.

Stiglitz, J. (2004, January 6). The broken promise of Nafta. *The New York Times.* Retrieved March 5, 2007, from http://www.nytimes.com.

Williams, G. (2002). *The other side of the popular: Neoliberalism and subalternity in Latin America.* Durham, NC: Duke University Press.

Williamson, J. (1997). *The Washington consensus revisited.* Washington, DC: Inter-American Development Bank.

World Bank (2000). *Working together: The World Bank's partnership with civil society* (Document 21644). The International Bank for Reconstruction and Development/World Bank.

Zarco Mera, C. (2000). Educación popular: Nuevos horizontes y renovación de compromisos. *La Piragua,* 18, 5–18.

CHAPTER 6

Afterword on Global Crises, Social Justice, and Education

MICHAEL W. APPLE

Pushing Back

In this book's first chapter, I pointed to the importance of two fundamental acts, seeing the world relationally and repositioning oneself. Any attempt at understanding the connections among the three terms which make up this book's title—global crises, social justice, and education—has its basis in these acts. And our roles in supporting serious attempts at interrupting the relations of dominance and subordination in so many regions and nations require that we push back against those ideological and social forces that are trying so very hard to destroy the collective memories, programs, and visions that things could be better than they are today.

At the outset of *Global Crises, Social Justice, and Education*, I outlined a set of tasks for the "organic" or "public" intellectual. Some of these are what we usually label as "academic," while others are related more to political, economic, cultural, and educational activism. These tasks are multiple and require a wide array of skills, some of which are already well-developed within critical educational communities, while others need to be relearned or developed. A key is connecting these tasks together so that they have coherence and are organized around a set of educational and social projects on which the "decentered unity" we are constantly trying to build can agree.

Let us be honest. Forming such a decentered unity will not be easy. Employing a wider range of critical theories and approaches—and thinking about them globally—is at times difficult enough. But respectfully engaging with the multiple political projects from which these theories arise and which they entail may be even harder. The fact that these political/educational projects may challenge us in what may be difficult ways, to ask us to inter-rogate where we stand on national and international issues about which we may have truly contradictory feelings or which position us as perhaps partly an oppressor, may make us very uncomfortable. But, so be it. We cannot ask others to listen carefully to our criticisms of the relations of dominance and subordination in the societies we examine in this book and to the voices of those who constantly organize and speak back against these relations, if we do not listen ourselves and if we do not struggle to overcome our own common sense.[1]

Becoming Literate

Listening carefully and speaking back also means asking different questions than those we commonly ask about educational policies and practices. For instance, one of the guiding questions within the field of education is a deceptively simple one: "What knowledge is of most worth?" Over the past four decades, an extensive tradition has grown around a restatement of that question. Rather than "*What* knowledge is of most worth?" the question has been reframed. It has become "*Whose* knowledge is of most worth?" (Apple 2000, 2004) There are dangers associated with such a move, of course, including impulses toward reductionism and essentialism. And the answer to this query may be different from nation to nation and from group to group. However, the question itself is crucial and the transformation of questions such as this and others has led to immense progress in our understanding of the cultural politics of education in general and of the relations among curricula, teaching, evaluation, and differential power.

In the process of making the conceptual, historical, and empirical gains associated with this move, there has been an accompanying international-ization of the issues involved. Thus, issues of the cultural assemblages associated with empire and previous and current imperial projects have become more visible. Hence, there has been an increasing recognition that critical educational studies must become much more truly global in their outlook(s), their approaches, in the issues with which they deal, and in their politics. This book is part of a growing a response to this recognition. Thus, for example, there has been a turn both to issues of the colonial imagination and to postcolonial approaches in order to come to grips with the complex and at times contradictory synchronic and diachronic relations between knowledge and power.

This more relational approach is significant in a number of ways, not the least of which was the growing understanding that even internal conflicts about what should be taught in, say, the United States and England bore and still bear the marks of global processes and politics. It has become ever clearer to those of us in education, for example, that the very notion of the canon of "official knowledge" had much of its history in a conscious attempt to "civilize" the working class, racialized and minoritized peoples, diasporic populations, and the "natives" of an expanding empire (Apple, 2000).

The very idea of teaching the "Other" was a significant change, of course.[2] For many years in Europe, for example, the fear of working-class literacy was very visible. This will be more than a little familiar to those with an interest in the history of the relationship among books, literacy, and popular movements. Books themselves, and one's ability to read them, have been inherently caught up in cultural politics. Take the case of Voltaire, that leader of the Enlightenment who so wanted to become a member of the nobility. For him, the Enlightenment should begin with the "grands." Only when it had captured the hearts and minds of society's commanding heights could it concern itself with the masses below. But, for Voltaire and many of his followers, one caution should be taken very seriously. One should take care to prevent the masses from learning to read (Darnton 1982, p. 130). This of course was reinscribed in often murderous ways in the prohibitions against teaching enslaved peoples how to read (although there is new historical evidence that documents that many enslaved people who were brought to the Americas were Muslim and may already have been literate in Arabic). It is also reinscribed in gendered ways in the current immensely damaging, and often violent, attempts by ultra-conservative activists to prevent women from going to school in a number of regions.[3]

Such changes in how education and literacy were thought about did not simply happen accidentally. As all of the chapters in this book demonstrate, they were (and are) the results of national and global struggles over who has the right to be called a person and a citizen, over what it means to be educated, over what counts as official or legitimate knowledge, and over who has the authority to speak to these issues (Young, 2003). And as all of the chapters in this book also demonstrate, these struggles need to be thought about using a range of critical tools, among them analyses based on economic transformations, the place of state formation in battles over identity and recognition, postcolonial theories, feminist understandings, the role of discursive politics, how racializing policies and practices operate, and the intersections of all of these. Clearly, then, as I noted earlier this requires a synthetic outlook, one that gives due respect to Fraser's arguments that both the politics of redistribution and the politics of recognition need to be combined, but always with caution so that they do not interrupt each other. How this might be done without losing one's core political principles in the process has been one of the aims of *Global Crises, Social Justice, and Education*.

Social Movements

One of the arguments underpinning a good deal of the material included in this book is the role of social movements as agents of radical change. If it is social movements acting for and against what is taken for granted as "correct," as common sense, that are often the driving forces behind major transformations in the ends and means of education—as I and others think it is (Apple, 2000, 2006; Anyon, 2005)—then more space must be given to the ways in which movements in civil society have an impact on what counts as legitimate issues and hence legitimate policies. Sandler and Mein offer a powerful example of this, as do the pro-immigration mobilizations discussed by Collin and Apple.

We know that the collective action of social movements has been one of the major weapons of the dispossessed and marginalized in society. For example, in Brazil currently one of the most powerful collective actors is the "landless movement." Given the immense inequalities in land ownership and distribution in Brazil—one of the most unequal nations in the world— thousands of poor people have developed tactics that include mass protests, occupying vacant land, and then building schools, health care centers, and similar things on the land that has been taken over so that permanence is more likely to be guaranteed. This has struck a responsive chord among many other groups in society and has generated cross-class alliances. Just as importantly, the tactics and strategies developed by the landless movement have been appropriated and used by other oppressed groups in their own struggles against racism, for example. Similar things have been found in the urban areas so clearly illuminated in Davis's book *Planet of Slums*, of which I spoke in Chapter 1.

Yet equally important are the ways in which what may be largely retrogressive movements and forces both within the state and civil society learn from progressive movements. In the United States, for example, authoritarian populist religious movements have taken both the discourse of cultural marginalization and many of the tactics of struggle from African American social movements and then rearticulated them into their own agenda, in the process calling themselves "the new oppressed." This says something crucial about the ability of conservative political alliances and social movements to learn from those who have considerably less economic, social, and cultural capital. This "poaching" is a fascinating arena for the study of how quickly more dominant groups learn to use movement strategies first developed by the least powerful members of a society in the conflicts over schooling and other institutions. The ability of dominant groups to disarticulate the language and issues developed by oppressed groups and to then rearticulate the language and issues—and sometimes the people who developed them—for use in restoring threatened hegemonic relations and structures is very visible today and is made clear in Takayama's chapter about how the Right in Japan has worked assiduously to create a new discourse and a larger alliance that supports its conservative ends inside and outside of education. The forces of "conservative modernization" are more than a little creative in working with and on the elements of "good sense" that people possess. We would do well to learn something from them about this (Apple, 2006).

How this works, for example, is clear in the United States as well as in Japan. In both nations, neoliberal proposals for marketization and privatization in education may be couched in the language of escaping from bureaucracy and "bad" state-supported schools, but the reality is that they constitute an attack on the state and on the entire public sphere. While the implications of these attacks are deeply troubling, the reality is that they have been more than a little successful in changing our common sense and in offering what are seemingly workable alternatives to even dispossessed groups. The power of the neoliberal agenda is visible in the hard and partly successful work that the Right has done in convincing some Black and Latino/Latina activist groups that neoliberal policies offer a more realistic hope for the future of their children than, say, existing state-supported schools (Apple, 2006; Pedroni, 2007).

Of course, in the face of this set of desocializing policies, the radical transformation of the public sphere into simply one more extension of the private is of no little concern. But, having said this, one should never romanticize the public sphere, as some people may do, since the public sphere has always been classed, gendered, and raced, with many groups being seen as less than persons and thus unable to participate in what counted as the public (Fraser, 1989; Mills, 1997). In fact, this may be one of the reasons that some aspects of neoliberal policies, with their vision of empowering the rational economic actor, may be attractive to racialized groups.

In societies where, say, Black people, indigenous people, or "despised" castes are tragically seen by dominant groups as irrational and dangerous— in essence as forms of pollution—the very idea of a set of policies that provides an identity *as fully rational* is partly counter-hegemonic. Thus, the reappropriation of neoliberal ideologies by oppressed people of color and minoritized groups is actually a fascinating, and contradictory, example of the ways in which dispossessed groups themselves disarticulate ideological positions from these positions' original site and then rearticulate them for use for their own purposes (Apple, 2006; Pedroni, 2007). For those of you who are familiar with Stuart Hall's work on the ways in which discourses and movements can be pulled under the umbrellas of groups that are very different from their origin, this very process of disarticulation and rearticulation sits at the heart of much of his political theory (see Morley & Chen,

1996) as well as our own. Like Stuart Hall, we too wish to focus on the creative processes used by dominant groups to attempt to radically alter the balance of forces in multiple nations and spaces. We do this in part because we believe that Gramsci's analysis of the importance of culture and consciousness is absolutely crucial for any attempt at forming counter-hegemonic alliances around the pressing social issues that concern people in their daily lives, educational issues included.

Disciplined Theoretical Bricolage

To understand this process of disarticulation and rearticulation, like others (see, e.g., Anyon et al., 2009) in this book we had to employ structural and poststructural theories. But our choice was based on a condition that they speak to each other and share a set of broad complementary goals. Thus, the chapter by Collin and Apple creatively appropriates both approaches while drawing for example on the work of Hart and Negri (2000) and their analysis of empire. We were taken with their firm grounding in an overtly anti-capitalist politics and a firm belief that the global "biopolitics" of empire is not only challengeable, but is being challenged right now in ways that have the potential to fundamentally subvert the logics of capitalist domination.

For Hardt and Negri, information production, circulation, and control are central to any understanding of the politics of empire. Their analysis of the centrality of these dynamics enables them to redefine what counts as counter-hegemonic action, who counts as counter-hegemonic actors, and what tools are increasingly available to challenge dominance. In the process, not only do they redefine and internationalize counter-hegemonic move-ments, making them a much larger set of groups, but they also see everyday life, geographic mobility, and cultural politics, among other things, as already creating the real conditions for the decline of dominant relations and structures. Thus, in the case of such movements included in this volume, youth in pro-immigrant groups, using a range of creative resources and tools, are showing us the possibility of difference. And the efforts to keep alive Palestinian histories, cultures, and memories in the face of diaspora and containment speaks to this as well.

We are not uncritical of Hardt and Negri's analysis. Indeed one of us has taken them to task for a number of their unwarranted political, theoretical, and empirical claims (Apple, 2003). However, as mentioned in Chapter 1, we are not in a church, so we are not worried about heresy. And as I suggested in the taxonomy of tasks included in that introductory chapter, we need to be open to multiple critical traditions, to keep them alive, and to use them to correct and amplify the questions and approaches we employ when reality and the politics generated out of it become ever more complex (see Apple, Au, and Gandin, 2009).[4]

Borrower Beware

There are, of course, dangers in using a range of theories. But this act of allowing oneself to be influenced by a more extensive set of critical perspectives is not the only danger involved in being open to influences from the "outside." Indeed, one of the most difficult dilemmas that educational actors in many nations face is a different kind of "borrowing," that of policy borrowing. Obviously, it would be wrong not to learn from the experiences of other nations. There will be times when what is being attempted in one country has been tried in another country—and learning more about such attempts can be important. However, one must be very cautious about appropriating the experiences of another country uncritically. Often, such "recontextualizations" (Bernstein, 2008) pull the reforms out of their context of intense debate that may characterize their development in the place where the policies originated.

Let me give a few examples of what I mean, one an example of interdisciplinary borrowing and the other an example of problems associated with international borrowing. The first concerns the very foundations of curriculum planning in the United States, foundations that spread throughout much of the world. The earliest curriculum planners in the United States drew their models from industrial and human engineering, especially from F. W. Taylor and his development of time and motion studies and task analysis (Kliebard, 1995). While these techniques seemed to guarantee efficiency and cost savings—and hence seemed to be crucial tools to be brought into educational planning—they also had their roots in anti-labor ideological forms, in the "popular eugenics" and anti-immigrant movements, and in models of top-down control that deskilled workers (see Apple, 1986, 1995; Selden, 1999). The appropriation of such methods into education also brought with it a set of interests that still to this day have had very negative consequences.

The second example is more current and more closely connected to the issues being dealt with in the chapters in this volume. As I have shown in *Educating the "Right" Way* (Apple, 2006) and as a number of the chapters included here have pointed out, the increasing pressure to move toward devolution, decentralization, marketization, privatization, and "choice" can be found in a considerable array of nations. Yet the historical and empirical evidence within schools and between schools and the larger society does not support a romantic vision about the effects of such policies. No nations—Japan, Israel/Palestine, Mexico, or any other—should take up such policies without a thorough examination of the debates surrounding them and of the ideological, economic, and political, and educational tendencies and effects of these movements.

This is not to say that nations should ignore the possibility that such reforms can be used for counter-hegemonic purposes. However, as in the past and in the context of differential power relations within the society, as I noted earlier in this chapter such reform agendas may actually be disarticulated from progressive movements and rearticulated to the neoliberal and neoconservative agendas. That is, while the goals of those who want more flexibility and a less bureaucratic state are ones I and the other authors included here tend to agree with and may be worthwhile in general, given the current balance of power and the growing power of neoliberal and neoconservative movements there is no guarantee that reforms such as voucher plans, charter schools, and "choice" will not be captured and used by the forces of conservative modernization. That this is what is happening in a many nations should make us even more cautious about the possible latent effects of the uncritical appropriation of such reforms.

I do not want to overstate this case. The reappropriation of seemingly "democratic" reforms by the forces of conservative modernization is not guaranteed to happen. Indeed, we have evidence that it is possible to resist such reappropriations and to defend thicker versions of democracy against the thinner versions sponsored by neoliberalism (see Apple et al., 2003). We also have compelling evidence that neoliberal discourse can be disarticulated from neoliberalism itself and rearticulated and used for progressive purposes—but *only* when there are large-scale and socially critical social movements that support and defend such counter-hegemonic moves (Apple et al., 2003). However, in the absence of such movements, as Takayama's chapter in this volume clearly shows, we are right to worry about what will happen when reforms such as these are instituted, about how they will be used, and about who will gain the most and the least from their institutionalization. These worries can only be dealt with if we understand the ways in which dominance and subordination work in our societies and if we connect the processes of school reforms to the growth of specific and identifiable ideological tendencies and movements in the larger society. This requires a nuanced sense of history and a more detailed understanding of the creative ways in which conservative modernization works than is often found within educational research and policy.

Keeping Real

One of the most powerful insights of a focus on globalization and its multiplicity is the valorization of knowledge not only from above but from *below*. This is particularly the case of the women's movements that were pointed to in Chapter 5. But it can and has been extended to all subaltern peoples. The issue is not whether "the subaltern speak," but whether they are listened to (Spivak, 1988; Apple & Buras, 2006).

Yet a focus on "knowledge and voices from below" has at times bordered on what Whitty has called "romantic possibilitarianism" (Whitty, 1974). It is all so cultural that it runs the risk of evacuating the gritty materialities of daily lives, of economic relations, and of the processes of marginalization and occupation. The analysis by Meshulam and myself of what has happened, and continues to happen, to Palestinians serves as a powerful reminder of the history of these gritty materialities. This speaks to a set of larger issues around which this entire book is organized.

The concepts that are so central to critical work on globalization, social justice, and education such as "neoliberalism," "neoconservatism," "the state and civil society," "hegemony," "counter-hegemony," "identity," hybridity," "marginalization," "subaltern," "resistance," and indeed the entire panoply of critical vocabulary, can be used in multiple ways. They are meant to signify an intense set of complex and contradictory historical, geographic, economic, and cultural relations, experiences, and realities. But what must *not* be lost in the process of using them is the inherently *political* nature of their own history and interests. Used well, there is no "safe" or "neutral" way of mobilizing them—and rightly so. They are meant to be radically counter-hegemonic and they are meant to challenge even how we think about and participate in counter-hegemonic movements—and even who the "we" is in the first place. How can we understand this, if we do not participate in such movements ourselves?

One thing that that they all have in common, however, is a recognition of the centrality of global power relations in understanding education both inside and outside of national borders. Recognition is not enough, of course. *How* one recognizes the global, for what purpose, for whose benefit—all of these are equally crucial. And this necessitates a searching critical examination of one's own structural location, one's own overt and tacit political commitments, and one's own embodied actions once this recognition in all its complexities and contradictions is taken as seriously as it deserves.

These complexities and contradictions may seem paralyzing to some. But they don't have to be. We have many examples where cultural, political, and economic struggles can be and are linked to critical actions in education in powerful and lasting ways. Certainly, the chapters in this book enable us to reflect on the limits and possibilities of such struggles, on what resources may be available, and on how they might be used. When they are added to the radical transformations that have been cemented in place in education and in daily life in places such as Porto Alegre, Brazil and elsewhere, they provide a window on to ways to demonstrate that coalitions can be built that interrupt dominance, that create institutional forms that are much more responsive to oppressed and marginalized people, and that redefine what counts as legitimate knowledge all at the same time (Apple et al., 2003; Apple & Buras, 2006).

In each of the locations, nations, and perhaps "nations-to-be" represented in this volume, there are powerful instances of counter-hegemonic work. In the United States, for example, this is more and more visible, even in the face of powerful neoliberal, neoconservative, authoritarian populist, and managerial impulses and policies. Thus, the hard but successful work within schools in the United States that are populated by students from oppressed groups and from multiple diasporic communities from all over the world also provides workable answers not only to the question of "Whose knowledge is of most worth?" and "How can education be organized around a deep and abiding commitment to social justice?" It also provides responses to the issues surrounding how we might continuously recreate the "common" and build critically reflexive "hybrid" educational experiences so that the voices and cultures from below are both present and have an impact (Apple & Beane, 2007).

Each of the chapters in *Global Crises, Social Justice, and Education* gives us reason for (at times cautious) hope. Given the inability of dominant groups now and in the past to totally control either the ideological terrain or the facts on the ground, no matter how hard they try, perhaps the best way of stating this is that we should be "unromantic optimists." Hegemonic powers always create counter-hegemonic spaces, actors, and movements. This is visible in the pro-immigrant movements seen in the chapter by Collin and Apple, in Takayama's discussion of the re-emergence of critical educational form and content in Japan, in Meshulam and Apple's interrogation of the constantly shifting terrain of struggles over orientalisms and marginalizations in Israel/Palestine, and in the resilience and creativity of the women's groups so clearly shown in Sandler and Mein's significant chapter.

Yet I want to make one other point. While we have done so here, the focus of such counter-hegemonic experiences should not be limited to oppressed groups. The growing attention to what might be called "critical pedagogy for the privileged"—where one works on and with the consciousness of advantaged groups on issues surrounding globalization, poverty, whiteness, masculinities, homophobia, disability, and similar crucial dynamics and structures—signifies a recognition that the sites of struggle are not "only" with those "below" but those "above" as well.[5] We shouldn't be overly romantic about the possible success of these efforts, but we can and must act as secretaries for movements and practices in both of these arenas.

This book has tried to work at multiple levels (perhaps sites is a better word, since it does not imply a hierarchy). It has employed a range of theories to deal with the complex politics of an education committed to social justice and the ways in which power circulates and is used. It also mobilizes these theoretical resources to better understand a politics of interruption, where multiple insurgent voices, activists, and movements—using a range of resources and tools—have acted on the terrain of both the state and civil society to counter dominance. The authors included here all agree that the best of these theories can be an immense help in understanding global and local relations and politics, their histories, their possible futures, and the differential positionings that are produced by these relations.

But if the range of critical approaches we use here—and the larger range of critical theories that could and must be used to complement them—remains simply one more set of rhetorical tropes, employed for purposes that represent mobility strategies within existing institutional and academic forms, we fear that once again the radical potential of insurgent theories and voices may be turned into something safer, something that will lose its potential to profoundly change "our" understandings of center and periphery, of "we" and "they," and of what needs to be done to alter these relations. That would be a distinct tragedy. Thus, we end *Global Crises, Social Justice, and Education* with one more task, to remember why we are engaged in doing it.

Notes

1   For a thoughtful discussion of the politics of this, see Dale and Robertson (2004).

2   The use of concepts such as "the Other" can have contradictory effects for progressive understandings as well, of course. It can cause those employing the concepts to focus on what is *different*, rather than on one's joint humanity. See Katz (2004) for an analysis of the oddly similar effects of global economic restructuring on children in both the Sudan and New York, an account that is useful as a reminder of why we must also ask what is the same, not what is different.

3   It is important not to engage in a process of stereotyping here. Women are not passive in the face of this and Muslim women often engage in strategic actions and compromises that are missed when we apply particular "Western" assumptions about their lives. For a treatment of these issues, see Afshar (1998).

4   We are aware that given the partly Foucauldian analysis of the importance of the concept of biopolitics, our arguments can undoubtedly be used by some postmodernists in education to continue their attacks on the supposedly irredeemably reductive and essentializing tendencies (again supposedly) within all Marxist-influenced work. Of course, all too many of these attacks are themselves strikingly naïve about the last three decades of neo-Marxist and neo-Gramscian work, to say nothing of the influences of people such as Stuart Hall and others on critical theories in education. It is unfortunate, but true, that a number of critiques of "the" neo-Marxist traditions in education have stereotyped these traditions in what are simply sloppy ways. Nor have they paid attention to the immensely interesting attempts at integrating neo-Gramscian, postmodern, and poststructural work together so that the sparks that fly when these traditions "rub against" each other illuminate mutually important relations (see, e.g., Apple et al., 2003).

5   I have drawn on discussions with Katy Swalwell for this point. A good practical example of how issues surrounding such things as globalization can be dealt with in classrooms can be found in Bigelow and Peterson (2002).

References

Afshar, H. (1998). *Islam and feminisms.* New York: St. Martin's Press.
Anyon, J. (2005). *Radical possibilities.* New York: Routledge.
Anyon, J. et al. (2009). *Theory and educational research.* New York: Routledge.
Apple, M. W. (1986). *Teachers and texts: A political economy of class and gender relations in education.* New York: Routledge.
Apple, M. W. (1995). *Education and power* (2nd ed.). New York: Routledge.
Apple, M. W. (2000). *Official knowledge* (2nd ed.). New York: Routledge.
Apple, M. W. (2003). Review of *Empire* (Hardt & Negri), *Globalisation, Societies and Education,* 1, 116–121.
Apple, M. W. (2004). *Ideology and curriculum* (3rd ed.). New York: Routledge
Apple, M. W. (2006). *Educating the "right" way: Markets, standards, God, and inequality* (2nd ed.). New York: Routledge.
Apple, M. W. & Beane, J. A. (Eds.) (2007). *Democratic schools: Lessons in powerful education* (2nd ed.). Portsmouth, NH: Heinemann.
Apple, M. W. & Buras, K. L. (Eds.) (2006). *The subaltern speak: Curriculum, power, and educational struggles.* New York: Routledge.
Apple, M. W., Au, W., & Gandin, L. A. (Eds.) (2009). *The Routledge international handbook of critical education.* New York: Routledge.
Apple, M. W., Aasen, P., Cho, M. K., Gandin, L. A., Oliver, A., Sung, Y-K., Tavares, H., & Wong, T-H. (2003). *The state and the politics of knowledge.* New York: Routledge.
Bernstein, B. (2008). *The structuring of pedagogic discourse.* London: Routledge.
Bigelow, B. & Peterson, B. (2002). *Rethinking globalization: Teaching for justice in an unjust world.* Milwaukee, WI: Rethinking Schools.
Dale, R. & Robertson, S. (2004). Interview with Boaventura de Sousa Santos, *Globalisation, Societies and Education,* 2, 147–160.
Darnton, R. (1982). *The literary underground of the old regime.* Cambridge, MA: Harvard University Press.
Fraser, N. (1989). *Unruly practices.* Minneapolis: University of Minnesota Press.
Fraser, N. (1997). *Justice interruptus.* New York: Routledge.
Hardt, M. & Negri, A. (2000). *Empire.* Cambridge, MA: Harvard University Press.
Katz, C. (2004). *Growing up global: Economic restructuring and children's everyday lives.* Minneapolis: University of Minnesota Press.
Kliebard, H. (1994). *The struggle for the American curriculum* (2nd ed.). New York: Routledge.
Mills, C. (1997). *The racial contract.* Ithaca, NY: Cornell University Press.
Morley, D. & Chen, K-H (Eds.) (1996). *Stuart Hall: Critical dialogues in cultural studies.* New York: Routledge.
Pedroni, T. (2007). *Market matters.* New York: Routledge.
Selden, S. (1999). *Inheriting shame.* New York: Teachers College Press.
Spivak, G. (1988). Can the subaltern speak? In C. Nelson and L. Grossberg (Eds.), *Marxism and the interpretation of culture* (pp. 271–313). Urbana: University of Illinois Press.
Whitty, G. (1974). Sociology and the problem of radical educational change. In M. Flude and J. Ahier (Eds.), *Educability, schools, and ideology* (pp. 112–137). London: Halstead Press.
Young, R. (2003). *Postcolonialism.* New York: Oxford University Press.

Author Biographies

Michael W. Apple is John Bascom Professor of Curriculum and Instruction and Educational Policy Studies at the University of Wisconsin-Madison. He has written extensively on the relationship among power, knowledge, and education, and on the contradictory effects of global educational reforms.

Ross Collin is assistant professor of literacy education at Manhattanville College in Purchase, New York. His research involves the examination of processes of schooling in times of socio-economic transformation.

Erika Mein is assistant professor of literacy education at the University of Texas at El Paso. Her research focuses on adolescent and adult literacies across educational contexts, including but not limited to community-based organizations in Latin America and the US–Mexico border.

Assaf Meshulam is a Ph.D. dissertator in the Department of Curriculum & Instruction at the University of Wisconsin-Madison. His research interests focus on democratic education and social justice. He worked as an educator for ten years in underprivileged communities.

Jen Sandler is currently a visiting assistant professor in educational studies at Trinity College in Hartford, Connecticut. She studies how people think about and attempt to shape social and educational reform in community, policy, and organizational contexts.

Keita Takayama is a lecturer in the School of Education, University of New England, Australia. His current research interests include global flows of educational knowledge, internationalizing critical studies of education, and postcolonial critiques of comparative education.

Index

Note: Page numbers followed by 'n' refer to notes.

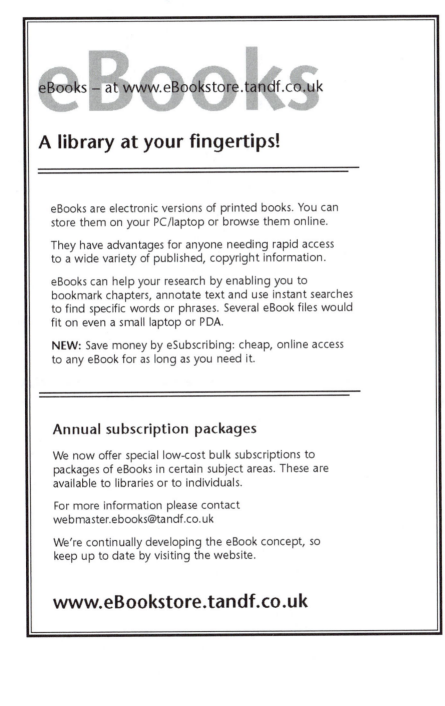